Cyber Commerce Reframing

Springer
Berlin
Heidelberg
New York
Barcelona
Hong Kong
London
Milan
Paris
Tokyo

Uwe G. Seebacher

Cyber Commerce Reframing

The End of Business Process Reengineering?

In Collaboration with
Lukas B. Juszczyk

Springer

Uwe G. Seebacher
179 Park Island
Lake Orion, MI 48362
USA
office@usp-consulting.cc

ISBN 3-540-42376-1 Springer-Verlag Berlin Heidelberg New York

Library of Congress Cataloging-in-Publication Data applied for
Die Deutsche Bibliothek – CIP-Einheitsaufnahme
Seebacher, Uwe G.: Cyber commerce reframing: the end of business process re-engineering? / Uwe G. Seebacher. With the assistence of Lukas B. Juszczyk. – Berlin; Heidelberg; New York; Barcelona; Hong Kong; London; Milan; Paris; Tokyo: Springer, 2002
ISBN 3-540-42376-1

Springer-Verlag Berlin Heidelberg New York
a member of BertelsmannSpringer Science+Business Media GmbH

http://www.springer.de

Printed in Germany

Hardcover-Design: design & production GmbH, Heidelberg

SPIN 10846880 42/2202-5 4 3 2 1 0 – Printed on acid-free paper

To my wife Sandra
and
my parents Christine and Bruno

Preface

The goal of this book is to create awareness for a change in mind-set that we will all have to face and go through. The necessity for this new mind-set is being driven by the situation that a completely new business world, a new reality, is being created at the point where the phenomenon commonly referred to as the "new economy" converges with the well-known old economy.

During the very late 1990s, this new reality was being driven by an almost incredible increase in yields in the financial markets, where conventional but value-driven and stable stocks such as Philip Morris, General Electric, or Bayer, did not attract as many investors as before – if we can call some of them investors at all. Companies in the high-tech or the new market segments are all part of the new economy.

This new economy has created new business ideas, business models, and a new reality, in which chief executive officers (CEOs) were in the mid twenties and had basically no clue as to what real business is and how much a dollar counts. Now, as this convergence is happening, the painful reality and the business rules of the old economy get us back down to earth. The CEOs become more senior, business plans are validated more carefully, and just having the famous ".com" in your company name does not get you any further or lead you to any of required money. We could say, the new economy had to learn to run on its own – to learn its lessons.

And this is the chance and opportunity where we have to take the pace, the dynamic, the enthusiasm, and all the other good things of the new economy and merge them with the understanding, the experience and the maturity of the old economy. This can lead us into a new world, where there is enough place for new ideas, start-ups, venture capitalists and catalysts, functioning jointly with the partly rigid but nonetheless challenging old economy.

But this requires us to broaden our horizon and to learn to understand the newly established rules of the game and to face dramatic changes, especially in the area of management science. Due to these changes, processes are no longer the one driving dimension. Several new ones have emerged as even more important and essential. This book leads you into a world where processes do not play the one dominating role any longer, as in the area of business process reengineering (BPR). A world where business survival and future business success will be the result of the intelligent convergence of strategy, technology, human resources, and processes. This is a business world in which companies will not invest millions of dollars in process optimization and process reengineering projects as these initiatives will neither lead to the pre-defined targets nor will they produce an acceptable return on investment.

Start to read this book by using and reflecting upon your own experience. Open up your mind to read about something you will find partly self-explanatory and partly new, and where you sometimes will find yourself having a feeling of *deja-vu*.

At the beginning I mentioned a new generation in a new business world. I am part of this new generation and, frankly speaking, I am proud of this generation and being part of it. Yet we all are part of it since there is no way around it.

No book is created solely by its authors. Let me take the opportunity to thank those individuals who helped make this book become a reality. First of all, Lukas Juszczyk, who had a tremendous impact on this publication and on the CCR approach. Furthermore one very special person, Mathias Nell, a dear friend of mine, whose experience, maturity, ability, and strength to deal with new challenges will always be kind of miraculous to me. Thanks as well to Alfred Taudes and Bernhard Weilharter for their support and advise. I also owe a debt of gratitude to colleagues and co-workers who served as sounding boards and exchange forums for new ideas and whose comments and critiques had essential impact on this book.

Many people played important roles in this book's evolution from an outline to a completed manuscript. Thanks to Ferdinand von Baumbach, Patty Bice, Marcus Englert, Dieter Ehrenberg, Ben Evetts, Peter Hackl, Michael Hiscocks, Gaby Leuchtenberger, Sonja Lo, Tor Lundgren, Chris Mabey, Bjoern Manstedten, Lothar Markowitsch, Ruth and Gary Matthews, Gerald Neumueller, Tobias Olbermann, Michael Schaub, Wilfried Scheer, Mark Selawry, Hans-Gerd Servatius and Peter Zschech. Special thanks to Werner Mueller and his team at Springer Heidelberg for his trustful and honest help and support throughout the whole project.

Munich/Lake Orion, April 2002 Uwe Seebacher

Table of Contents

Preface .... **VII**

Table of Contents .... **IX**

CHAPTER 1: Cyber-Commerce Reframing: A New Paradigm? **1**

Introduction 1
The Cyber-Economy 1
The Upcoming Cyber-Challenge 2
BPR: The Shortcomings 2
Reframing, Not Optimizing 3
Cyber-Commerce Reframing: The Approach 3
The New Role of Information Technology 4
The Human Resource Challenge 5
CCR for Which Companies? 5
Cyber-Assessment as the Starting Point 6
CCR Case Studies 7

CHAPTER 2: The Cyber-Economy **9**

The Development of IT in the Context of the Internet 9
The World Wide Web (WWW) and Its Implications 13
The Evolution of the Cyber-Economy 16
The Definition of Cyber (C-)Commerce 19
Changing Environmental Factors 24
Electronic-Commerce 26
Mobile Commerce 27
Television Commerce 30
Pervasive Commerce 32

CHAPTER 3: The Upcoming Cyber-Challenge **35**

Cyber-Challenge: Dreams and Reality 36
B2C: The Cyber-Flop 40
Yet Another Cyber-Debacle: B2B 45
Human Resources: The Cyber-Key 48
The Financial Imperative 49

CHAPTER 4: BPR: The Shortcomings....................53

The Basic Framework for Reengineering....................54
The Managerial Roots of Reengineering....................55
The Reengineering Story....................58
BPR and the Merging Paradigm Shift....................61
The BPR and ERP Success Story....................62
BPR Will Not Save the New Economy....................64
BPR and the Technical Shortcomings....................65
BPR and Strategic Human Resource Management (SHRM)....................66

CHAPTER 5: Reframing, Not Optimizing....................67

Talking about Optimization....................67
The Limitations of ISO 9000....................68
The Limitations of Total Quality Management (TQM)....................69
The Limitations of Six Sigma....................70
The Limitations of Operations Research....................71
The "Pareto Rule" as a Test of the Limitations of Optimization Activities....................74
CCR versus Optimization and Reengineering....................75

CHAPTER 6: Cyber-Commerce Reframing: The Approach....................81

The Praetorians of CCR....................81
The Issues with Surveys and Opinions....................82
Awareness as a Facilitator for Understanding CCR....................84
Bad Experience for Good Stuff....................85
The Dimension-Impact Matrix (DIM) of CCR....................86
The Structure of CCR....................88
The CCR Horizontals....................89
Conclusion....................108

CHAPTER 7: The New Role of Information Technology....................111

The "E-volution" of IT....................111
The Driving Economic Role of IT....................113
Trends and Observations....................119
Special, Technological Requirements for CCR....................120
CCR – Understanding of Application Architecture in Iterated Markets....................121
CCR Framework for Analysis of IT System Components....................122
Analyzing the IT Side of Web Solutions Using the Framework....................123
Cluster Computing as Enabler for CCR....................125

CHAPTER 8: The Human Resource Challenge **127**

Setting the Agenda 127
Modified Organizational Structures 132
Developing and Maintaining Human Capital in the Cyber-Economy 139
Cyber Competences and Capabilities 148
Evaluating HR Initiatives and People in the Cyber-Economy 149

CHAPTER 9: CCR: For Which Companies? **153**

Successful CCR Implementations of the Past Leading the Way 153
Different Departments: One CCR Approach Used 155
Are CCR Projects Suitable for All Industries? 157
CCR: Helping all C-Business Initiatives to Be Successful? 159
CCR in the Area of E-Procurement 160
CCR and E-Selling 164
CCR and Customer Relationship Management 166
CCR and the E-Marketplace 169
CCR and E-Billing 171
CCR Mythology for All Companies – for All Purposes? 173

CHAPTER 10: Cyber-Assessment as a Starting Point **175**

Cyber-Assessment: The Methodology 176
Module One: Industry Analysis 176
Module Two: Internal Analysis 178
Module Three: Analysis and Evaluation of Cyber-Commerce Projects and Options 180
Module Four: Strategic Recommendation for Decision-Making 183

Case Study: eZoka Group **185**

SupplierLinx: CCR in the Area of Collaborative e-Procurement 185
The Strategy 186
The Process 186
The Technology 188
The People 188
Conclusion 189

Case Study: Multi-national IT Company **191**

CCR in the Area of Procurement 191
The Strategy 191
The Process 193

The Technology 193
The People 194
The Results 195
The Future 196

Case Study: US-Based Internet Start-up 199

CCR Helping Internet Start-ups to Grow up 199
The Assessment 200
The Strategy 201
The Process 202
The Technology 203
The People 203
The Future 204

Epilogue 205

Further Reading 207

Index 231

CHAPTER 1

Cyber-Commerce Reframing: A New Paradigm?

Introduction

This chapter aims to give an overview of the book and elaborate why and how it has been written. In this chapter, I will also define the book's perspective and my intentions in order to set the context.

The Cyber-Economy

Chapter 2 describes the Cyber-Economy, setting the stage for the new paradigm of *cyber-commerce reframing*. After discussing the development of information technology (IT) in the context of the Internet, I will reflect on the history, the current status, and the future development of the Internet, as well as on the implications of the World Wide Web with specific focus on those developments causing the required paradigm shift. I then address the evolution of the *cyber-economy*, and advance an important thesis: "The question is not how the technology will change but how people will be able to manage the process of change and evolution?"

The second part of Chap. 2 explains the different forms of commerce, namely direct commerce, indirect commerce, and no commerce. It also describes the different facets of *cyber-commerce* (c-commerce) which are:

- Electronic (e-)commerce
- Mobile (m-)commerce
- Television (t-)commerce
- Pervasive (p-)commerce

This description makes it possible to find a common understanding of the relevant terms and possible trends. I then go on to explain why the days of money overflow in every sort of New-Economy company are over and clearly position CCR – as distinct from *business process reengineering* – as a tool to optimally use and integrate already existing components and systems, one of the main advantages of the new paradigm of CCR.

The Upcoming Cyber-Challenge

The first part of the third chapter focuses on the *c-commerce* bubble, which burst in March 2000. The fear of possibly missing the bandwagon led many companies to invest millions of dollars in quick and dirty implementation of solutions that are now not fulfilling the expectations set in them in terms of providing a specific contribution to turnover. By using practical examples, I describe how harsh business reality destroyed the ambitious dreams of the leaders of the New Economy. I also tackle the reasons for the failure of many former dot-com wonders in the business-to-business and business-to-consumer spheres.

Chapter 3 focuses, furthermore, on experience gained from real projects to illustrate the issues and problems facing the real world. An essential part of this chapter concerns the misunderstandings existing in the market that *c-commerce* is the miracle of the new millennium and that it replaces all the processes and structures of enterprises developed in past decades. The chapter concludes with a discussion of key areas such as finance and human resources, which represent the major challenges for the future of the New Economy.

BPR: The Shortcomings

"A company is a value chain and interacts with other companies in the market." The first part of this chapter focuses on the origins of this insight, starting from Taylor's scientific management approach to Mayo and Homan and their *Principles of Group Behaviour*. These value chains provide the framework for the famous *business process reengineering* (BPR) approach, which forms the basis of this chapter. I will provide a general background on the managerial roots of the BPR paradigm and its basic theoretical concept. I will also discuss environmental factors such as:

- Market challenges
- Increasing competition
- Companies' consequent cost-cutting orientation

all of which led to the increased popularity of *enterprise resource planning* (ERP-) systems and, thus, BPR.

The second part of Chap. 4 focuses on developing and discussing arguments, as well as reasons, why the classic BPR approach is now, in all likelihood, no longer adequate for solving the problems either of the New Economy as such or of the New Economy as a part of the Old Economy. References to relevant publications are made to discuss the hypothesis of a requisite shift from the old BPR paradigm to the new CCR paradigm.

Reframing, Not Optimizing

I open this chapter with an overview of my understanding of reframing. I will attempt to make a clear distinction between the reengineering and optimization orientation of BPR and the reframing orientation of CCR, and outline the pitfalls of different optimization tools such as *total quality management* (TQM), the ISO 9000-norm, Six Sigma, and, in particular, of operations research. With particular regard to operations research, I will refer to problem areas such as competition, research, system design, and planning. Clear definitions of the latter terms and techniques, as well as of BPR in particular, are being established in order to create a better awareness and understanding of why a paradigm shift away from BPR to CCR has become inevitable.

Based on the discussion of the above-mentioned topics, it will be possible to create an understanding of the need to challenge conventional thinking in a real sense. This means that the manifold components of a *c-commerce* solution need to be challenged at the outset of a CCR initiative, thus enabling subsequent reframing and ultimately leading to a successful *c-commerce* solution.

Cyber-Commerce Reframing: The Approach

This "core" chapter of the book describes the CCR model and approach. I will reflect on the praetorians of the CCR approach and provide a detailed description of the process by which this new approach has been created. I will then present the *dimension-impact-matrix* (DIM), which is at the core of CCR. Chapter 6 also provides a detailed description of both the verticals of the DIM, such as:

- Strategy
- Processes
- Technology
- People

as well as of the horizontals of the DIM, which include:

- Focus and Objectives
- As-is Assessment
- Definition of gaps
- Development of CCR plan
- Implementation of CCR plan
- Web-based performance measurement

Since CCR is not only a methodology but also a high-level thinking model, this underlying concept will be discussed on a meta-level, focusing on issues and topics important for successful CCR initiatives. In this chapter, I will also attempt to establish a structure for a CCR initiative, but do not claim to provide a perfect process model. In addition, I have chosen to support the CCR paradigm by integrating my own experience gained during various CCR projects.

The New Role of Information Technology

Technology has become a driving force in the New Economy. Chapter 7 discusses the technology (r)evolution from its very beginnings to its current state as a driving force, once more highlighting only those developments and events which have caused, however directly or indirectly, the proclaimed paradigm shift away from BPR to CCR. I will describe how technology is driving *micro*- and *macroeconomic* factors. Using BPR as a basis, this new role of IT is described as an important part of the shift to the new CCR paradigm. This chapter also provides information on interesting trends currently impacting the business world and IT systems, such as application clustering, customer-centric systems, as well as integration and outsourcing. Chapter 7 also takes a more detailed look at the following components:

- Systems and communication components
- Security components
- Information and payment components
- News and exchange components
- Components for servicing applications
- Front-end application management components

Furthermore, the impact of CCR initiatives on the process level of the approach are determined. Chapter 7 concludes with a CCR framework for the analysis of IT system components.

The Human Resource Challenge

Human capital has become the most valuable asset in the New Economy. This chapter discusses changes in the area of *human resources* (HR) and how CCR can help in terms of strategic HR repositioning. It addresses topics such as changing demographics and the emergence of the *Internet generation*. I focus on the impact of these changes on businesses operating in this new environment. Specific problems discussed in the chapter include the management of human capital, change, and innovation. In this context, I critically keynote lean and process-based management approaches and the emerging need for flexibility and learning on different levels, i.e., both on the individual level and on the company or organization level.

In addition, the chapter elaborates on problems related to cultural diversity, strategic outsourcing, and maintaining, developing, and motivating human capital. It also discusses learning in terms of both the individual and organizations. Moreover, I have taken the opportunity to analyze the different types of competencies required in the New Economy and conclude with various methods for assessing *human resources* initiatives and people.

CCR for Which Companies?

While the previous chapters discussed the "whys" and "hows" of the CCR approach, this chapter addresses the question of "who" and "where." It elucidates the areas in which the implementation and use of CCR makes sense. I will support my discussion with reference to successfully implemented CCR projects, the reasons for their success, and why CCR makes sense not only for large multinational players, but also for small start-up companies. I will provide explanations of various *e-business* initiatives in operational as well as administrative areas. Simultaneous to that, I will explain why the use of CCR, which was originally created as a tool for reframing such *e-business* solutions and organizations, can also be adapted to a rethinking and reframing of other types of web-enabled commerce solutions as part of *c-commerce*. CCR is not restricted to New Economy companies.

The second part of this chapter addresses concrete *e-business* initiatives and demonstrates how CCR has enabled pre-set goals, which formerly remained unachieved, to be finally realized. For this purpose, and to provide a more practical perspective of CCR, actual CCR projects which have already been realized are presented as brief case studies.

The first CCR project to be discussed in detail is the reframing of an existing *e-procurement* solution. After explaining the basic principles and advantages of *e-procurement*, I will go on to explain the different levels and dimensions, such as front or back end, at which integration and reframing can take place. Other *e-business* solutions to be discussed include *e-selling* and *customer relationship management* (CRM). In a business environment where competition is tough, CRM solutions have become an important competitive weapon. Unfortunately, their implementation has all too often been rash and, as a consequence, the solutions have not lived up to expectations.

Another *e-business* solution to be discussed in this chapter is *e-billing*, the concept of smart billing processes made possible by the Internet. CCR can be used as a tool to ensure the seamless fit of *e-billing* into a company's solution set.

Further mini-case studies in the area of *m-commerce* serve to underline CCR's versatility, enabling its application in other areas of *c-commerce*. Once again, experience drawn from successfully implemented reframing projects is presented to promote a deeper understanding of operational CCR projects.

Cyber-Assessment as the Starting Point

Chapter 10, which is also the last conceptual chapter in the book, describes *cyber (c-)assessment*, the starting point for CCR and today an integral part of the CCR approach. *C-assessment* refers to the procedure by which current and prospective *c-commerce* activities are analyzed and evaluated. It is used to establish whether a project will enhance or reduce a company's value. After a description of the methodology of *c-assessment*, I will introduce the four different modules of *c-assessment* in detail.

The first module deals with "industry analysis." After explaining the increased need for this module in the New Economy, I move on to a step-by-step explanation of the methodology of this module. The second module, "internal analysis", relates to the analysis and optimization of a company's core processes. I will describe the creation of a so-called *project master plan* and a *value driver analysis*, and explain how, when combined, they can be used to identify value-enhancing and value-reducing activities.

The third module, "analysis and evaluation of *c-commerce* projects and options," discusses the issue of prioritizing projects and options in order to achieve maximum benefit. For the purposes of efficiency, overlaps should be avoided. I will describe not only quantitative, but also qualitative analyses of projects, as well as the evaluation of project fit and involved risk.

The last module, "strategic recommendation for decision making," addresses the dilemma of whether to realize a project in a partnership or whether to realize it within the company. I will take the opportunity to define critical success factors, which should help to solve this question.

CCR Case Studies

Based on examples taken from successfully implemented CCR projects, I have selected three case studies for detailed presentation in order to describe the application of the new approach and promote a deeper understanding of it and its conceptual model. The case studies have been written based on CCR engagements to ensure a realistic and pragmatic description of the activities undertaken. Although I felt it necessary to keep two cases anonymous due to competitional issues, I have nevertheless included them as I found this information valuable to enable you the reader to deepen your understanding of the application of the CCR methodology. I have therefore tried to describe all the relevant details of the CCR process. In addition, Chap. 11 discusses specific issues and dangers, as well as success factors and quick wins.

CHAPTER 2

The Cyber-Economy

Technology defines to a great extent the possibilities that companies have at their disposal for strategy reframing. For this reason, I will take a closer look at the development of information technology (IT), with emphasis on web-empowering technology and the potential leading role it currently holds in the world of the Cyber-Economy (*c-economy*).

The Development of IT in the Context of the Internet

Since most of you, I assume, are more or less familiar with IT through everyday use of the Internet, the World Wide Web, databases, and other empowering, efficiency-enhancing tools, one does not need to start with the *Babbage Machine* to formulate a convincing argument that IT has and will continue to play an ever more dominant role in business. The description of some elementary historical developments, however, is essential for a profound understanding of IT's and the Internet's tremendous potential in the present, as well as the future.

The Internet has revolutionized the computer and communications world like nothing else before it.[1] On the basis of, and in combination with, earlier momentous inventions – namely, the telegraph, telephone, radio, and computer – capabilities could be integrated and a medium created that would enable enhanced collaboration and interaction between individuals and their computers regardless of geographic location.

Its influence does not stop at the outer boundaries of technical computer communications, but spreads out through history as we move toward increased use of online tools to accomplish e-commerce, information acquisition, and community operations.

---

[1] Mougayar, W.: "New Rules. New Metrics. Keeping Score in the New Economy", Business 2.0, September 1998

Origins of the Internet

In October 1962, a computer research program was initiated at the United States' Defense Advanced Research Projects Agency (DARPA) and headed by J.C.R. Licklider, who had first envisioned a globally interconnected set of computers through which everyone could quickly access data and programs from any site during his earlier time at the Massachusetts Institute of Technology (MIT).. DARPA's objective was to develop a decentralized, virtually indestructible *wide area network* (*WAN*), later termed *ARPANET* (Advanced Research Agency Projects Agency Net), which would maintain communication between networked computers, even in the event of some nodes failing.

The U.S. military wished to have a tool on hand that would enable faster and more reliable communication and information exchange between various departments, command units, and intelligence. By implementing this version of a *WAN*, designed to survive a military strike targeting many key facilities, the U.S. military also tried to increase the essential accuracy of information, thereby ultimately enabling a more informed decision-making process. As a consequence, not only troops could be deployed faster, but also resources could be moved with increased speed to where they were needed.

By the end of 1969, and after extensive research on the ARPANET's structure, architectural design, and functions was completed, four host computers[2] were connected up to constitute the initial ARPANET. Computers were quickly added to the ARPANET during the following years, and work proceeded on completing a functionally complete *host-to-host* protocol and other network software.

For the purpose of making the ARPANET work better, communication protocols were needed which would allow networked computers to communicate transparently across multiple, linked packet networks, and could thus meet the needs of an *open-architecture networ*k environment. Therefore, in 1973, DARPA initiated a research program to investigate techniques and technologies for interlinking packet networks of numerous kinds. This was called the *Internetting* project and the systems of networks

[2] Network Measurement Center at the University of California at Los Angeles (UCLA), Stanford Research Institute (SRI), University of California at Santa Barbara (UCSB) and the University of Utah

that emerged from the research were known as the "Internet." The system of protocols which was developed over the course of this research effort became known as the *TCP/IP Protocol Suite*, after the two initial protocols developed: Transmission Control Protocol (TCP) and Internet Protocol (IP).

The TCP was designed to split transferable data into single packets. The IP should generate an "electronic envelope" specifying the sender's as well as the recipient's address. These encoded packets would then be sent to the recipient, sometimes taking various routes, where they would then be decoded with the aid of the TCP/IP information.[3]

One of the focal primary motivations for both the ARPANET and the Internet was resource sharing which, when the two were connected, was far more economical than duplicating the requisite, and extremely expensive, computers. Powerful computers and the existence or construction of infrastructural telecommunication facilities were crucial for technological development. But they alone would not set the stage for an IT revolution. For this to happen, computers needed to be able to communicate with each other. This sort of communication was made possible by the TCP/IP protocol suite.

However, while file transfer and remote login (*Telnet*; *Teletype Network*) were very important applications, electronic mail (*e-mail*) has probably had the most significant impact of all the innovations from that era. E-mail provided a new model of how people could communicate with each other and changed the nature of collaboration, first in the construction of the Internet itself, and later for much of society. A key concept of the Internet is that it was not designed for just one application, but as a general infrastructure on which new applications could be conceived, as illustrated later by the emergence of the *World Wide Web* (WWW).

A crucial change in the development of the Internet was introduced as a consequence of the commercialization of the "network of networks". A great deal of support for the Internet community came from the U.S. Federal Government, since the Internet was originally part of a federally-funded research program and, subsequently, became a major part of the U.S. research infrastructure. During the late 1980s, however, the popula-

[3] Stevens, R. W.: "TCP/IP Illustrated", Addison Wesley Professional Computing Series, January 1994

tion of Internet users and network constituents expanded internationally and began to include commercial facilities. Indeed, the bulk of the system today is made up of private networking facilities in educational and research institutions, businesses, and government organizations across the globe.

In the last couple of years, a new phase of commercialization has taken place. Initially, commercial efforts mainly comprised vendors providing the basic networking products and service providers offering the connectivity and basic Internet services. The Internet has now become almost a "commodity" service, and much of the recent attention has been on the use of this global information infrastructure as a means to support other commercial services.

This has been tremendously accelerated by the widespread and rapid adoption of browsers and WWW technology, allowing users easy access to information linked throughout the globe. Products are available to enable easy provision of information and many of the latest technological developments have been aimed at providing increasingly sophisticated information services over and above basic Internet data communications.

The history and development of the Internet is an exciting story that is by no means over yet. It is astonishing how a network, originally envisioned to support functions ranging from file sharing, made possible by *FTP* (*File Transfer Protocol*),[4] and remote login to resource sharing and collaboration, could in due course have grown to be a commercial success with billions of dollars of annual investment.

The Internet is not destined to wane. New, applicable technologies such as broadband residential access and satellites will bring us new applications. Technology will certainly improve and broaden the Internet and thus – from a technological perspective – ensure its future existence.

There is no single group that manages or finances the Internet. Providers on different levels, however, have merged to form interest groups such as the Internet Society (ISOC), the Internet Activities Board (IAB), the Internet Engineering Task Force (IETF), the Réseaux Associeés pour la Recherche Européene (RARE), or the World Wide Web Consortium (W3C).

---

[4] Robinson, D.: "All about Internet FTP", Library Solution Press, January 1995

They, among others, coordinate standards and collectively pursue international Internet activities

The most pressing question, therefore, is not how the technology will change, but how the process of change and evolution itself will be managed. If the Internet stumbles, it will not be because we lack technology, vision, or motivation. It will be because we cannot set a direction and march collectively into the future. With currently over 50,000 local networks, more than 20 million computers, and 100 million users, this is not an easy task.

The World Wide Web (WWW) and Its Implications

In addition to the fundamental Internet services such as Telnet, FTP, news, and e-mail, the WWW is arguably the most important feature of the Internet. Its development paved the way for the emergence of various commercial, net-based activities, information exchange on a global scale, as well as of worldwide, unlimited communication in the form of chatting, instant messaging, and other tools for quick communication.

The WWW was innovated in 1989 by Tim Berners-Lee and Robert Cailliau of the European Organization for Nuclear Research (*CERN*), Geneva, Switzerland. The idea behind it was to facilitate communication between the CERN's extensive community that today includes about 80 countries and roughly 6,500 scientists who use the CERN facilities.

The chief objective was to provide quick and free access to crucial information such as research projects, experiments, and scientific reports. Moreover, electronic information exchange, coupled with the traditional channels for the exchange of ideas such as at conferences, in coffee rooms, or in front of the blackboard, would complete the spectrum of communication alternatives vital to guarantee smooth interaction.

In 1991, essentially two browsers enabling the download of information on any connected computer were presented to the high-energy physics community via the CERN program library, enabling a whole range of universities and research laboratories to start using them. Many joined in Berners-Lee's plea to develop more sophisticated, user-friendly browsers. The driving force in the improvement of browsers was the *National Center for*

Supercomputing Applications (*NCSA*)[5] at the University of Illinois which, in 1993, released its first version of the so-called Mosaic browser that would run in the X Window System environment.

Shortly thereafter, NCSA also released a version for PC and Macintosh environments. Thus, browsers were made available to a wide range of users and the exponential growth in the use of browsers, and therefore the WWW, was initiated. With the emergence of a common standard know as *hyper text markup language* (HTML)[6], by late 1993, there were over 500 known servers, and the WWW accounted for 1% of Internet traffic – a phenomenal achievement considering the WWW's comparatively recent inception and limited circle of users at that time.

The introduction of HTML brought with it not only the possibility to put information on the WWW, but also new and exciting dimensions opened up for creative web-page design, dimensions which were still unexplored at that time.

Companies became aware of the possibilities (although perhaps not of the opportunities which were to emerge in the future) that the Internet, and with it the WWW, offered them at least in terms of publishing company and product information to a large audience at minimal cost. But they did not have the necessary knowledge to set up attractive or sophisticated web pages. Thus, more and more service companies specializing in web design and web graphics, as well as web creation and web programming emerged. Consultancy companies also recognized this new trend, and climbed on the bandwagon by providing web-consultancy services.

The WWW started to become an economic issue, even though nobody at that time could or would realistically predict the degree to which the web would ultimately change the very nature of almost every company. But the benefits were already evident: e-mail would provide faster, more reliable, and more frequent communication internally, as well as with the outside world. E-mail was the perfect solution for a clearer, quicker, but less intrusive, communication channel. The WWW would ensure, at least in a virtual sense, the company's global presence, and thus greater customer awareness.

---

[5] http://www.ncsa.uiuc.edu/Indices/InsideNCSA/NCSAbrief.html

[6] Musciano, C.; Kennedy, B.: "HTML & XHTML: The Definitive Guide", O'Reilly and Associates, August 2000

The tremendous increase in acceptance and use of information offered via the WWW (by the end of 1994, the Web had 10,000 servers, of which 2,000 were commercial, and 10 million users) demanded better structure and organization of information. Companies such as Yahoo! and Alta Vista appeared, offering web-search engines. For the first time, measurable added value was created as these *portals* (start or entry pages for all kinds of users) provided tools and algorithms for optimizing research work and information search via web-based databases.

An avalanche, with all its destructive force, started to threaten businesses that did not take the WWW seriously, shunned it, or had watched its progress from the sidelines. They ran the risk of being perceived as slow, averse to innovation, and simply "untrendy". A decision had to be made and most opted to catch up with the thought leaders such as IBM or Siemens. Both the Internet and the WWW started to stimulate widespread, large investments.

The number of organizations seeking assistance overwhelmed consultancy companies. They themselves did not really know what the WWW required of businesses and, under time pressure, often incomplete and poorly structured web initiatives were implemented. While some companies were struggling to get their first page on the Web, some tech wizards and visionaries developed the first engines and applications enabling various transactions to be conducted on the Web. Soon, the know-how was transferred to different industry segments. The first segment where such transaction engines were used broadly was the *business-to-consumer* (B2C)[7] segment. When Amazon.com launched its site in 1995, everybody was taken by surprise. Business had never taken place on the Web on this scale since its development in 1989.

Everybody expected the B2C segment to be the one essential web-based business opportunity that would bring about unheard-of revenue streams and incredible growth figures. Two main factors were driving this assumption: On the one hand, companies could market and sell their products worldwide, leading to economies of scale creating additional profit margins; on the other hand, the Internet would bring down the cost of sales and marketing to a minimum.

---

[7] Whitepaper: "The World Wide Scam – Reality Check on Dot.Com Retail Trends", The Standish Group International, April 2001

But companies, still driven to a great extent by consultants, did not realize that the Internet and the WWW represented in actual fact another channel of distribution, and thus had to be an inherent part of the company's overall strategy (i.e., sales and marketing or procurement).

In addition to the progression from passive information dissemination to active transactions via the Internet, a shift from B2C towards *business-to-business* (B2B) occurred. Soon, subsequent terms such as *business-to-government* (B2G), *business-to-associates* (B2A), and *business-to-employees* (B2E), on which I will later expand, would emerge. The stage was set for the evolution of the Cyber-Economy!

The Evolution of the Cyber-Economy

You have no doubt heard and read a lot about the so-called *New Economy*. In general, this term refers to the improved macroeconomic performance of recent years, more favorable inflation and unemployment figures, as well as the apparent acceleration of productivity growth as a result of IT in general, and of the Internet in particular.

On a microeconomic level[8], the New Economy describes a new business world of

- Incubators[9]
- Start-up companies
- Business angels[10]
- Venture capitalists[11]
- "Lock in" phenomenon[12]

---

[8] Spulber, D. F.: "Market Microstructure – Intermediaries and the Theory of the Firm", Cambridge Univ. Press, 1999

[9] Hayhow, S.: "A Comprehensive Guide to Business Incubation", National Business Incubation Association, December 1995

[10] Coveney, P.: "Business Angels: Securing Startup Finance", John Wiley & Sons, June 1998

[11] Laurie, D.: "Venture Capitalist: The Five Stages to Explosive Corporate Growth", Perseus Books, February 2001

[12] Shapiro, C.; Varian, H.R.: "Information Rules a Strategic Guide to the Network Economy", Harvard Business School Press, 1999

- Board members, sometimes barely 25 years old, but earning more than the president of the United States of America

But some of you may ask: What is the Cyber-Economy? Wherein lie the differences of the New Economy? How did it emerge?

The Cyber-Economy is an integral part of the New Economy, the latter constituting the framework within which the former has come into existence and operates. Each is inseparable from the other and, through a mesmerizing interplay, the New Economy and the Cyber-Economy reciprocally influence their respective architecture, design, and development, not to mention their existence. The Cyber-Economy is the centerpiece, the heart of the New Economy, and supplies it with life-essential blood, carrying with it new ideas and ventures, risk-friendly businessmen and women, new technologies, and fresh sources of finance.

The Cyber-Economy comprises the many facets and types of web-based commerce. In a general sense, the following four key terms make up what we called the Cyber-Economy (by the time this book is published, several new forms will already be under discussion and development):

- Electronic (e-) Commerce
- Mobile (m-) Commerce
- Television (t-) Commerce
- Pervasive (p-) Commerce

We are going to discuss each of the above terms in a later part of this chapter.

The Cyber-Economy is driven by a new generation of strategies, technologies, individuals, processes and rules. Neuronal nets will be capable of updating and retrieving essential information automatically; processes will be automated. Machines, for instance, will undertake their own maintenance without the need for any human involvement, thus creating additional value.

What may sound simple is not at all so in reality. Large and long-established companies may find it all but impossible to change their strategies according to the enormous speed with which the increasing use and importance of IT is spurring the economy. Moreover, they may also find that their employees – their human capital – are not sufficiently trained to cope with the new challenges arising.

Start-ups and young companies may find this task easier since their managers and employees might be less averse to risk. But often the lack of management skills and experience in leading a company steers them into "fast and dirty" strategy implementation as pressure from investors for profits mounts.

The Cyber-Economy includes numerous existing, evolving, and yet-to-be-innovated web-based or –enabled businesses. A central factor, and one closely correlated with new contingency factors such as age, education or networking competencies, is the individual and his or her talent and ideas.

While a couple of months ago, the Cyber-Economy was driven mainly by young hotshots selling jobs (i.e., getting the message to the audience and presenting a more or less valid and plausible business case), which would then provide them with the necessary funds to finance their ventures, right now, we have gone back to a more realistic and down-to-earth Cyber-Economy in which business and financial criteria from the so-called *Old Economy* such as turnover, annual profit, and return on investment (ROI) are increasingly used to evaluate *cyber-businesses*. The Old Economy seems to be catching up with the New Economy. Three main factors have initiated this change:

- Impatience with start-up companies
- Intensive e-business competition among traditional companies
- Existing market dominance of traditional firms

After a slow start – which can partly be attributed to traditional companies' large, and pending investment projects for Euro[13] compliance, as well as the introduction of ERP (Enterprise Resource Planning) software – Old Economy organizations have woken up and learned to combine their strengths, such as market power and brand, with new, Internet-driven forces.

Though not alone anymore, the Cyber-Economy is still dominated by young players not afraid to spend millions of dollars for the one *cyber-idea* they believe in. But access to funds has become limited, as investors become more cautious. The economy has become more realistic; but it has lost neither its momentum nor its fascination.

[13] Hellweg, E.: "A Global Guide to Y2K", Business 2.0, January 1999

Given all the enthusiasm and exuberance with which the advent of the New Economy was welcomed by consultants, investment bankers, and other self-proclaimed Internet-literate groups, the term *e-commerce* has often been narrowly, or even incorrectly, defined as a result of time pressure, convenience, or expediency in various customer-winning strategies. Moreover, rapid changes in the Internet and continuously evolving technologies have made it not only unrealistic, but also pointless to reach a permanent definition of *e-commerce*.

The fascination about the potential of the Internet lies in its flexibility: its ability to grow, change, and to improve every second through the input of millions of users and ideas. The nature of the Internet consequently demands a definition of the type of commerce conducted via its medium that does justice to its very nature.

For the purposes of successful *cyber-commerce reframing* (CCR), *e-commerce* would not only be too narrow and rigid a definition, but it also serves little use since it is no longer considered a euphemism for "potential", "immensity", or "the future". New forms of Internet-based or -empowered businesses have already evolved – at least to a certain level of maturity – and will continue to do so over the next few years and beyond; and as such, *e-commerce* as a term is neither adequate nor satisfactory to take into account all future progress of web-based businesses such as mobile (*m*-), television (*t*-) and pervasive (*p*-) commerce.

For these reasons, we are concerned with establishing a definition of the term *cyber-commerce* (not least because a definition of something as intangible as Cyber-Commerce is imperative) in an open-minded and flexible way – in a way that grasps the essential nature of the medium and thus enables its redefinition as it follows its miraculous course over the next few of years.

The Definition of Cyber (C-)Commerce

In a business world where information flow is no longer hindered by geography and where business transactions are increasingly loosening their restrictions across national borders and suffering the ensuing adverse side-effects, changes in the environment in which businesses and organizations operate are constantly taking place. No business model, however perfect it may seem to its creators, is guaranteed to survive the onslaught of ever changing factors directly or indirectly influencing the company's role in the business environment.

Companies, therefore, feel the need to develop strategies that evolve in harmony with changing circumstances; concepts to provide flexibility are required; the approaches projects take to goals, and the objectives themselves, must be variable in order to cope with new challenges. New ways of conducting business – and among them the most preeminent, web-based commerce – are creating opportunities as well as hazards for organizations whose ability to transform is put to a hard and unforgiving test. In such a harsh environment, pursuing plans and initiatives in a resolute way without allowing much space for flexibility may be equivalent to steering a company into insolvency and ultimately into bankruptcy.

E-commerce is about to enter a stage in which it will possibly become rigid, and therefore a threat for companies, since e-commerce covers only a small fraction of the spectrum of business activities that are, and will become, possible through the combination and interaction of various types of technology-based and web-enabled devices. But it is overly applied and existing e-commerce initiatives and solutions are becoming increasingly unsuitable for other forms of commerce combining various types of technologies with the web. One only has to look at the current problems being experienced by various telecommunication companies who invested vast sums of money in obtaining *3G* (third generation)[14] licenses, only to discover that, silently, *SMS* (short message service) has become a trend and is preferred over expensive and slow internet services such as e-mail via a mobile phone. Of course, once mobile Internet access has improved (see Japan's NTT *DoCoMo*),[15] consumers may start using it. But for now, SMS, which has existed since the first mobile phone came on the market, is outperforming its electronic counterpart by generating tremendous revenues. The prefix "*e*" proved not to be the solution for all the telecoms' problems!

In the beginning of the New Economy, there were mainly e-commerce solutions. M-, t-, and p-commerce, however, are demanding ever more comprehensive know-how. But e-commerce is only the basis of electronic business conducted in the New Economy. Because of the variety of freshly

---

[14] Poe, R., "Next-Generation Wireless: No Panacea", Business 2.0, November 2000

[15] Seamus, P., "Who Needs a PC?", Business 2.0, November 2000

developing types of applications, the term *cyber-commerce* (c-commerce) was brought to life.

C-commerce takes into account the whole range of already existing, evolving, and future types of web-supported applications. Cyber-commerce reframing (CCR) is thus a designation for a proactive approach towards new business models and ideas evolving around web-supported applications. It allows small-, medium-, and large-sized companies alike to rethink their strategies in the light of the flexibility necessitated by the speed with which the Internet changes contingency factors.

CCR does not throw a company's existing concepts and strategies overboard, along with its products. It seeks rather to build new starting points, a new basis, including the promising old elements, from which the company can improve its strategies, concepts, infrastructure, and processes. Investments already made within the framework of CCR projects – in particular those in cost-sensitive technology – must not become obsolete.

CCR – in contrast to classic business process reengineering (BPR)[16] – takes up the challenge to optimally use and integrate already existing system and infrastructural components and solutions after the process of rethinking, redesigning, and reframing the original business model.

To truly understand the terms *Cyber-Commerce* – and ultimately *Reframing* – it is essential to discuss each word individually.

Cyber refers to virtual space. Unlike the environment we are working in everyday, where deals are closed with a handshake or exchanging goods and services are exchanged for coins and notes, the Internet is an intangible medium. Information is encoded in bits and bytes, packeted and sent to whoever requests it by either typing a "WWW" address or clicking on a hyper-link. Finally, those packets of information are again decoded. True, without the physical infrastructure, this kind of exchange would be impossible. But devices such as desktop PCs, notebooks, mobile phones, or even the glass-fiber cables transmitting information, are only tools or infrastructural facilities to build the space (virtual marketplace) in which business transactions are conducted.

---

[16] Hammer, M.; Champy, J.: "Reengineering the Corporation – A Manifesto for Business Revolution", HarperBusiness, New York, 1st edition, 1984.

Cyber therefore refers to the space that physical, web-supported devices create and in which we actively interact with other participants.

Commerce in the *Cyber-Economy* takes place in three ways, which will be described in detail below.

Direct Commerce

Direct commerce refers to the type of business activities that most of you may already be familiar with. It comprises "traditional" e-commerce activities such as

- business-to-consumer (B2C)
- business-to-business (B2B)[17]
- business-to-government (B2G)[18]
- business-to-associates (B2A)
- business-to-employees (B2E)[19]

More recently, other forms of web- and telecommunication technology-based activities, namely m-, t-, and p-commerce have emerged. These three, along with e-commerce will be discussed later in this section.

Direct commerce involves two or more parties that, as a consequence of their commercial activities, immediately produce a revenue stream for one or more participants.

Indirect Commerce

Indirect Commerce is found in search engines (Alta Vista, Excite, Yahoo!), free ISPs (Internet Service Provider), online newspapers, and other service providers that may offer something for free. The customer him- or herself is not charged anything for the services provided. He or she, however, may be continuously exposed to advertisements in the form of

[17] Whitepaper: "The Value Propositions of Business-to-Business Dynamic Comerce", Moai Technologies, May 2001

[18] Whitepaper: "Automation of B2G, G2B, C2G, G2C & G2G Payments in the US: The Federal Government Leads the Way", Tower Group, November 2000

[19] Whitepaper: "Knowledge Management Solutions with a B2E, B2B and B2C focus", IDC, July 2000

- Banners
- E-mail newsletters
- Pop-up ads
- Site sponsoring
- Other web-oriented marketing tools

This type of service creates an indirect revenue stream for the company. It is paid not by the customer but by the firm trying to reach potential customers through miscellaneous channels of communication.

But traditional forms of online marketing, in particular banners, have become much less attractive to companies. While almost 8 years ago the first banner on the web site of the Internet magazine "Hot Wired" (whereby visitors were asked to click on a box and then immediately taken to the Internet site of the beer brewery *Zima*) had a hit rate of over 50%, the number today has shrunk to as little as 0,5% overall. Moreover, 64% of all American Internet users opt not to click on any banners at all.[20]

But this does not mean that Internet marketing is about to become obsolete; indeed, quite the contrary. According to the US market research firm *Jupiter*, the Internet will take the fourth spot – just behind TV, radio, and newspaper – in the ranking of advertising channels. Growing online-marketing expenditure reflects this trend. Between 1996 and 2000, companies in the United States increased their spending for online advertising by almost 2000%, from 267 million US dollars to roughly 5.3 billion dollars. Thus, online advertising has become an essential ingredient in companies' marketing mix.

So what's the deal with online marketing? Where is it heading?

New forms of advertising in the Internet have emerged as new technologies, such as *DHTML*, have been developed. Thanks to DHTML, for instance, freely movable elements, such as a dog running across your screen, are possible. Specialist firms like DoubleKlick, which still generates 70% of its sales with banners, expect pop-up ads and site sponsoring to gain in importance.

---

[20] Judge, P. C., "Will Online Ads ever Click?", FastCompany, March 2001, page 182

A pop-up is a small browser window that builds itself up during the downloading process of an Internet site. Unlike the infamous intermissive ads, a pop-up window does not disturb the intended download and can be closed voluntarily. The browser window contains graphics, animations, and sound elements. Well-designed pop-ups reach click rates of 5% and more.

Site sponsoring is relatively new but, according to a research study conducted by PriceWaterhouseCoopers, has already taken up 27% of online-advertising revenues. It is not uncontroversial, however, since on journalistically oriented web pages, the line between editorial content and advertisement is blurred.

E-mail newsletters are another powerful online-marketing tool available to companies. Since Internet users must subscribe to e-mail newsletter services, which are themselves very specific, advertisements can be perfectly tailored to target particular groups.

There are various ways to advertise online. The key to success, however, is to strategically harmonize these new forms of advertising with classic ones such as direct marketing.

No Commerce

Even though no business transaction as such takes place, and as a result no revenue stream exists, organizations, groups of people, as well as individuals may provide information for free. These groups may have philanthropic or other disinterested motives for doing so. Organizations (including not-for-profit and non-governmental organizations), however, may use the web as a billboard for attracting and recruiting people or getting potential customers interested in their products. In this sense, one can also speak of commerce.

Changing Environmental Factors

The organizational environment – the combination of factors or elements that influence the way an organization functions[21] – is becoming ever more complex and dynamic and thus challenges managers like never before.

[21] Mosley, D.; Petri, P.; Megginson, L.: "Management – Leadership in Action", 1996 Collins Harper; p. 77

Even though general environment factors, such as legal/political or economic factors have been relatively stable (the latter at least until recently), changing social (demographic and social forces), international, and technological factors have largely contributed to the dynamics that have kept the business world in motion. While environmental forecasting has grown dramatically in importance, is has also grown in vagueness.

As we saw earlier, technological progress is the driving force of the New Economy; but it is also guilty of making the commercial environment almost impossible to forecast, as well as terrifyingly unmanageable. Technological advances threaten companies that, for decades, have dominated the production and distribution of music, movies, and books; intermediaries are struggling as the Internet and virtual market places are threatening their function in the microeconomic business structure; and former post and telecommunications monopolies are finding it increasingly difficult to keep up with young and dynamic enterprises, both in terms of service and price.

The Internet is transforming and revolutionizing businesses in every sphere imaginable. Suppliers are discovering new customers as the network of networks brings them closer on a virtual level, thus easing negotiations. Competitors are popping up like mushrooms since entry barriers, such as capital or know-how, have been lowered by a new generation of risk-friendly venture capitalists and talented individuals. Employees, who are no longer satisfied with their jobs, simply quit to find professional fulfillment in another, more permissive company. Customers have become increasingly selective as the Internet allows them to compare goods and services at low cost.

The speed of change in a connected economy forces companies to rethink and reframe their whole business models and strategies. Whoever is not capable of using the New Economy to his or her advantage, will find themselves left behind faster than a blink of the eye.

As we have seen, the Cyber-Economy is, up to this moment, made up of e-, m-, t-, and p-commerce activities. Therefore, we will now take a closer look to each of these four forms.

Electronic-Commerce

E-commerce has already been extensively discussed in various books and studies, and therefore we shall only dwell briefly on this topic.

E-commerce refers to all Internet-based, commercial services such as purchasing, selling, and offering goods and services. It must not be confused with e-business, which refers to the support of business processes with the help of the Internet.

Several segments of e-commerce have evolved, the most well known being business-to-business (B2B) and business-to-consumer (B2C).

B2B is relatively self-explanatory; it describes web-based, interorganizational commerce that is supported by technologies such as CORBA (Common Object Request Broker Architecture)[22] and EDI (Electronic Data Interchange), or EDIFACT (Electronic Data Interchange for Administration, Commerce and Transport). As a consequence of B2B, numerous virtual market places such as COVISINT (http://www.covisint.com), an electronic procurement (e-procurement) platform for the automobile manufacturers General Motors, Ford, DaimlerChrysler and Renault/Nissan, have, materialized more or less successfully.

The B2C segment is based on business transactions between businesses and consumers facilitated by Internet technologies. Consumers can shop online for virtually every item on display in traditional bricks-and-mortar stores. Information can be retrieved just by one mouse-click.

B2B and B2C built the basis for all further types of electronic commerce such as business-to-government (B2G)[23], business-to-employees (B2E)[24], and business-to-associates (B2A)[25].

The most interesting, not to mention profitable, of the three is arguably B2G. Governments all across the globe are heavily investing in the technological architecture and infrastructure that will ultimately provide them the

[22] Overview of Cobra at: http://www.cs.wustl.edu/~schmidt/corba-overview.html

[23] Konrad, R., "Will B2G Become the Next 'Big Thing?'", CNET News.com, June 2000

[24] Ransdell, E., "Portals for the People", FastCompany, May 2000, page 366

[25] Seebacher, U.G.: "Anbindung von Handels und Geschäftskonzepten" Speech at the Management Cycle Event, Frankfurt, April 2000

cost benefit of procuring office supplies online, thus circumventing expensive intermediaries, and sending or receiving tax or administrative forms, as well as tax bills via e-mail, thus saving a lot of paper and ink.

E-commerce is by far the most mature of web-based business activities. It laid the foundations for all other currently developing forms – m-commerce, t-commerce, and p-commerce – as well as the ones to come.

Let us now turn our attention to the other three current forms of web-based business.

We will start with mobile (m-)commerce.

Mobile Commerce[26]

Imagine a rainy day in your summer vacation; you have actually planned to spend the day outside in a park with your children playing ball and having a barbecue. The weather forecast, however, is pessimistic and there is no chance of a rain-free park later in the day. Thus, you decide to change your plans. One hour later, you are off with your loved-ones, driving to a large, exciting mall that is one-and-a-half hours away.

But you know that this mall will be crowded on a bad-weather day. And you do not even want to think of the parking situation. You take your mobile phone and reserve a parking lot on the mall's web page you bookmarked earlier. You ask your children what they would like to have for lunch; pizza is the preferred choice. So, on an Italian restaurant's web site, you reserve a table and order a Diavolo and a Quattro Fromaggio, to be ready at 12 o'clock, paying in advance by pressing a few buttons on your mobile phone. In all that hurry, you take the wrong exit and finally find yourself somewhere you have never been before. Once again, your cell phone helps you out by giving you the correct driving directions.

Those are just three of the myriad ways in which a mobile device like a mobile telephone can already partly, and will increasingly, be used in the near future. Companies, having more or less successfully managed to transform in order to take advantage of e-commerce, are now gearing up

[26] Seebacher, U.G.; Büchsenmann, K.: Mobil Commerce – Synonym für Mehwert?, Information Management & Consulting, 2001/2, p. 24 – 27.

for a new challenge: mobile (m-) commerce, i.e., e-commerce conducted with the help of mobile devices.

In the not-so-distant future, many of us will be doing business via cell phones[27] and other personal devices such as digital organizers like the Palm VII. These devices will enable us to do business without the use of a personal computer and are thus about to become wireless wallets.

On the consumer level, there are four main broad categories of m-commerce applications currently emerging: voice recognition, location-based services, wireless portals, and instant messaging.

Voice Recognition

A cell phone, like any other handheld device, is naturally very small. Typing an e-mail or the address of a web page is a very dull and irksome task, as is reading a message on a screen often not larger than a newborn baby's hand. Therefore, a number of m-commerce companies, like BeVocal and Quack, are working on improving voice-recognition programs, especially speech-to-text technologies, for wireless devices. Soon, sending an e-mail may not take much longer than placing a call.

Location-Based Services

The Federal Communications Commission (FCC) required cell-phone carriers to be able to locate any mobile-phone user by the end of October 2001, for the primary purpose of letting 911 operators know where a possible emergency call is coming from. This capacity necessitates the use of either global positioning satellite receivers, triangulation (whereby a cell phone's location can be calculated by examining signals from three different cell-phone towers,), or a combination of technologies.

The clue behind all this is that if wireless carriers can give this information to 911 operators, they could also sell it to businesses of all kind, and in particular to m-commerce companies.

Whenever the whereabouts of a mobile-phone user can be identified, an m-commerce service provider would send advertisements for nearby

[27] Seebacher, U.G.; Büchsenmann K.: Mobile Rechner für Vertreter, Versicherungswirtschaft, 8/2001, p. 580 - 583

clothes shops, grocery stores, or restaurants in the form of an SMS, or any other digital format, to the user's cell phone. Similar, hyper-tailored marketing initiatives are possible once Internet-car-radio has taken off. Movie theaters, fun parks, museums, discotheques, and bars, just to name a few, could then have their adverts on air exactly when the driver is within proximity.

Wireless Portals

At present, surfing the web with a hand-held device is not very convenient, nor very exciting due to enduringly mediocre graphics and bad navigation. But as technology improves, so will wireless web design. One should not assume, however, that wireless Internet traffic will be as high or as frequent as its wired counterpart. Users will prefer to search for a portal – such as Yahoo! or Excite@Home – that perfectly suits their information needs (news, stock quotes and market reports, weather forecasts, etc.), as well as other services such as online flight booking, ticket reservation, or comparison shopping. Some companies (MyAladdin, Visto, and Yodlee) even offer their customers the option to build their own site.

Instant Messaging

Unlike in Japan or Europe, where a single network standard guarantees the compatibility of text messages, US phone service providers still use a handful of incompatible messaging technologies. Moreover, being online wirelessly in the United States costs as much as placing a phone call. (Japan's NTT charges only for data sent.) Both factors have contributed to a reluctance to send messages instantly. Instant messaging's popularity via a PC, however, suggests that there is great potential for businesses once a uniform standard has been introduced and going online has become cheaper than rates charged for a phone call.

On a business level, myriad other m-commerce applications are flourishing. The most prominent are:

- *Mobile inventory management* (enabling businesses to track the location of goods and services such as boxes, packets, or cattle)
- *Proactive service management* (providing applications to collect information on user needs and send it to vendors)
- *Product location* (locating certain items such as TVs, VCRs, or cars)

- *Wireless reframing* (improving business services such as claims adjustment or insurance)

Once several functional components, such as appropriate display, sufficient memory, and communications functionalities, have been introduced and underlying technologies have been improved, m-commerce could really take off. With roughly 350 million mobile devices in use worldwide, 80 million of them in the United States (as of 2000), and projections for this number to rise to 1 billion in the next few years, the foundations for m-commerce have certainly been laid. According to the GartnerGroup, one of the leading market research firms, at least 40% of C2B e-commerce will come from smart phones using the wireless application protocol (WAP) by 2004. Wireless Data and Computing Service (WDCS) projects the annual mobile market to have risen to $ 200 billion by that time.

M-commerce is the next tidal wave that is already shaking up the business world. Would you have ever guessed that banking would be conducted with the help of mobile devices alone? Well, this is happening; take, for example, the German *MobilCom* which, ahead of all other international financial service companies, is gearing up to establish its mobile bank called *MobilBank*.

Television Commerce

Television has thus far been a rather passive medium. With the exception of choosing a program or using the remote control, little active engagement has been sought from viewers. Its potential for active interaction, and therefore also commerce, however, is tremendous.

Let's consider the following example. A television set with broadband cable is connected to the Internet and hooked up to a network of video stores, which themselves have made their movie catalogues available on the web. The viewer could enter his preferred movie, say *The Matrix*, and let a search engine find the stores that have the film in stock and offer the best price. Once the video store is chosen, the viewer could rent the movie by using his advanced remote control, and have it sent directly to his television set via a cable connection. Payment would be done via the screen with a credit card – or, in all likelihood, using a mobile phone!

This model would make it easier for the viewer to rent a movie, as he or she would not even need to leave his home. In addition, video stores could (if they chose to) dispense with cost-intensive physical outlets and instead store all their movies in digital form. This would also enable them to "rent out" movies to any number of people. Moreover, price transparency would ensure a service-based and fair fee. (Subscription would also be possible.)

Interactive TV (ITV)[28] is about to enter the stage. In combination with web technology, a television set is not destined to remain an uncustomized medium of hundreds of options. Signing up for a special service that tracks viewing habits and creates corresponding profiles (much like cookies), a viewer watching the news would be made aware, for instance by pop-up windows on the TV screen, that his or her favorite talk show is currently on air on another channel. Participating in that talk show's discussion would be possible by instant messaging. But at the same time, a brand new song by your son's favorite group is being shown on MTV; by clicking on a banner, you could instantly buy the new track at CDNow or download it directly from that page onto your MP3-player.

As we can see, the possibilities for ITV are virtually limitless. Relatively new, ITV is still in its development. For ITV to become exciting and entertaining, the following guiding principles may be of use.

ITV requires smooth navigation and relevant search results. Thus, a search system and the content it searches should be designed together in order to provide relevant information or products that closely match viewers' needs. The theory behind t-commerce is that video creates the mood and interactivity gives viewers the opportunity to buy. But without the right navigation systems, this positive attitude towards shopping might be lost, as viewers feel confused about where they are taken and the time required to order a specific item. Therefore, t-commerce requires the creation of innovative formats that combine the best of interactivity and conventional television. "Point and click" shopping must incorporate narrative and characters that involve and entertain viewers.

If everything goes right, Forrester Research predicts that by 2004, Interactive TV could already generate $20 billion in revenue. A total of $11 billion would come from advertising, $7 billion from commerce, and $2 billion from subscription fees. For the $91 -billion TV industry, interactive services are a great opportunity.

---

[28] Winfield, G. T.; Lawrence, C. S., "Designing Systems for Internet Commerce", Addison-Wesley Longman, 1998

Pervasive Commerce

Pervasive (p-)Commerce is by far the youngest child of the c-commerce family. Some of you may have never heard this term before; therefore, it needs thorough explanation.

P-commerce refers to business integration of machines, means of transportation, appliances, and the like enabling their self-managed maintenance, as well as repair through automatic, electronic procurement of spare parts, for instance. Moreover, p-commerce comprises an appliance's (i.e., a refrigerator's) ability to order and pay for new, necessary items (groceries) via the Internet without human intervention.

This sounds very much like a robot! In a technical sense, this is true. The key difference, however, lies in communication and decision-making processes.

At *Bayer*, a multinational German pharmaceuticals company, robots search the Internet for the best deal for office supplies. These robots then communicate their results to humans who ultimately make the purchasing decision.

In the new field of p-commerce, robots at Bayer would communicate their results to each other (not to humans) and compare the decision alternatives. Following certain guidelines, the robots would automatically order necessary office supplies, as indicated by inventory robots. Valuable, human working-time would be saved and thus costs reduced in the long-term.

To really understand what is meant by p-commerce, it is helpful to discuss it in the context of the following two examples.

A refrigerator, equipped with a couple of weight-responsive sensors, is programmed to contain a specified variety of basic groceries (milk, bottled water, salad, yogurt, cheese, eggs, etc.) that are placed in a particular area in the refrigerator. The refrigerator is connected to a network of grocery stores. Whenever a certain item is close to being consumed (measured by its weight), the refrigerator automatically orders it anew, searching for the best deal offered by one of the networked grocery stores. A couple of hours later, the new item would be delivered.

After a certain service life, adjusted for intensity of use, the refrigerator could, for instance, also order a new cooling system to be installed by a specialist.

In the aviation and automotive industries, p-commerce finds myriad applications. With the help of *Bragg-Lattice-Sensors*, found in the core of glass-fiber cables, critical and often inaccessible spots in engines can be tested for deformations, stretches, and vibrations. (Bragg-Lattice-Sensors possess one crucial advantage, their *multiplex-capability*: with only one conduction, hundreds of sensors can be approached.) These sensors could automatically detect signs of depreciation (even during a flight) and communicate their results via satellite not only to the next airport's ground staff (mechanics), but also to a contracted supplier of spare parts who would deliver the necessary parts to the targeted airport.

In an industry, like aviation, that incurs huge costs and requires a lot of time for maintenance and repair, the use of intelligent sensors and automation of procurement processes would be a great leap forward. Not only towards full capacity but also towards customer satisfaction.

P-commerce is still in its early development. For it to be a success, it has to be made as easy and convenient as possible. Certainly, one does not wish to program the level of consumption at which the refrigerator should re-order the gallon of milk or the piece of cheese. Moreover, since we probably like changing the type of groceries we consume, re-programming should be convenient. This could be done with the help of a laser pointer translating codes into physical units.

P-commerce definitely requires profound perceptive changes in the way we shop or businesses conduct the maintenance and repair of machines, engines, and equipment. Foremost, we have to put our trust in technology's capabilities. Therefore, it will undoubtedly take some time until p-commerce will be recognized as a great alternative to traditional ways of procurement. But its advantages are clear and definite, and therefore business will adopt p-commerce.

Several interesting and innovative ideas and concepts have likely emerged in the time between writing this book and it finally reaching the reader. Most likely, some of the ideas and concepts described here as new and innovative will probably already have been adopted as an integral part of a New Economy which is gathering ever greater momentum.[29]

[29] Amor, D., "Internet Future Strategies: How Pervasive Computing Will Change the World", Prentice Hall Computer Books, August 2000

CHAPTER 3

The Upcoming Cyber-Challenge

Within a year, the NASDAQ Composite lost more than 50% of its value when dark clouds over both Wall Street and Times Square first shadowed the golden horizon of *New Economy investors*. Companies, organized or re-organized around the Internet all across the globe (but in the United States in particular), finally saw themselves in the middle of a grandiose financial hurricane that down-to-earth economists and analysts had long been predicting. Hope, exuberance, arrogance, as well as insatiable appetite for ever more of investors' money, made them deaf to rationale. Finally, most investors and businesses in the world got in contact with reality again. *Bang!* Welcome to the cyber-challenge!

Did anyone of you invest in the so-called *New Economy* sector (Internet, information technology, telecommunications, etc.) prior to March 2000? Did you invest in Internet start-ups or Internet supplier or software companies producing, for example, *customer relationship management* (CRM)[1], or electronic (e-) procurement[2] software in particular? If you did so and you did not withdraw your money before March 2000 then let me welcome you to the big international community of people first surprised, then worried, and finally desperate as the *big bang* happened on NASDAQ in the days of March 2000.

Within the last couple of years, a second industrial revolution has taken place. Famous scientists, sociologists, and economists had predicted its advent, but even they were surprised by the revolution's dynamics.

It was back in 1989 that some publications first wrote about the World Wide Web (WWW), raised it to the zenith of computer science, and called it the miracle of the 1990s enabling quicker research, communication, and information exchange. But would these authors have imagined that, within such a short period of time, the WWW would be the starting point for such

---

[1] Brown, S. A.: "Customer Relationship Management: A Strategic Imperative in the World of E-Business", John Wiley & Sons, May 2000

[2] Neef, D.: "E-Procurement: From Strategy to Implementation", Prentice Hall PTR/Sun Microsystems Press, May 2001

profound social, political, technological, as well as economic changes as can be witnessed today? Probably not. The "inventors" and initial beneficiaries of the Internet and the WWW certainly were visionaries. They did not, however, anticipate that their combined efforts would trigger a revolution affecting so many spheres of life.

As the Internet and the WWW developed, grew, and improved, more and more people – spurred by widespread enthusiasm and hardly paying any attention to the reasons – realized that a train they had to jump on was starting to leave the station. Everybody was apparently talking about the Internet, the WWW, e-mail, and new terms such as e-procurement, e-selling, and the like.

Companies' IT departments were asked by senior managers to develop or acquire the required know-how to get the company up to speed with the train. Technicians were expected to check what had to be done to get into a position to use the Internet and to develop concepts of how to take advantage of this new medium. They themselves started to become visionaries in their respective fields of interest, generating amazing, though naturally incomplete, ideas. The Internet and the WWW were still mainly analyzed from a technical perspective. Other essential aspects were neglected.

Given the recent battering sustained by any stocks even superficially related to the Internet, you may wonder what has happened to the computer and business communities' dreams and wishes? Therefore, I would like to present my view of these developments below in the first part of this chapter. This will be followed by a consideration of the two most prominent cyber-challenges: Human resources and finance. Whereas the latter challenge will be discussed in more detail, I will provide only a sketch of the former, since a later chapter, Chap. 8, is dedicated to this subject.

Cyber-Challenge: Dreams and Reality

To the great masses, new inventions and the ensuing social, political, or economic changes, have never announced themselves with much fanfare. They just happened, and suddenly one found him- or herself in the middle of some more or less deep transformation process. Thus it was with the Internet, and later the WWW.

One day, I read a newspaper article about the Internet. I tried to get some more information on it and, above all, I wanted to see what the Internet looked like. While the former task was not that difficult, the latter proved to be more problematic given that only research or educational centers and big companies had access to the Internet. As so many other people apparently did, I gave up on the Internet and concentrated on what at the time appeared to be far more interesting computing issues (MS Office, for instance). However, when tools (i.e., browsers) like MOSAIC became available and made surfing the WWW easy, I regained my interest in the Internet and the WWW – and so did a lot of multinationals.

First movers in creating web pages were the big companies such as IBM, General Electric, Ford, as well as small "one-man-shows". As we saw in Chap. 2, they initially developed simple-structured, low-end graphic Internet appearances for their companies. Lacking the know-how, technology and software companies were consulted to design and webmaster more sophisticated sites. These software companies were either working on software facilitating HTML programming like *Pixelpark* [3], or on the know-how to develop high-end web pages for other companies such as *Razorfish*.

Initially, emphasis was put mainly on design. The goal was to be perceived as a thought-leader, an innovator. Internet initiatives and projects were set in motion and soon other benefits and business opportunities were discovered. Nevertheless, the sites did not produce anything but costs. The impact of individual web pages on consumer behavior could be neither tracked nor measured. The media started to condemn the Internet as a useless money-sucker.

All of a sudden, surprising news arrived: Some Internet entrepreneurs were generating a turnover! By creating traffic on their sites and selling advertisements on the basis of a ratio of potential viewers to traffic, some companies developed a business model that apparently worked. The business age of the Internet had arrived and with it its *irrational exuberance* [4].

Since then (1994), huge Internet projects have been realized with varying degrees of success, big contracts signed, and billions of dollars invested in software and IT, all with the primary aim of getting the biggest piece of the

[3] www.pixelpark.com

[4] Shiller, R.: "Irrational Exuberance", Broadway Books, April 2001

Internet "pie". In 2000 alone, European businesses spent over $533 million on e-commerce software.[5]

Were there any business models? Of course! Or have you ever heard of anybody closing a million-dollar deal without such an essential piece of information? Most of the business models that were developed on the basis of Internet concepts, however, were already obsolete by the time they were presented to the board or investors. This was not only because of market dynamics – although they played an important role as well – but rather because unrealistic growth projections for e-business were used since nobody had either any long-term experience with the Internet or a clue where it was heading. (This realization was also reflected in 2001 whereby many research companies were becoming increasingly defensive and less bullish when asked about figures on the future potential of B2C, B2B, B2E, B2G and B2A markets.)

Market dynamics are a second factor largely contributing to the failure of many business models. Due to the pace at which the Internet changed the business world day by day, business models that were developed at the beginning of Internet projects would easily become invalid by the time the "solution" – a portal or a marketplace – went live. The prerequisites for making the model work, and ultimately profitable, simply changed without organizations recognizing it.

But why, then, did so many people invest so much money in projects that were, by most standards, mere adventures?

A survey[6] conducted among IT specialists in large European companies revealed something very surprising: Most of the IT experts did not really know what the company's strategic goals were and could not act accordingly. Moreover, executive managers, facing a situation in which young companies like AOL were buying old behemoths like Time Warner, were forced by the overall market hype to implement Internet-related projects without much planning or regard for how these projects would fit into the company's overall strategy, or any clear understanding of the results.[7] And who would really think about the costs when investors' punishment for no

[5] Frost & Sullivan Report 3887 (09/00), Press Release September 2000

[6] CIN, Software & Computing Magazine 20/2000 (May)

[7] CAP Gemini, Computerwoche 20/2000 and FORSA, Advertising & Selling 05/23/2000

e-action – which, as was seen happening to others, could wipe off millions of dollars in market capitalization within a few minutes – was hanging over one's head like a Damocles sword?

This applied to *Old Economy* companies. But what about the start-ups? How did they help to create the financial mess we are currently experiencing? Two companies are "exemplary".

Some of you may recall the story of boo.com, a UK based apparel company that sold mainly sport clothes via its page on the WWW to end consumers. After boo.com had been operating for a couple of months, the star of the New Economy ceased to shine as brightly and eventually closed down, selling off all its assets including the URL (uniform resource locator) domain.

What happened? Boo's goods were not really cheaper than those in physical stores because shipping and handling was quite expensive. Additionally, logistics and distribution did not work well either. Above all, boo's strategy of entering almost every European country's market swallowed a lot of money. Of course, staff did not dispense with much luxury either. Grandiose meetings, rather resembling parties, were held regularly at different places all around the globe. Naturally, staff would travel first-class.

Boo.com burned cash crazily. After some time, the company had simply run out of money.

BeautyScene.com happened to experience the same brutal fate as boo.com. This U.S. company sold cosmetic products as well as fragrances via its Internet site. BeautyScene had to deal with increasing competition and powerful, hard-playing companies like L'Oreal. Decisive in its failure, however, was its unusual finance strategy. Entirely financed by private investors, BeautyScene.com started operating before it had raised all the necessary funds. When prospects for the company turned bleak, BeautyScene did not succeed in raising additional money. Finally, it simply starved of cash.

Both business cases share two characteristics that determined their collapse. First, positions at the top managerial levels of both companies were held by relatively young and inexperienced people whose only reason for going into business (and public) was probably the expectation of being bought by a big company and receiving a fat compensation package. Second, their financial strategy was superficial. Boo.com and BeautyScene thought that they could tap the capital market again whenever they ran out of money. This proved to be a false, highly arrogant, and ultimately suicidal assumption.

Boo.com and BeautyScene.com were the forerunners to a development that forced the business-to-consumer segment to its knees and triggered the freefall in e-businesses' share prices.

B2C: The Cyber-Flop

Since March 2000, the business world has resembled a financial slaughterhouse. Billions of dollars have been wiped off the wealth of companies and individual investors as a result of the major international indexes' terrible decline. Skepticism about everything either starting with the formerly magic prefix "*e*" or including a "dot" and a "com", which has ultimately led to the destructive tidal wave sweeping the NASDAQ or Germany's *Neuer Markt* (*NEMAX*), was triggered largely, though not exclusively, by overall profit warnings from the B2C segment of e-commerce. Boo.com and BeautyScene.com were just the first two of myriad Internet start-ups that, for one reason or another, did not manage to steer themselves correctly in the New Economy. Other B2C behemoths (beyond.com, pets.com, e-toys.com, and lastminute.com), previously considered unwaveringly settled and positioned in the New Economy, followed suit. By the beginning of 2001, almost every B2C company was affected by investors' unforgiving reluctance to expose themselves to any further risk. In February 2001, the last ship, which had always been perceived as unsinkable, amazon.com, showed cracks in its hull.

But what went wrong with B2C business models? Were there not brilliant ideas underlying and bright people behind those *business-to-consumer* initiatives? How could it happen that something thus praised by the business community just two years previously, would ultimately disrupt and halt the United States' longest peacetime expansion?

B2C is not all bad. Within this segment, there lie great opportunities and benefits for businesses and customers alike. Companies jumping into the cold water without any warm-up, however, did not think about the countless possible hurdles and how to approach them. Already in full speed and backed by the claim of *new economists* that the business cycle was dead and new rules would apply, they seemed to prefer to drag the obstacles along rather than jump over them.

The main obstacles to B2C were:

- Experience
- Security
- Technology (speed and capacity)
- Costs
- Distribution
- Strategy

All of the above reasons for the troubles encountered by B2C companies are closely interrelated. Technology affects experience and security as it does costs; distribution determines strategy and vice versa and largely influences costs.

Experience

The "shopping experience" on the Internet is a rather mediocre one. Of course, ordering a CD or a book online and then having it delivered 24 hours later for the first time is definitely exciting. (I still recall the first time I ordered online with Amazon. It was indeed a good experience.) But the fascination runs thinner with every additional order or click via the Internet. Online stores such as amazon.com or e-toys.com have certainly changed their web-page design several times since their inception. The former has even stretched its brand and now offers drugs, toys, and home appliances beside the traditional products (books, CDs, and videos). But shopping on sites such as amazon.com's has essentially remained the same dull process of clicking on an intangible, graphic item and ordering it with the support of a keyboard and a mouse.

Online shopping cannot replicate the social functions usually associated with "real" shopping. One does not bump into friends with whom one can chat, maybe about Hugo Boss's new fragrance one just purchased; neither does the smell of a fresh slice of pizza from the food court awaken your appetite; nor are you instantly gratified by your purchase since virtual shopping requires you to wait for at least a couple of hours. These reasons merge into one conclusion: Online shopping cannot and will not replace real shopping any time soon. The assumption that most of the Internet users will conduct their shopping online is illusory. The initial hype has given way to reality. Companies engaged in business-to-consumer transactions failed to generate a constant revenue stream leading to much needed profits.[8]

Security

Security has long been a key issue for online shopping. Even though there has been no major case of credit-card abuse to date, and new forms of online payment such as smart cards and digicash have been developed (though their use is not widespread), people are reluctant to enter their credit card information online. Particularly people in their 40's and 50's are skeptical. Hence, their children, who would constitute the broadest customer base for online retailers, are not allowed to shop online either.

Online security is an issue currently receiving intensive attention and will not remain on the priority list for long. But it has also slowed down acceptance, and thus the profitability, of online shopping.[9]

Technology

Technology is naturally a decisive factor for electronic retailers (*e-retailers* or *e-sellers*). It has been essential for both the "shopping experience" and "security" discussed earlier and, in consequence, has shaped online shopping's unrealized success. Two factors have played a defining role: Speed and capacity.

In the early days of e-retailing or e-selling, most Internet users were still hooked up to the network of networks via a dial-up modem. Slow and unreliable, much of the potential attractiveness of Web pages in terms of *Flash* graphics or other eye-catching Web-design software applications was lost. (The rapid spread in the use of cable modems or DSL lines will in due course eliminate this problem.) Yet, start-up e-retailers failed to meet customers' expectations.[10]

---

[8] Daniel-Falk, L.: "Merchandising Strategies for the Competitive Nineties 2: Creating the Total Shopping Experience for the Savvy Nineties Shopper", RTW review, June 1997

[9] "Online Shopping Worries: UK Style", eMarketer, December 2000

[10] McLaughlin, L.: "Broadband Usage Spikes", Business 2.0, February 2001

Costs

Online retailers and other B2C businesses were convinced that their business models must be profitable because of the sheer fact that they would cut shopfront costs and intermediaries and distribution would be cheaper. They (and unquestionably their consultants as well), however, oversaw the huge costs involved in servicing a Web site and ensuring its reliability. Moreover, the success of an e-commerce venture depends heavily on smooth logistics and distribution. Acquiring and maintaining the right channels of distribution is not only a very complex and time-intensive task, it is also extremely costly. Furthermore, there are also considerable marketing expenses. The only asset online shops had was a dot.com in their name; this fact alone would not make customers aware of their respective brands in the ever-increasing jungle of start-ups and *IPOs* (initial public offering). E-sellers needed to spend fortunes on customer-acquisition activities. These were all costs that consultants and investment bankers apparently did not expect or neglected – but they broke the neck of most B2C businesses.[11]

Distribution

Distribution is without a doubt the key element of a retailer's triumphant online strategy. Christmas 1999, however, showed that most e-tailers did not incorporate (and to some extent still have not) satisfactory delivery processes in their business model.

Lacking the energy and know-how, most online retailers initially outsourced the whole tiresome business of order checking and distribution. Outsourcing proved to be neither very cost-effective, nor did traditional systems of distribution work for online retailing. Here, items were not delivered in palettes and in bulk to shops. E-tailing required single items such as books, CDs, flacons, and the like to be shipped quickly and with utmost care. Unspecialized logistics firms failed in doing both, and failed expensively.

Passing additional costs on to the customers was not an option since online retailers needed to convince Internet users that they would benefit financially from ordering online. Charging extra for better service was not an option, added to which more and more cases of late or no delivery oc-

[11] Welte, J.: "Be True to Your School", Business 2.0, August 2000

curred. Foremost, customers would not hesitate to change retailers as they could easily compare prices via the Internet.

The "natural" conclusion for B2C businesses was to take care of distribution themselves. Amazon started to erect the next of what would become seven warehouses in total in America, while *Webvan*, an online grocery store, drafted plans for 21 warehouses across the nation. Gigantic expenses were underway.[12]

Strategy

Thousands of consultants were employed to draft sound and promising e-business plans and strategies. Spurred by *e-nthusiasm* and fat fees, a lot of these consultants' plans rather resembled the ones *James Bond* characters such as *Dr. No* or *Goldfinger* would aspire to in pursuit of world domination. Some businesses were smart and started operating locally to test their business models and customer response (HomeRuns.com and Streamline.com in Boston). The majority of B2C businesses, however, wanted to spin their net around the world without delay, all the while lacking a comprehensive understanding of the diverse cultures and naturally varying tastes of international customers. The Internet was understood to be a universal, cosmopolitan medium without regard to national boundaries; and so were its users (customers).

During meetings with consultants, were there any emergency plans, fallback positions, or at least alternatives, discussed? Probably not. With so many, virtually inexhaustible sources of finance (venture capitalists, business angels, corporate and individual investors, banks), there was no need for alternatives. Presumably, money would be provided until the original strategy would generate profit. This assumption proved to be hazardously wrong!

All of the factors cited above – mediocre "shopping experience," security concerns, technology bottlenecks, costs incurred for servicing a Web page and marketing, various distribution dilemmas, as well as incomplete strategies – made B2C companies, especially e-tailers, fail in their ventures.

---

[12] Scheuermann, M.: "Manufacturing & Distribution in the New Economy", Speech held at the Marriott Thruway, June 2000

As investors realized that their beloved business-to-consumer companies were going bust, new investment alternatives within the Cyber-Economy were sought. B2C was expelled from investors' hearts and business-to-business (B2B) took its place.

Yet Another Cyber-Debacle: B2B

In early 2000, investors were already weary about the long-term viability of business-to-business e-marketplaces. Throughout most of 2000, former *golden calves* such as Ventro Corporation[13] were closing down electronic exchanges as venture capitalists sought to redefine their strategies for funding B2B marketplaces and other investors were withdrawing financial sources.

Suprisingly for many of you may be the following example of CommerceOne (C1). Heavily investing in marketing, annoying partner companies as well as clients with almost weekly and very colorful emails inviting to join for the cyber cafe – in order to hear more about their products and become for another time victim for their marketing force. C1 was broadly promoting their global marketplace and one was to a certain extent believing C1 is a special new economy firm. But I cannot forget one meeting, it was a huge C1 conference in Berlin in 2001. During this meeting I was introduced to Mark Hoffmann, CEO at C1. As we were talking Mark gave me his C1 business card and in the same instance another one showing his name but another company. He just said: "...and that's my new company, I am starting!" This to me answered a lot, reflecting the overall idea for C1, similar to many other start-ups: Blow it up and just get rid of it! No more than that.

B2B is yet another example of companies' failed e-business models and strategies, as well as their implementation.

There were numerous reasons for many B2B marketplaces to fall short of expectations.

[13] Welte, J.: "Ventro's Hopes for Bailout", Business 2.0, February 2001

Cyber-Darwinism

The simplest reason was that there were too many e-marketplaces for every single industry. One had only to name an industry and could be sure that it would have at least one, if not two, three, or even ten B2B exchanges. Too many B2B exchanges were chasing too few transactions. Industries were fragmented and corporations did not know with whom to do business. Naturally, the weakest and most ill-prepared e-marketplaces fell victim to the Darwinian rule that the fittest would survive. The fittest proved to be the ones that were generating enough content and traffic to thrive. Industry giants were obviously favored in both aspects.

Incomplete and Marginal Transactions

For various reasons, some transactions, mostly settled offline between the buyer and the supplier, were never completed. According to Frank Florence, vice president and general manager at Interwoven Inc., Sunnyvale, California, only 4%–5% of Web marketplaces were doing a fully integrated transaction, tied into the back end and deleting from inventory.

Financial, as well as technical, strains made full integration of enterprise resource planning (ERP) systems or supply chain software difficult. The result was that integration was implemented superficially as back-end accounting, inventory, and other systems were often not tied perfectly to the exchange. The consequent transaction problems scared a lot of potential participants away from digital marketplaces and back to traditional ones.

According to the *Economist* magazine, an estimated 80%–90% of all business goods and services are traded through long-term contracts (one year or more). The public "spot" markets, on which too many B2B exchanges focused, constitute just a tiny fraction of one-to-one contract deals. These deals are difficult to conduct via the Internet.

A lot of B2B marketplaces thus built their business models around only a marginal segment of transactions. Consequently, the big companies that would ultimately provide vital revenue streams and liquidity stayed away and continued to negotiate deals as usual.[14]

[14] Kellher, R.: "Group Predicts B2B Market Collapse", The Irish Times, July 14th 2000

Big Brother

The Federal Trade Commission (FTC), as well as the European Commission, made very thorough investigations into some of the big digital exchanges such as COVISINT[15] – *Big Three's* version – for potential antitrust violations. Although undoubtedly necessary, these investigations worried many of the smaller and less powerful participants who did not want to see themselves being held legally accountable for the bigger players' possible temptation to fix prices.

The Human Factor

Beside the issues of technology, cost, and regulation, there was another, often underestimated yet crucial reason for the malfunction of B2B exchanges.

Suppliers were not only skeptical and disbelieving that they would profit as much as the big-name buyers; they worried that exchanges would erode their margins as price transparency and comparison was made extremely easy (and cheap) via the Internet.

Byers were equally concerned. They knew about the technological and financial troubles of suppliers to integrate ERP, customer relationship management, and supply chain management systems into the trading exchange and were therefore worried about suppliers' unreliability and inability to fulfill commitments.

The advent of B2B marketplaces required organizations and people to change the way they had been doing business for generations. With so many venture capitalists and investors fleeing B2B, they opted instead to do business as usual.

These four reasons – cyber-Darwinism, incomplete and marginal transactions (technology), big brother, and the human factor – coupled with

- Unrealistic budget forecasts
- Immature standards
- Political infighting
- Lack of consensus[16]

made B2B the next bitter disappointment of the Cyber-Economy.

---

[15] www.covisint.com

[16] Source: AMR Research Inc.

In recent years, we have seen companies that funded more and more projects, spending – and in some cases wasting – millions of dollars. Inaccurate forecasts and market dynamics were the most important factors leading to superficially planned and realized Internet solutions. Marketing and "me-tooism" motivated decision-makers to go for highly risky strategies without much consideration. As a consequence of high investment, unrealistic expectations were nurtured. But, of course, the bubble had to burst, which it did – and for good. Now is the time to reframe these B2B solutions in a cost-oriented and contingent way!

In addition to myriad other factors – be they political, legal, or environmental – companies in the Cyber-Economy are facing two overwhelming yet critical *cyber-challenges*: The *human resource challenge* and the *financial imperative*. Since the former will be discussed in greater detail in Chap. 8, I will only sketch the main problems in this chapter. I will take more time to elaborate on the financial cyber-challenge.

Human Resources: The Cyber-Key

As we have just seen, the *human factor* – among others – played a determining role in the downfall of both B2C and B2B.

Whereas in the case of B2C it was the customers who were disappointed with how the goods and services were offered, B2B went "bankrupt" because suppliers, distributors, and other key participants did not want to make the changes required by the advent of digital marketplaces.

A company, however, does not have to deal only with its task environment. Its internal human resource (i.e., employees) is a, if not *the*, essential component. Employees do not only perform their designated tasks – be they physical or mental in nature. They also shape a company's culture and directly influence the general public's, the customers', as well as potential employees' perception of the company through interaction with theses groups on various communication levels and via various channels. Moreover, employees can undoubtedly be valued as any company's most precious asset. The combination of their know-how, skills, character, and network makes them unique and irreplaceable. Effective *human resource management* (HRM), which refers to the process of planning, organizing, leading, and controlling personnel, is consequently needed to put the company in a good market position and keep it there.

The Cyber-Economy, however, challenges HRM in each of its aspects and requires it to be re-framed in order to preserve, or even enhance, its essential function within an economy dominated by technology and scarcity in numbers of skilled people.

For a more detailed analysis of the *Human Resource Challenge*, please see Chap. 8.

The Financial Imperative

With investors fleeing turbulent stock markets and seeking shelter once again with bonds, funds, and other securer forms of investment during the past years, around $4 trillion has been wiped off the value of American shares alone, it becomes gradually more strenuous for start-ups and companies targeting the e-business market to raise the necessary capital to finance their ventures. Besides, traditional sources of finance – banks, in particular – are closing their once wide-open doors to young entrepreneurs in the light of the huge piles of bad debts they have been left to confront. There has been a clear deterioration in the quality of lending and default rates are the highest since the last recession.

In theory, America's double-pillared financial system, with its well developed capital markets, should make it easier for firms to switch sources of finance. If banks were to decrease lending, capital markets could be tapped and vice versa. The burst of the tech bubble, however, has dealt a heavy blow to both pillars, leaving nothing but financial drought.

The deteriorating state of the banks is of particular concern since banking is supposed to be the more rational of America's two financial pillars. While in the last year the stock markets have been driven by a lot of psychology – and increasingly so since individual investors, often without proper knowledge in trading shares, have appeared on the scene – the credit sector was meant to be stabilized by economically (thus rationally) thinking professionals.

Distress in the derivatives[17] market and deteriorating credit quality, both for marketable debt and bank loans, have left banks vulnerable to further squeezes.

[17] Derosa, D. F.: „Currency Derivatives: Pricing Theory, Exotic Options, and Hedging Applications", John Wiley & Sons, October 1998

Corporate lending to players in the *Old Economy* is still in relatively good shape. Firms operating in the IT, telecommunications, Internet, and logistics sectors have been shunned and denied necessary credit.

As we saw in Chap. 2, IT has played a key role in the emergence and later in the development of the Cyber-Economy. Investment in, and the promising application of, new technologies did not only spur the credit markets, but it also naturally boosted the technology-laden indexes, NASDAQ and NEMAX. A virtuous cycle came into being.

Credit would make investment in IT possible; IT, in turn, would enhance companies' effectiveness and efficiency. On a macroeconomic level, productivity would be raised by the application of (information) technology.[18] (Although the productivity issue is still disputed, talk about it in the media and among economists contributed to the cycle's completion.) The widespread assumption that IT raises productivity, and thus lowers unit costs and consequently inflation, lured investors to pump ever more money into the stock market as they were made to believe that the traditional business cycle had been blown to pieces. Increasing market capitalization through the stock markets' boom was sufficient "collateral" for banks to extend loans. The cycle was about to start again.

This virtuous cycle, which turned rather vicious, had not only widespread economic, but also political and social implications which will be dealt with in greater detail in Chap. 7, *The New Role of Information Technology*.

Let us return, however, to the financial imperative.

The challenge for start-ups in the Cyber-Economy, therefore, lies in regaining the trust of the capital markets – especially also taking September 11 in to consideration, an event striking down the existing level of trust back down again dramatically – as well as of banks, once the latter's messy situation has been turned around. Convincing business models and strategies, as well as flexible implementation, are required to get business going again and to avert the harmful effects of the current economic situation on both enterprise, investor action, and innovation.

[18] Stamp, D.: „The Invisible Assembly Line: Boosting White-Collar Productivity in the New Economy", Amacom, 1995

The Matchmakers

An important role in the process of matching start-ups and potential investors in the Cyber-Economy, as well as in reanimating it, is played by so-called *catalysts*. Unlike fundraisers who are actively engaged in the process of searching for sources of finance, catalysts are people who use their extensive network of people to bring potential investors in contact with start-ups. Given the nature of their work, consultants are particularly well suited for the tasks of a catalyst.

Large consulting firms are approached by various kinds of businesses seeking advice in corporate, political, or legal affairs. The background information most consultants have on their clients (or "accounts") can indeed be helpful in bringing together, say, a bank and a software firm. Consultants would screen both companies and could then decide whether a win-win situation with profound synergy effects would be created or not.

A positive effect of consultants doing the job of catalysts is that they analyze companies more scrupulously in an attempt to avoid the negative effects that recommending a "poor match" could have on their own network. A long-term approach to project implementation would follow. Based on the described contingency situation a new generation of small firms providing excellent corporate finance services for start-ups, technology driven companies as well as SMEs of other sectors is emerging. These companies are focusing on funding management – raising money from public parties such as regional fundings or sector specific fundings, venture management, and sales and distribution consulting.

This book constitutes a sound guide for developing new concepts and re-framing existing ones. In the following chapter, I will present arguments to highlight the shortcomings of an existing tool: *business process reengineering* (BPR).

Chapter 4

BPR: The Shortcomings

For any description of the history of reengineering, it is crucial to provide a general understanding of the basic theoretical concept of the term "*reengineering*": A company is a value chain and interacts with other companies in the markets[1].

Where did this understanding originate? Some explanation is necessary.

Let us start in the past with F.W. Taylor and his definition of scientific management[2], followed by scientists like H. Fayol and their point of view, especially the administrative theory of management[3], to identify the roots of cyber-commerce reframing (CCR) and business process reengineering (BPR). Of course, we must not forget Mayo and Homan, who studied and defined principles of group behavior[4]. Finally, we will talk about management ideas which defined key inputs for the reengineering process in the late 1980s, and which are still influencing us today: The theory of behavioral principles for individuals and groups[5]; the system theory; describing a company as a complex of co-operating entities in correlation with external entities[6]; the influence of situation-based conditions on the definition of business strategies[7]; statistical surveys among top companies in the 1980s which helped to define critical success factors; and, finally, the IT revolution and its influence on managerial thinking.

While we are taking a brief look at these concepts that ultimately had an enormous impact on the development of BPR as a management principle and idea, we should not forget that business has become truly global in

---

[1] Becker, W.: "Strategisches Management, 2nd edition", Bamberg 1995
[2] Taylor, F. W.: "The Principles of Scientific Management", New York 1911
[3] Fayol, H.: "Administration Industrielle et Générale", Paris 1916
[4] Mayo, G.E.; Homan, G.C.: "Principles of Group Behaviour"
[5] Roethlisberger, F.J.; Dickson, W.: "Management and the Worker", Boston 1934
[6] Barnard, C. I.: "The Functions of Executive", Cambridge 1938
[7] Stoner, J. A.: "Management, 2nd edition", Engelwood Cliffs 1982

recent years.[8] Older business ideas were developed in an isolated way, influenced by regional thinking and cultural ideals. Today, business management scientists are still talking about specific, regionally-based business models that are to a certain extent very different (e.g., the U.S., Japanese, and Arabian business models, among others[9]).

Ultimately, it is important to understand the business management models as products of their time. These models were generated by people thinking and acting in specific situations that were themselves based on specific contingency situations[10]. A perfect example would be the production concept of Henry Ford. Using production lines and a work force that was trained to follow only very few but highly specific production steps in a short time, mass production was first established in times of upcoming mass markets and unified consumption wishes. These times are over and, today, mass products are confronted with millions of different consumer needs and requirements that have to be met on an individual and equal basis.[11]

Let us return to the main ideas of reengineering. I will give an overview of reengineering: the ideas behind it, its aims, and its importance for businesses. I will also briefly discuss experiences made by businessmen and women all over the world, and my personal impressions after reengineering's 11 years of existence .

The Basic Framework for Reengineering

How can we imagine companies acting in markets and being the basis for all managerial thinking? From my point of view, when referring to economic processes, we are talking about places where an exchange of goods takes place[12]. The word "goods" stands for manufactured goods like cars, but also for financial goods and information – generally referred to as services.

---

[8] O'Mera, P.; Mehlinger, H.; Krain, M.: „Globalization and Challenges of the New Century", Indiana University, May 2000

[9] Macharzina, K.: "Unternehmensführung, 2. Auflage", Wiesbaden 1995

[10] Fiedler, F. E.; Chiemmers, M. M.: "Improving Leadership Effectiveness, 2nd edition", New York 1984

[11] Fickel, L.: „Know Your Customer", CIO Magazine, August 1999

[12] Becker, W., Strategisches Management, 2nd edition, Bamberg 1995

Places where such exchanges take place are markets in which the companies are operating. Companies themselves, however, can also be seen as places of exchange, where various kinds of inputs (raw materials, commodities, data, etc.) are taken and assembled to transform them into outputs (finished goods, information, services, etc.). In a car company, for instance, different metals, plastics, glass, and other subsystems are transformed into a car.

Naturally, a company is not isolated in a market as such. Companies have to deal with numerous suppliers, clients, alliances, and competitors. One of the most famous theoretical analyses of this situation is the theoretical work of M. Porter[13,14] who developed a "strategic diamond" to show and define the interdependencies of companies in markets.

Porter also conducted essential research on the interaction processes within companies and those of companies in the markets. One basic construct was the value chain that ordered all activities of a company in a value adding process.

Two types of activities can be distinguished: activities that directly add value (e.g., procurement, production, sales, service), and activities that support the creation of value (e.g., human resources, management). From a high-level perspective, markets can be seen as an arrangement of value chains: One company's output is another company's input. This also requires companies to permanently review their current self-production and purchasing activities; they constantly need to make decisions on whether outsourcing or self-production adds more value and is ultimately more profitable. This idea of an integrated value chain is the basic theoretical input for the reengineering idea.

The Managerial Roots of Reengineering

The starting point of modern management ideas and concepts was the involvement of engineering concepts in managerial thinking. Well known examples for these first modern ideas were the rational optimization ideas of H. Ford (see above) or the "Principles of Scientific Management" by

[13] Porter, M. E.: "Competitive strategy," 9th edition, New York – London 1997

[14] Porter, M. E.: "Competitive advantage", New York – London 1985

F.W. Taylor[15]. The dominating idea of these concepts was the quantitative analysis and optimization of production processes. The work had to be done more effectively and in a shorter time. Production flows were measured and analyzed step by step, making use of time-analysis methods. The result was the fragmentation of work flow into small isolated activities that were performed by a specialized work force. Today's operations research models are based on these thoughts[16,17].

These concepts were followed by administrative management ideas in the late 1920s. H. Fayol[18] established management principles for organizations by defining the activities of planning, organizing, leading, and controlling as the basic functions of management. The new ideas were not only focused on concentrating the management efforts on production, but also to manage the administrative areas of a business, integrating rationale in management processes.

Parallel, M. Weber[19] indicated three possible sources of power for organizations: Individuals can have power as a result of tradition, law, or simple charisma.

At the same time G.E. Mayo and G.C. Homan[20] made physiological and psychological studies of employees in an attempt to answer the question of how working conditions influence an individual's output (productivity). Another important question for which an answer was sought was the impact of social factors on group behavior. This and later works in this area are summarized today in the so-called behavioral management theory[21]. The main idea is that the behavior of individuals within and without groups depends on social, cognitive, and emotional aspects.

When speaking about modern management ideas, I am referring to management concepts that were developed and further evolved after World

---

[15] Taylor, F. W.: "The Principles of Scientific Management", New York 1911

[16] "The Journal of Operational Research Society", Oxford, U.K. since 1950

[17] Neumann, K.: "OR-Verfahren, 3 Bände", München-Wien 1975 - 77

[18] Fayol, H.: "Administration Industrielle et Générale", Paris 1916

[19] Weber, M.: "Wirtschaft und Gesellschaft – Grundriss der verstehenden Soziologie, Band 1 und 2, 5. Auflage", Tübingen 1980

[20] Roethlisberger, F.J.; Dickson, W.: "Management and the Worker", Boston 1934

[21] Conger, J. A.; Karungo, R. N.: "Towards a Behavioral Theory of Charismatic Leadership in Organizational Settings", Academy of Management Review, 1987

War II. I would like to concentrate on the main ideas of these concepts, indicating the closer origins of the BPR concept.

In the late 1930s, Bernard[22] first drew a parallel between biological systems and businesses within the economy, declaring a company to be a socio-technological system, that stands in a steady interdependency with the surrounding environment. This system is a collection of components that interact with each other, exchanging goods, information, and money. Interaction of a business system with its environment means that connections to other systems (companies, governments, unions, the environment) are prevalent. The main point of this theory is the changing managerial focus from an internal company orientation to an understanding of a company within a complex net of relations and markets[23]. A term that came up was the so-called contingency theory or approach[24].

Based on criticism of the system-oriented theory, a situation-based theory was developed in the mid 1960s. Within the system theory, a definition of clearly defined management instructions for the success of a company was almost impossible, because of the complexity of the systems. Company or business case-specific instructions were developed, based on predefined economic and business contexts[25]. The definition of important influencing factors for a specific company and the description of interdependencies between such factors is unfortunately no small challenge.

Management models based on statistics were of great influence, especially for Anglo-Saxon management theories. One of the most important statistical models was developed by Peters and Waterman[26] in the mid 1980s. They conducted an important survey over several years, mainly within U.S. companies, asking decision-makers about what they considered the most relevant success factors. Based on the survey's results, Peters and Waterman defined critical success factors for companies which were highly recognized for a certain period of time. The main factors were that

---

[22] Barnard, C. I.: "The Functions of Executive", Cambridge 1938

[23] Ulrich, H.; Krieg, W.: "St.-Gallen Management Modell," 3rd edition, Bern – Stuttgart 1990

[24] Fiedler, F. E.; Chiemmers, M. M.: "Improving Leadership effectiveness," 2nd edition, New York 1984

[25] Stoner, J. A.: "Management," 2nd Edition, Engelwood Cliffs 1982

[26] Peters, T. J.; Waterman, R. U. Jr.: "In Search of Excellence", New York et al. 1982

companies that wanted to succeed needed to be action- and customer-oriented, and they should support an autonomous workforce.

Finally, it is essential for an understanding of BPR's history to underline the increasing importance of IT components and systems during the last 50 years. After the times of isolated IT solutions for specific problems, IT started to answer more and more sophisticated questions and provided real support in the solving of primarily financial problems[27].

Nowadays, sophisticated systems that can be handled in a convenient way, like People Soft[28] or SAP[29], are the central nerve system of most companies. The development of these systems, and the possibilities inherent in them, helped companies to start rethinking their activities and forced them to focus on cost cutting.

The Reengineering Story

In the early 1990s, a new managerial model was born. "You have the choice: Either you decide to reengineer your company – or you can close down your business," was the slogan of Morris and Barndon[30] who first established the reengineering standards, together with Hammer and Champy.[31,32,33] The idea was simple: Companies had to undergo radical changes to be successful. The main idea was to concentrate on business process optimization, improving the speed of a company's business proc-

---

[27] Ferstl, O. K.; Sinz E. J.: „Grundlagen der Wirtschaftsinformatik, Band 1, 2. Auflage", München 1994

[28] People Soft provides enterprise application software for customer relationship management, E-commerce, human resources management, financial management, supply chain management and enterprise performance management.

[29] SAP AG is a provider of collaborative e-business solutions. The solutions are designed to allow customers, partners and employees to work in an open collaborative internet environment.

[30] Morris, D.; Brandon, J.: "Re-engineering Your Business", New York et al. 1993

[31] Hammer, M.: "Reengineering Work – Don't Automate, Obliterate", in: Harvard Business Review, 68. Jg., Heft 4, 1990, S. 104 – 112

[32] Hammer, M.; Champy, J.: "Reengineering the Corporation", London 1993

[33] Hammer, M., Stanton, S. A.: "The Reengineering Revolution", New York 1995

esses and cost situation, and therefore improving shareholder value[34] and customer orientation.[35] The changes had to be radical to be successful, which meant that all former business rules had to be left behind.

Shareholder value and customer satisfaction were defined as the overwhelming objectives of reengineering. All efforts had to be judged on the basis of these objectives. To reach them, it was claimed to be necessary to adhere to the following seven main principles of reengineering (see footnote 33, p.70, and footnote 35, p.22):

- Critical analysis of all business structures and processes. All non-value adding activities must be eliminated
- Quality, service, and productivity must be improved, led by the idea that time is the most critical success factor in the markets
- Processes are the orientation for future organization
- Reengineering work should be conducted by high performance teams
- During reorganization, optimal personnel must be the focus of the reorganization process
- Reengineering must define a completely new role for communication and information technology
- Top management must indicate the reorganization and repositioning
- Additionally, it is necessary to live the reengineering process even after initial reengineering, making it an on-going process

The starting point of a reengineering initiative in any one particular case had to be an analysis of main competencies and business perspectives based on critical success factors. Defined fields with best prospects had to be the future competencies of the company. Radical organizational changes and a strict focus on core processes were the next steps.

The grade of radical reorganization and repositioning was not clearly defined: American business experts aimed for the most radical changes pos-

---

[34] Morin, R. A.; Jarrel, S. L.: "Driving Shareholder Value: Value-Building Techniques for Creating Shareholder Wealth", McGraw-Hill Professional Publishing, January 2001

[35] Talwar, R.: "Business Reengineering – A Strategy Driven Approach", Long Range Planning, vol. 26, 6, 1993, S. 22 – 40

sible. Meanwhile, European experts identified changes that should not be so radical in nature, in order to help personnel to gradually become accustomed to new situations.

The methodical framework of reengineering was only one of several very similar concepts based on the idea of process-oriented changes in companies. These concepts were called: renewing, relocating, or revitalizing.[36] Reengineering, or BPR, was the most radical and most complete theoretical concept.

Enormous market challenges, strong competition, and therefore cost cutting orientation of companies supported the success of the reengineering idea. Originating in American businesses, the idea was soon spread around the world, supported by a successful marketing campaign.

But the business world was really surprised by the results reengineering promised everyone: in particular, consulting firms promised turnover improvements of over 40%, productivity improvements of over 20%, and stock decreases of over 40%.[37] Up until today, most of the Fortune 500[38] companies like ABB, BMW, HP, BASF, etc., have conducted reengineering efforts. Reengineering is a true success story – at least for its creators and consultants.

But these efforts also demonstrated problems with reengineering. One of the biggest challenges was that there was no clear definition as to which areas of a company, in what detail, and within which time frame a reengineering project should be conducted. Experts and scientists only agreed on the point that these issues had to be defined case by case.

Radical reengineering stands for a totally new beginning in terms of thinking and acting within a company. This means that mature structures, cultures, and rules are thrown away. Moreover, it means a radical break with concepts, projects, and investments of the past.

---

[36] Servatius, H.-G.: "Reengineering-Programme umsetzen – Von erstarrten Strukturen zu fließenden Prozessen", Stuttgart 1994

[37] Strittmatter, F. J.: "Ich habe meine Firma auf den Kopf gestellt", Impulse, Issue 6, 1994, pp. 94 - 105

[38] www.fortune.com

Within reengineering projects, there have often been additional challenges, which were managed by competent and experienced program management. In one case, while the technical aspect of the reengineering program was predominant (customizing the SAP system was the main topic of one important reengineering program), the resistance of staff and middle management created serious problems, and the isolation of core processes was highly political.

The day-to-day handling of these challenges, along with ever increasing competition even for companies who had undergone reengineering efforts, made me think about something different to reengineering. Most of all, I was confronted with the strong wish to save the efforts and investments of the past. But a radical cut, as proposed by reengineering theories, would nullify these efforts, while at the same time harming top management's credibility with the shareholders. Moreover, in an environment driven by fierce competition, nobody really wants to make a radical cut with the past and blow millions of dollars to the wind.

BPR and the Merging Paradigm Shift

When I joined one of the big five consulting companies, as I still remember very well, the first thing I received as a welcome present was the consulting bible – Michael Hammer's "Business Process Reengineering." One of the partners told me: "This is what it is all about!"

I can tell you something: I did not even read the Hammer/Champy book given to me by one of the partners of my firm at that time. There was no need to, since I got into all kinds of different projects with valuable research resources, research centers, and libraries providing all the relevant information for specific client problems. Years later, at a certain time, it happened that the first customers began to approach us asking for assistance to reengineer their e-commerce solutions. I remembered receiving the consulting bible years earlier.

When I got home from a project one night, I started to search for that book, found it, and started reading. It was a fascinating experience, as I learned to understand what was behind the famous three letters BPR. I found out about how BPR was developed, what was so innovative about it, why the world was urgently awaiting such a methodology, and what the added value using this kind of model would be sinse, in a sense, BPR is something abstract and there is no real project structure behind it.

The authors of BPR structured and wrote a book on a thing many people were already doing. The only difference was that there was nobody labeling these kinds of activities as the authors did. To label and structure something is absolutely essential, since many more people then get the chance to understand, in a structured way, what has to be done and, therefore, are able to adopt and apply this know-how, know-how which becomes a methodology when structured and written down.

The BPR and ERP Success Story

In any discussion of the shortcomings of BPR in the age of the Cyber-Economy, it is essential to briefly analyze the development and content of the BPR model itself. BPR came up when the first enterprise resource planning (ERP[39]) systems had reached a certain level of development and stability, and therefore were implemented in more and more multinational, as well as medium-sized, companies. As these ERP systems were meant to automate the processes of these companies, they enabled the realization of huge saving potentials. The only problem these companies faced was that the ERP systems did not allow their specific processes, which had likely been in place for years, to be directly transferred to the ERP system. What could be done about it?

The challenge was to find the right way through it – the golden path. A compromise between the old processes and the process or industry prints offered and supported by the new generation of ERP systems had to be identified; otherwise, the customers would have never bought an ERP system, knowing that they would have to remove all their current processes and redevelop their work flows. To address this issue, the suppliers of ERP systems developed prototypes of industry-specific processes to facilitate transition from old processes to new ERP-supported processes as the clients now would have the target process, which helped to identify the previously mentioned golden path between the old world and the new.

BPR was the tool leading the way from the old processes to the new ones. The reengineering of the processes was ultimately the transformation of

[39] White Paper: "ERP and Business Continuity", December 2000

the relevant processes into processes that would be enabled by the target ERP system. The consultants who were involved in such BPR projects now faced several challenges. First of all, they had to convince their clients' employees to identify problems and weaknesses inherent in existing processes with which they actually felt quite comfortable. Then the consultants, on the basis of information gathered, told the clients how bad the existing processes were. This was the point at which employees were motivated to forget their old processes and work flows and help the consultants reengineer them. This was done by using the industry-specific process prototypes provided by the ERP-system suppliers to enable efficient and quick transition and ERP-system implementation.

Frankly speaking, these reengineered processes were not as good or as optimized as they were supposed to be. Just take a look at different surveys carried out in the 1990s. Most of the reengineering projects (which showed an approximate failure rate of 60%) failed because they did not meet the defined targets. In retrospect, one now gets the impression that BPR was probably developed or initiated by the big ERP-system suppliers to make the markets and clients believe that running a BPR-project in tandem with an ERP-system implementation would solve all their problems. Moreover, these companies trusted in the BPR projects and the know-how of the engaged consultants to really develop the most efficient and most competitive processes.

Today, most companies use ERP systems of all different sizes and on various levels, parts, and units of their organization. Today, BPR has become more and more unimportant, as almost all processes have been somehow optimized, reengineered, and adapted to the new requirements. Most companies are today facing new challenges. The challenge to stay competitive in a new world – the Cyber-Economy.

Processes and work flows have reached a certain level of optimization where further reengineering activities would not achieve proportional added value relative to the investments and costs for the reengineering effort. Here, the famous *Pareto Rule* of the 80:20 comes into play. This can as well be seen on a more generic macroeconomic level. Our economies are highly developed and the needs of companies have changed. Promoting BPR in the 1990s with the chief focus on cost reduction and process optimization went along well with the contingency situation of those days, when increasing automation enabled competitive advantages for companies even in industries facing decreasing turnovers and margins.

BPR Will Not Save the New Economy

Today, our highly developed industries are still facing decreasing margins and increasing competition due to internationalization, globalization[40], and – as a result of the reengineering of the 1980s and early 1990s – decreasing first mover advantages. These are caused by decreasing time-to-market and production processes, which count in relation to imitating the competitor's products. The issue with the processes is that they are already pretty sophisticated and have reached a very high level of quality.

This leads us to the point at which we should become aware of further process optimization initiatives which do not really culminate in essential gains in terms of either time or money. Again, the Pareto rule comes into play: Investing big amounts of money will not lead to improvements following a considerable input-output relation. More and more organizations will get to the point where they will understand the issue of BPR projects not leading to the expected results. This understanding will facilitate the successful management of companies in the so-called New Economy. Managers have to face the changing requirements and they need to realize that, due to its shortcomings, BPR is no longer an adequate approach to deal with the problems occurring in the world of the New Economy. This is also reflected by the fact that the godfathers of BPR are already in the act of thinking about how to reframe BPR in order to make it valuable once again for companies in the time when the old and new economies are converging.

Furthermore, BPR did not even define a clear procedure of how to really achieve optimized procedures and processes since the model remained on a high level. Almost all consulting companies developed their own models for BPR projects. Frankly speaking, they all looked much the same! And all these consulting companies partnered up with the big ERP suppliers, in the end becoming their distribution arms and following the suppliers' strategy of heavily pushing the products in the market.

Companies must learn to understand that processes as such are not the core factors or problems anymore, since continuous process improvement and optimization have become a commodity. Moreover, all companies have the required resources and know-how at their disposal to run their activities in their given area without the assistance of any external service companies.

---

[40] Matzke, P.: "Challenges for Global E-Business", Whitepaper, 2001

Here we are getting to the crucial issue: Processes as such are not a core topic anymore and BPR focused processes and their optimization and implementation absolutely into some kind of ERP or IT system. And this ERP or IT system had to be conceptualized, developed, and implemented. Most components were bought at that time. Huge investments in hard- and software were made. This was absolutely essential to ultimately be able to use the new ERP systems with all their new add-ons, modules, and tools.

Based on these huge investments, BPR did not have to focus on technical issues of re-using existing and old systems as efficiently as possible. The idea was to get rid of the antique systems and programs to ensure a consistent IT infrastructure and architecture. This was possible from the point of view of chief financial officers (CFOs), as these old systems and programs had already depreciated completely and therefore could have been eliminated or easily sold.

BPR and the Technical Shortcomings

This section addresses the next major shortcoming of BPR. Today, we are facing new and sophisticated IT infrastructures and components that were bought six months or one year ago at maximum. What does this mean? All these investments are brand new and not at all depreciated!

Using BPR to optimize existing cyber-commerce solutions would mean to focus on the back-end processes, neglecting the issues of ensuring consistency of new processes and existing systems. This implies a significant risk, since the existing systems have certain parameters enabling only specific kinds of transactions, transmission, etc., and would probably not support the new, optimized processes. This would result in a gap between processes and required and existing IT systems, and would consequently mean further investment – on top of the investments made six months or one year ago.

Because of BPR's origin in relatively operational topics such as processes and IT, there are also strategic shortcomings. BPR, undoubtedly, did not focus on long-term organizational aspects. It tackled more the short- to mid-term issues and aspects since new processes and organizational structures would have an impact on the company's development. But BPR neglected to consider real management and strategic aspects such as vision, mission, or external market development – to name but a few. One might say that BPR was not a strategic topic. I would agree. But in the New

Economy, dealing with all the problems described in Chap. 2, reframing unsuccessful cyber-commerce solutions has to be considered as a strategic task, as companies' long-term development and future heavily depend on the outcome of such CCR initiatives.

BPR and Strategic Human Resource Management (SHRM)

Last but not least, one additional issue merits attention: People. I intend to only discuss it briefly here, focusing on the shortcomings of BPR in that specific area; a later chapter, Chap. 8, will focus on the broader issue of the new role of *strategic human resource management* (SHRM) within the New Economy.

Essentially, in terms of human resources, BPR did not have as many shortcomings as it did with processes, IT, and strategy, as discussed above. As BPR was developed in the United States of America, there was already a greater awareness of human resources becoming more and more a strategic factor in the development of a company. This was the reason why all existing methodologies of the consulting companies included some kind of so-called *change management*[41] – some were even more creative, using the term of *change leadership*. Once in a while, we would really like to ex-*change* our own *leadership*.

So, change management was a consolidation of activities in the field of leadership, project management, project teams, communications, etc., all activities based on theories and methodologies taken from SHRM. SHRM becomes more and more important and organizations increasingly learn to understand the role of up-to-date human resource management leading the way to demand-driven SHRM and enabling companies to realize their defined strategy. Furthermore, SHRM implies that the overall strategy will evolve on the basis of a two-way linkage – a continuous exchange or involvement of top managers and HR manager(s).

Here CCR fully supports the SHRM approach and acknowledges the importance of adequate people management to enable a reframed cyber-commerce solution, promoted by the aligned acceptance and commitment of all parties and stakeholders involved.

---

[41] Bridges, W. P.: "Managing Transitions: Making the Most of Change", Perseus Publishing, September 1991

CHAPTER 5

Reframing, Not Optimizing

In this section of the book I will try to provide enough information and facts to enable you, first, to get a correct understanding of the CCR approach and, second, to internalize the reframing feature.

Very often clients, journalists, friends, and other interested people approach me with the request: "Tell me more about the new model – the optimization of unsuccessful cyber-commerce solutions." Having been asked several times about "optimization", I understood how important it would be to tackle the issue in this book, as this is the key to CCR and to understanding the whole methodology. One essential distinction between BPR and CCR is represented by the term "reframing" as such, and therefore it is of utmost importance to accept this word as an inherent part of the new approach.

Once you have read this chapter, you will understand that CCR is not about optimizing unsuccessful cyber-commerce solutions, as this would be a totally inappropriate way of talking about this new paradigm that is replacing BPR.

Talking about Optimization

To optimize means to *improve an existing object or to design it in the best possible way.*[1] This implies that optimization is the final improvement of a solution to make it perfect. Thus, optimization needs an almost perfect solution to begin with, to make it maximally perfect in a final effort. The solutions that I was dealing with, however, were far from being final or almost perfect. So I am definitely not talking about optimizing unsuccessful cyber-commerce solutions, as this would create no added value for clients. Nevertheless, let us take a closer look at optimization and its limitations.

---

[1] "The Advanced Learner's Dictionary of Current English", Oxford 1975

Since every action a company takes can be referred to as a process, naturally, all actions can be optimized in one way or another. There are several parameters that influence a process, and improving them can optimize the process. They are:

- Cost
- Quality
- Time
- Value creation

Optimization should therefore result in the two-dimensional elevation of a company's processes towards *effectiveness* and *efficiency*. Optimizing is meant to enhance the way a process works so that it produces the intended results *and* operates quickly in an organized manner, which, in turn, should lead to an increase in profits.

A discussion of the numerous optimization tools that exist would be beyond the scope of this book. I would therefore like to take a closer look at the most prominent of these tools – *ISO 9000*, *Total Quality Management* (TQM), *Six Sigma*, and *Operations Research* (OR), on which I will focus in particular – to show that optimization is by no means the best way to tackle cyber-commerce issues.

The Limitations of ISO 9000

ISO 9000 was established in 1987 by the *International Standards Organization* (ISO) and has been accepted by over 70 countries. The chief objective of the ISO 9000 norm[2,3,4] is to ensure that manufacturers and service providers produce their goods and services according to minimal standards set by the ISO.

---

[2] There is a row of regular norms (ISO 9001 to 9003) and two leading norms (ISO 9000 and ISO 9004). For reasons of simplicity, however, I summarize them in one term: ISO 9000.

[3] Ketola, J.; Roberts, K.: "ISO 9000: 2000 in a Nutshell," 2nd edition, Paton, January 2001

[4] Brauer, J.: "Die EN ISO 9000–9004 umsetzen," Hanser Wissenschaft, München 1997

The ISO norm series had emerged from the manufacturing industry, though. During the following years it was more and more the idea to use these process quality standards for the service industry – the ISO 9004 norm was developed. Nonetheless, most of the companies especially in the service industry had tremendous problems to apply the 9004 series and to gain financial advantages from implementing a cost-intensive ISO 9004 quality system.

Subject to various controls by accredited auditors and to the manufacturer's declaration that his/her products conform with EN (European Norm) ISO 9000, the manufacturer is granted a certificate of product quality for a period of 3 years.

There is some criticism, however, to the effect that EN ISO 9000 includes only minimum requirements and cannot keep up with the well-known American *Malcom-Baldrige Award* [5] or the *European Quality Award* [6]. The fact is criticized, for instance, that the norm does not focus enough on customers and employees, which would be important, as only (intrinsically) motivated employees on every hierarchical layer can provide quality.

Additionally, EN ISO 9000 is more about the *image* of quality than about anything else. Real improvement in quality is not an automatic consequence of the certificate.

The Limitations of Total Quality Management (TQM)

Total quality management means that a corporation's culture is defined by and supports the constant attainment of customer satisfaction through an integrated system of tools, techniques, and training.[7] TQM should enable ultimate customer satisfaction. TQM does not originate in one department only; rather, it is the result of optimal harmonization of the value chain.[8]

---

[5] Heaphy, M. S.; Gruska, G.: "The Malcolm Baldrige National Quality Award: A Yardstick for Quality Growth", Addison Wesley Longman Company, May 1995

[6] Zink, K. J.: "Successful TQM: Inside Stories from European Quality Award Winners", John Wiley & Sons, May 1997

[7] Mosley; Pietri; Megginson: "Management – Leadership in Action," 3rd edition, Harper Collins

[8] Creech, B.: "The 5 Pillars of TQM: How to Make Total Quality Management Work for You", Plume, December 1995

Though it sounds very promising, and many companies have been involved in quality initiatives, TQM has many shortcomings.

Often, TQM is not supported by upper management because the company's reward system is not harmonized with improvements brought by TQM. Moreover, the lack of support can be traced back to the hostility of businesses toward innovation and change. Their philosophy rather resembles the saying: "If it ain't broken, don't fix it." Many TQM projects are frozen because management is expecting too much too soon. The search for a quick fix often causes promising initiatives to be abandoned because of management's excessive focus on costs. It does not understand that TQM is a philosophy that needs time to be incorporated, not only in the organization but also in the minds of its employees.

The Limitations of Six Sigma

Two of the leading proponents of Six Sigma, Mikel Harry and Richard Schroeder, define Six Sigma in their book[9] as "a business process that allows companies to drastically improve their bottom line by designing and monitoring everyday business activities in ways that minimize waste and resources while increasing customer satisfaction."

Six Sigma, however, is just a conceptual development of already existing management systems – *failure mode and effect analysis* (FMEA),[10] for instance, or the *eight-discipline approach to problem solving*[11]. It does not present anything new to the field of defect prevention, as quality improvement and cost efficiency can be attained with other tested initiatives, such as benchmarking, that can improve a company's bottom line by at least 30%.

There is of course besides others one company having been very successful in aligning the Six Sigma approach for its specific needs – General Electric (GE). This organization further developed the Six Sigma methodology, originally implemented at Motorola, and now uses it as global basis

---

[9] Harry, M.; Schroeder, R.: "Six Sigma – The Breakthrough Management Strategy Revolutionizing the World's Top Corporations", 2000

[10] McDermott, R. E.; Mikulak, R. J.; Beauregard, M. R.: "The Basics of FMEA", Productivity Inc. 1996

[11] Stamatis, D. H.: "Who Needs Six Sigma, Anyway?", Quality Digest, 2000

for internal standards and procedures. This approach is undoubtedly on of the success factors, that enabled GE to integrate new firms all over the world into the structure of the Group very efficiently and even more to realize synergies.

Like TQM, Six Sigma misses the point that optimization is not so much about tools and methodologies or statistics, but rather about management support and employees internalizing the quality mind-set.

The Limitations of Operations Research

Operations research attempts to provide those who manage organized systems, such as business entities, with an objective and quantitative basis for making decisions.[12] OR draws on many different disciplines – logic, mathematics, and statistics, as well as communications theory, decision theory, organization theory, general systems theory, and the behavioral sciences – to find how managerial decisions are and should be made.[13]

Since its first application in business, OR has helped to solve a large variety of managerial and administrative problems. A comparatively stable environment and, to a large degree, isolated micro- as well as macroeconomic systems were beneficial to its success. In the *cyber-economy*, however, stability and isolation are nonexistent because information technology has the effect of wiring the business world and making its players more vulnerable to global changes.

As OR is relying very much on mathematics and statistics dealing with variables and input/output relations to define optimum production functions, this does not cover the need of companies working in the convergence of the old and new economy – driven by increasing pace, intangible know-how and innovative production procedures.

The Problem with Competition

Problems of competition are classifiable as certain, risky, or uncertain, depending on the knowledge available to a decision-maker regarding his opponents' choices. Under conditions of certainty, it is quite easy to calcu-

[12] Encyclopaedia Britannica, 2001

[13] Rardin, R. L.: "Optimization in Operations Research", Prentice Hall, July 1997

late how to maximize gain or minimize loss. Solving risky competition problems, however, requires the use of statistical analysis.

Certainly most difficult is the task of estimating the probabilities of competitors' choices. Game theory[14] has provided a remedy for making decisions in an uncertain environment. Nevertheless, I doubt that such a sophisticated science as game theory can follow the pace at which globalization is changing the business world: Every second, thousands of people with diverse cultural backgrounds – to name just one factor influencing the decision-making process – are making decisions, and new companies, which may be present exclusively online, represent increasing competition for every organization.

One input for the OR model will thus be incomplete or, at best, distorted.

The Problem with Search

Obtaining essential information is key to making any decision. Two kinds of errors are involved in the search process, however: observation and sampling.[15] The problem with observation is that one can see something that is not there and not see something that is there. Finding the right sample size is also crucial to receiving the right information. Samples, though, are connected to costs, and the larger and more accurate the sample, the higher the cost.

Even though the costs involved in samples are important, observation may be more so. In the *cyber-economy*, the possibility of omitting essential facts is very high as, once again, too many decisions are taken at various levels and therefore cannot be isolated. Yet another input for operations research models may be incomplete or simply nonexistent.

The Problem with Planning

Most problems do not arise in isolation but are part of an interacting system. Finding interrelated solutions to a set of interdependent problems requires major planning efforts that are very costly. Moreover, the solutions desired are becoming more and more elusive, as the internal and external environments of an organization often change dramatically and un-

[14] Fudenberg, D.; Tirole, J.: "Game Theory", MIT Press, October 1991

[15] Deming, W.E.: "Some Theory of Sampling", Dover Publications, July 1984

expectedly. As the capitalization of a company's market depends increasingly on its performance on a stock market, for instance, organizations have become exposed to wide fluctuations which, in turn, make long-term planning a very difficult task.

The planning problem is closely related to one of the main deficiencies of OR: system design.

The Problem with System Design

OR systems try to solve specific problems. However, they do not predict and prevent future problems. Neither might these systems be accurate once they are implemented. Consequently, they often lack the ability to identify and solve current problems and cannot implement and maintain solutions under changing conditions.

The Problem with Organizations' Aversion to Change

Most organizations resist changes in their operations or management. Optimizing is about change, though it is certainly less drastic than reengineering. Often, an organization's need for a complete and more efficient turnaround is not as pressing as its need to make maximum use of what it already knows. Many solutions are therefore not even implemented, and those that are probably do not survive for long the widespread tendency of an organization to return to older problem-solving methods.

The last of the five major problems with OR is probably the most important, for it expresses the desire of many organizations not to lose the time and money they have already invested in preceding efforts at finding a solution. Coupled with an unrealistic precondition of complete information to make OR systems work satisfactorily, the general reluctance of many companies to initiate far-reaching change made me aware that reframing was the only plausible and reasonable answer to optimization. As we will see later, cyber-commerce reframing is also about change. CCR, however, pays attention to an organization's worries about cutting too deeply with the past. It is thus inherently more acceptable to companies.

Another area that deals explicitly with optimization is the *Profit Impact of Market Strategy* (PIMS)[16,17] program. Within the PIMS program, a tool

[16] Developed in 1960 by General Electric and the Harvard Business School to spot so-called *rules of the marketplace*

named "optimum strategy report" makes it possible to simulate the impact of different clustered strategic actions taken by a specific company, for example, on its profitability. Thus, again, the optimization of existing business solutions is a scientific task. Science, however, has difficulties in evaluating the human factor and therefore often produces results that are of little use to companies that are run by people. Optimization is not the key, because it does not allow for human flexibility. Reframing does!

The "Pareto Rule" as a Test of the Limitations of Optimization Activities

Now that we have discussed optimization in the scientific sense, we can look critically at the sense of optimization activities in the era of the cyber-economy. This next step will focus more on the business side and the impact on the cash-flow of an organization, a business unit, a profit center, or a single process.

For those who dealt in the past with existing cyber-business ideas, it was easy to gain the impression that once business ideas were transferred from scratch into "real life", the greatest potentials for optimization had already been realized and probably exhausted. Within the big Fortune-500 companies, after the first "Internet – me-too" wave had hit the shores of business dreamland and the initial costs had shocked the responsible management, the potential for optimization was depleted. Bright and sometimes brilliant people from the best business schools and leading companies around the world, however, were of course able to define optimization potentials and take the necessary action.

But at a certain stage, the effect of the famous 80/20 rule of Vilfredo Pareto[18] was felt by these same bright people. The Pareto rule[19] says that at some point the efforts needed to optimize an existing solution outweigh the benefits of the expected results. In business English: The costs of an optimization effort rise so much that the loan taken to initiate the optimization effort is no longer productive. Using the well-known 80/20 relation: 80% of the optimization is achieved with 20% of the costs. Then the relation

[17] Buzzel, R.D.; Bradley, T.G.: "The PIMS Principles: Linking Strategy to Performance", Free Press, August 1987

[18] An economist, born in France in 1848, who emigrated to Italy in 1852.

[19] Pareto, V.: "Manuel d'Economie Politique"

reverses, and the remaining 20% of the optimization efforts are swallowing 80% of the costs.

Finally, two equally damaging "options" stood at managers' disposal: First, they could totally withdraw from the optimization efforts and freeze all ongoing projects. Second, they could press further with optimization at any cost. Managers found themselves in a situation similar to the well-known prisoner's dilemma.[20] Choosing the first option would reposition the company back where it started from and would additionally make large investments simply evaporate. Opting for the second would probably bring some desired results but would leave the company in financial distress. And both would probably cost the managers their heads. Optimization was a zero-sum game.

CCR versus Optimization and Reengineering

We have already discussed business process reengineering in Chap. 4. In this chapter, however, I will discuss it in the context of optimization.

Hammer defines reengineering as "the fundamental rethinking and radical redesign of business processes to bring about dramatic improvements in performance."[21] This definition conveys the message that reengineering is a very radical step for a business to take. Reengineering stands for a break with the past and, at the same time, for a focus on processes.

Later interpretations of Hammer's words and concepts tried to bring these thoughts down to an operational level, from the initially quite generic one, and involved strategic components of a company's ongoing reengineering projects. By initiating the reengineering process, markets and companies' core competencies should be analyzed and reengineered up front. But the real world often understood reengineering as the first step to implementing company-wide legacy systems like SAP or People Soft. So the reengineering concentrated on processes and technology. As of today, there is no reengineering methodology providing operational hints on how to deal with the strategic parts of reengineering and optimization projects. In the end, the technological restrictions became the main driver of the reengi-

---

[20] Heylighen, F.: "The Prisoner's Dilemma", Principa Cybernetica Web, April 1995

[21] Hammer, M.; Stanton, S.A.: "The Reengineering Revolution", New York 1995

neering efforts. You probably remember the words often heard during a reengineering project: "Sorry. This process is not possible the way you are designing it. SAP cannot do that."

What is CCR about? "Cyber-commerce", as discussed in Chap. 2, includes all different kinds of new commerce channels enabled by web technology already existing today and those to come in the future. These channels offer organizations new opportunities to get into:

- New markets
- New segments
- New product areas

The word "reframing" needs some explanation as well. To "frame" means to give something the adequate surrounding, keeping it together in the right manner – from a three-dimensional perspective; e.g., a picture or a painting can be framed. If you do not like the current frame anymore or if the current frame is no longer fitting or adequate, you will probably change the frame or re-frame the picture or the painting.

Transferring this verb into the word "re-framing" by adding the "re" to indicate something happening again is by no means the creation of an artificial word. It stands for giving something a new direction, a new perspective, or a new and adequate framework, i.e., keeping something together and restoring it to its original glamour or beauty. This little generic description should give you an impression of what reframing is all about.

Turning again to CCR, reframing means to estimate and to evaluate existing things – the cyber-commerce solution, including all aspects such as high-level thinking about the direction a company's efforts should take, be it vision, mission, or competitive strategy, but also about all different technical components, be they hardware, software, or the systems architecture. In particular, CCR involves a thorough look at ongoing initiatives and investments.

CCR means to evaluate and reconsider all these factors because the cyber-commerce solution that is already in place is not successful, for various reasons that have to be identified throughout the CCR project.

One of the main focuses in CCR projects is on understanding the past development of an existing cyber-solution in a particular company. This means that one tries to monitor where and how the idea originated, what the initial aims and who the key players were, following the path until the present. The development and implementation of related technical parts and of systems is monitored, too.

Let us now pose ourselves the main question: Where does reframing stand compared with optimization and reengineering?

Optimizing is sometimes not radical enough, whereas reframing is quite radical but at the same time requires that specific parts have to remain as they are. What does this imply? Talking about optimizing leads us back to the beginning of industrial engineering when Taylor first implemented work-splitting, trying to speed up the manufacturing process in his production halls. Big improvements were then made by Ford, which introduced new ways of manufacturing using assembly lines and piecework. Taylor's first reframing efforts moved economic thinking forward in giant steps. These early steps were essential to the development of our economy.

Of course, optimizing is a part of CCR; several processes or technical solutions just need to be slightly improved. Not everything has to be discarded, however, as Hammer was inclined to suggest in his definition of reengineering. The difference is that CCR goes further and takes much more into consideration. It is more profound and has a broader reach.

Reengineering stands for new processes, new roles, new systems, and new types of work flow. In brief, the focus was mainly on introducing new things and leaving the "old world" behind. A dramatic cut with the past was necessary. Therefore, the idea of reusing technological systems like hardware and software was really not very popular. Viewed in the historical context, this becomes clear. During the first big reengineering wave, new systems were implemented. The old host-based systems and fragmented solutions that were running on old hardware were outdated anyway, so no one seriously considered reusing those systems.

So where do the differences between reengineering and CCR lie? CCR calls for radical cuts only if they are really necessary. CCR wants you to analyze the situation in detail before you decide to make a cut with the past. Perhaps optimization is sufficient, or even leaving things as they are is the best you can do in several areas of your cyber-solution (the latter, though unexciting, is very probable because CCR projects operate under great pressure to be fast and successful). However, the most important thing about CCR in comparison to reengineering is that its principal goal is to save as much of past investments as possible! Reframing is positioned between two extremes: optimization and reengineering.

Reframing acknowledges that there are useful parts which do not need to be replaced in the course of redesigning existing processes. This understanding evolved as I was approached by CFOs who had invested millions of dollars in a brand new infrastructure, in systems and components, and whose staff had spent months to get things running. These CFOs wanted no further investments to be made, and they expected me to deliver results that would enable them to tell their investors that things would soon work as planned.

The definitions and differences given above sound very theoretical. What does CCR mean in "real life"? To answer this question, it is necessary to talk about data we collected while working with our clients and experiences we gained from these partnerships.

We ran an internal survey to document the importance of the four CCR project horizontals:

- Strategy
- Process
- Technology
- People

The base was a typical CCR, divided into project phases which we brought into correlation with the verticals. The main issue was to help the pragmatics to decide which topics should receive the principal focus during the project in order to make it a success. Parallel to this, we defined answers to the question above: "What is special about CCR?"

One finding was that the importance of a horizontal varies during the project fulfillment time; e.g., strategy is of crucial importance at the beginning and of minor relevance by the end of the project, during the implementation of defined results. The survey results were presented using a special tool we developed: the Dimension Impact Matrix (see Chart 6.1, p. 87).

The matrix indicates the impact of the different layers during the flow of a project based on the colors, from bright, meaning "low impact – not crucial", to dark, meaning "high impact – crucial and critical".

This matrix can be used to support our finding about the difference between conventional "optimization" and CCR:

Optimization tasks typically concentrate on one of the horizontals, while involving other aspects slightly. If a technical solution were optimized, the curve representing the horizontals strategy and people –would be in the bright area or below during the whole project. The curve representing processes might reach the dark area at some points, and the curve demonstrating the importance of the horizontal technology would be in dark area during the entire project.

Moreover, optimization projects already start with a *gap definition*, not even trying to understand more than necessary. So the project phases that are crucial to the success of a CCR solution are missing in an optimization project.

Using this matrix also helps to understand the difference from conventional BPR:

- In a typical BPR project the curve representing the horizontal "process" would be in the dark area during phases 2 and 3, and the one representing the horizontal "technology" would move into the dark area during phases 4 and 5.
- In addition to differing in terms of the impact of the project, the rough structure of BPR initiatives can be easily distinguished from CCR on the basis of the evolved phase-scheme for CCR projects.

In today's highly competitive markets, where more and more players are operating at a speed that is hard to grasp for people and systems alike, optimizing is not the right answer. First, it would not bring the desired results, owing to incomplete information – as shown in the example of operations research, and, second, it would not go far enough in terms of change. Additionally, optimization does not consider the efficient reuse of investments already made. In contrast, reengineering would be *too* rigorous because of the radical cut with past investments and the missing focus on strategic components. The natural choice is a measure that lies in between both extremes: reframing! Reframing allows companies to rethink and redesign their processes in a flexible way with maximum attention paid to saving past investments. It helps a company win back its shareholders' trust[22] and confidence by delivering promised results.

[22] Saracevic, A.: "Vulture Capitalists", Business 2.0, November 2000

CHAPTER 6

Cyber-Commerce Reframing: The Approach

Having discussed and described the contingency situation in detail, including the various challenges, risks, and potential, we are now in a position to deal with cyber-commerce reframing (CCR).

Some of you initially may have had trouble with this new term, the underlying methodology, and its thought model, as in this book I am trying to describe something that is for the moment quite unreasonable, especially for people whose daily business is to implement successful e-commerce solutions[1] or, worse, who are already fire-fighting within their own company to minimize damage caused by unsuccessful implementations in the area of c-commerce.

The Praetorians of CCR

While carrying our research for this book, I was astonished at the divergent feedback received and emotions aroused by my questions. Frankly, some discussions were rather controversial, but that was what I was looking for: that is, people who would challenge my approach, who would argue with me, and who would directly tackle the issues and concerns. Their criticism enabled me to further evolve the approach to the next stage of industrial development, where we will face millions of web-based solutions that do not fulfill and meet predefined expectations and financial targets.

At this point of the book I would like to take the opportunity to thank all these people for their contributions. Now, having developed the CCR approach thus far, I have come to realize how important and essential their opinions were and still are. Their input gave me valuable insight as to what people were expecting of the book and this made it much easier to put my

[1] Lientz, B.; Rea, K.: "Dynamic E-Business Implementation Management: How to Effectively Manage E-Business Implementation," Academic Press, New York, July 2000.

thoughts on paper. These people also encouraged me to write this book; after all the different discussions they had learned to understand the problems and needs and therefore had developed the awareness needed for something completely new.

By getting involved, these people played the role of praetorians, spreading the CCR approach further and in turn engaging in other discussions to consequently build their own network of praetorians.

In time more and more people learned about CCR and, importantly for me, started to understand the challenges posed by the thousands of unsuccessful web-based solutions we will face during the next two to three years.

Especially, I would like to mention one person who helped me throughout the development of this book: Lukas Juszczyk. A colleague from my last company, Lukas was someone who aimed to express problems and issues in simple terms. He understood completely the message and the method of the CCR approach. For hours we would sit in bars and restaurants in various places, depending on where we were working. I was always surprised at how long we could sit in a restaurant without ordering because we were discussing and arguing various points about CCR. Waiters would often come before we finally ordered something.

Lukas, with his charming way of challenging me throughout this period, became a close friend whose aim was to discover and understand the core message of the CCR approach. And with his in-depth operational knowledge and experience he was therefore adequately qualified to play the role of a sparring-partner – even though I sometimes wanted to avoid addressing his more direct questions and astute concerns.

When at times I despaired that I would not be able to drive my thinking forward, developing and optimizing the CCR approach, I would often recall Lukas's arguments and look for explanations and ways of realigning the approach using the huge potential of my friend's experience.

The Issues with Surveys and Opinions

Many companies now are involved in and committed to the conceptualization and implementation of c-commerce solutions. Nobody dares to guess what the future will be in more than two years' time. Only in surveys do companies take this risk by talking to and interviewing managers who are working on the implementation of their c-commerce solutions. Undoubtedly, these managers are the ones to talk to when it comes to asking questions about further developments and what the market will look like in a few years.

Nonetheless, we have to appreciate that these managers are encouraged by their CEOs, CFOs, CIOs, etc., to explore the cutting edge of c-commerce. And this is the very problem. Do we really believe that such managers, working on tasks set by the board, would say that before any kind of c-commerce solution can be implemented, it is necessary to face the fact that most solutions are not working and not fulfilling pre-set expectations and financial targets?

This would of course not happen. At this stage of development, all kinds of surveys are being published, featuring the development of c-commerce solutions that have a dramatic impact on our macro- and microeconomic systems. But these surveys cannot create an awareness of what will happen within the next few years. Will we face an increasing number of unsuccessful cyber-commerce solutions – as already indicated – which will require a suitable approach to handle such solutions?

At present, whole industries are seizing the opportunity to grow their businesses by selling in the area of c-commerce without paying much attention to the long run. Such shortsightedness, however, could have – probably since March 2000 already has – a very negative consequence for economies, organizations, and, probably the weakest part, employees. What I am referring to becomes obvious when one opens a newspaper and reads the daily financial market news. More and more companies are confronted with tremendous problems as financial markets decline and do not show any sign of reversing the trend. More so, some are already talking about recession signals.

In searching for the reason, we can admit to ourselves that the hype about the New Economy[2] caused the dilemma. During 1999 and 2000 we became used to increases and gains on shares on the order of 50 percent and above. The New Economy was in superficially good shape and shares were growing steadily. Everybody was happy: companies invested, venture capitalists readily invested their money, and start-ups entered a competition about

[2] Kelly, K.: "New Economy? What New Economy?" Wired, May 1998.

who would have the highest cash-burn rate.[3] Those days are gone,[4] but we have to keep in mind that the effects of this New Economy bubble[5] – and there will be some for sure – will accompany us well into the future if we do not actively work to minimize the damage already caused.

Awareness as a Facilitator for Understanding CCR

At this stage of the book I hope that you have acquired enough background information to understand what I mean by CCR and to deal with it in the right manner.

CCR is new and probably three years too early. Some may say that it is just a new brand of something old. But consider this: imagine that you were approached 15 years ago by somebody asking for your opinion of business process reengineering (BPR). What would you have said? If at all, you might have asked: "What is it really? Tell me more about it." After a brief explanation you might have said: "Process reengineering – isn't that kind of the same as process optimization or improvement? This doesn't seem to be new to me personally as we've already undertaken all kinds of improvement and optimization activities." You would have been proud of yourself, your company, and the fact that you were working for such a great company doing then what some smart guys are only now, years later, bringing to the market!

What I want to emphasize is the fact that years ago it was the same kind of story with BPR. People considered BPR to be nothing new, as organizations had always optimized their processes and workflows. Basically, people had to learn to appreciate that BPR was an approach for something new, for structuring activities their organizations were already up to, not really aware of what they were doing as such.

Remember this example when you read the following section on the approach because it is an essential part of the awareness you must have to get the most out of this book and, indirectly, out of the time spent with your

---

[3] Green, D.: "Cash Burn May Lead E-Commerce Stars to Crash 'n Burn," Infowar.com, April 2000.

[4] Armbruster, B.: "Handbook of Nasdaq Stocks Fall 2000," Financial Information Services, November 2000.

[5] Horvath, J.: "New Economy Bubble in No Trouble?" Telepolis, December 2000.

respective company. If CCR is probably something that has already been done partly in your organization, then you are one of the few who are at the leading edge, ensuring long-term success for their companies. If you are not in this group, then this section should help you to initiate the paradigm shift from BPR toward CCR.

Bad Experience for Good Stuff

When we first started to realize CCR projects, my colleagues and I were by no means clear about how we should structure our work and our workflow as such. Our attempts to reframe existing c-commerce solutions were not as successful as our business ethics and our client orientation would oblige them to be. During this time we tried to apply different theoretical frameworks, methodologies, and concepts, including BPR. We soon realized that we had to dramatically change our procedure if we did not want to risk losing our credibility.

Therefore, we set up a series of internal meetings to consolidate all our experience and expertise. We spent weeks with different project teams, account members, and, of course, clients. We had one clear goal: find out why these initiatives were not working! Initially, we had problems communicating our goal as everybody involved was unhappy about agreeing to deliver the intended output, but at least this was the basis for an open and creative process.

We approached project leaders who wanted to participate in our internal engagement, to develop something completely new. Soon this initiative became recognized internally and everybody was encouraged to make contributions. We developed a clear workshop structure to ensure the consistent and compatible flow of information. The structure of the workshops was roughly as follows:

1. Strategic assessment
2. Brief description of aligned objectives
3. Presentation of achieved goals
4. Presentation and discussion of methodologies and tools
5. Presentation and discussion of problems and crucial issues from an internal perspective
6. Presentation and discussion of problems and crucial issues from a client perspective

7. Consolidation of lessons learned
8. Alignment of methodology based on lessons learned

Working through all eight items on the agenda took two to five days depending on the size of each project. Nevertheless, these days were both interesting and at times tough. We had to develop the self-discipline to pursue something we were convinced to be right for our clients. Sometimes clients were as surprised about our initiative as they were happy with our results. But soon they understood what we were aiming for and added value by sparing their time to work and discuss matters with us.

After six months of intensive sessions, we finally completed work on those projects that had been considered as extraordinarily relevant for our initiative. Overall, we screened several projects, some large-scale and some smaller engagements from different parts of the world. During the following weeks we consolidated our collected expertise and summarized the lessons learned. Looking back, the most essential part of the job was to align or optimize the methodologies used, as this was the basis for the new approach to fill the gaps between the various methodologies, including BPR.

The Dimension-Impact Matrix (DIM) of CCR

In consolidating our results we recognized one crucial aspect about the focus on the projects and activities investigated: all activities were concentrating primarily on process issues and neglecting the relevance of other dimensions. Due to this fact we continued to work in the specific area and ran a study aiming to verify or deny this key message which could be seen as a hypothesis. We developed a certain set of questions and ran standardized interviews with many clients and account team members.

The key question was to examine the potential diverging relevance of four dimensions that we called horizontals. These horizontals were:

A. Strategy
B. Processes
C. Technology
D. People

As such they do not represent innovation, but they are certainly four areas that companies – both private companies and those operating in the not-for-profit sector – are driven by. The innovative aspects are actually located within these horizontals comprising of not less than 19 modules consisting of 99 underlying activity packages, and indirectly within the following six "verticals:"

Vertical 1: Focus and Objectives
Vertical 2: As-Is Assessment
Vertical 3: Definition of Gaps
Vertical 4: Development of CCR Plan
Vertical 5: Implementation of CCR Plan
Vertical 6: E-Performance Measurement and Management

This two-dimensional framework is the structure behind the framework for CCR initiatives and was also essential for our internal study to verify our hypothesis of the diverging impact of the verticals in correlation with the horizontals. Having conducted these interviews, we analyzed the results and developed the dimension–impact matrix (DIM) basically underpinning our CCR approach.

The DIM enabled us to understand the problems we were facing in our projects as we could verify the varying impact of the verticals on the pro-

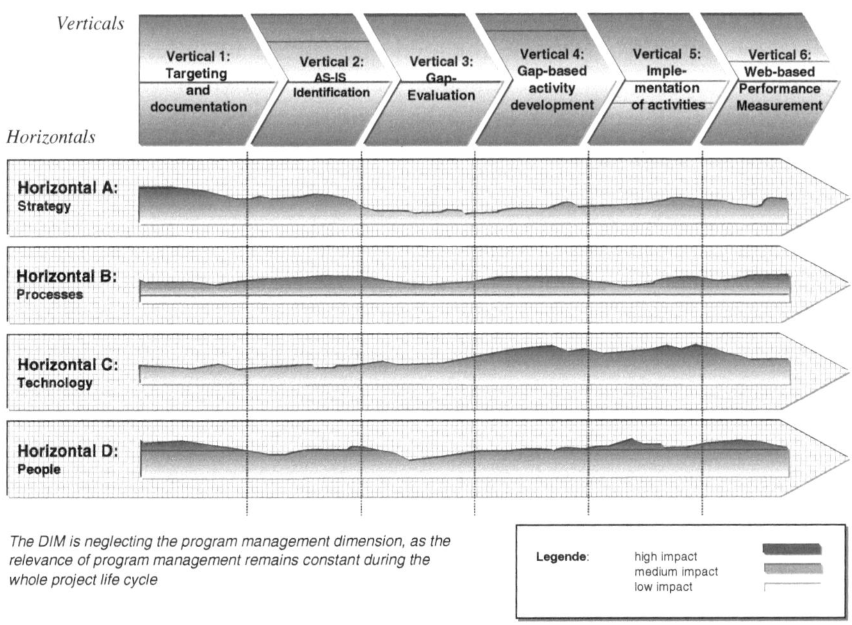

Chart 6.1 Dimension-Impact Matrix (DIM)

ject flows along the horizontals. The DIM also represents another difference between CCR and BPR. BPR primarily focused on processes and neglected the other horizontals – besides the target ERP systems – but this issue has already been discussed in Chap. 4. In our workshop sessions, we consolidated the relevant information concerning further input for the theory underlying the DIM and obtained consistent results. At this stage we realized that we had identified the core problem caused by the New Economy and the changed contingency situation, why conventional methodologies and management approaches would not be working anymore as such.

The Structure of CCR

Based on the workshops and core projects where we reframed an unsuccessful e-commerce solution, we were able to develop the framework for CCR and now have a prototype methodology compatible with the needs of the c-economy. The findings are closely linked with the information provided in Chap. 4, as we identified some key problems caused by an exaggerated focus on processes and reengineering. And undoubtedly these terms are closely linked with BPR as indicated in that chapter.

This generic prototype was located – regarding its content, level of detail, and grade of operationalization – on a level comparable to that of the first publications on BPR, when it emerged and spread to different business segments. Our aim was to continuously contrast our findings against the conventional BPR approach as the benchmark concerning the extent of innovation provided by our CCR approach and of course the problem CCR was developed to solve.

Essential to this work was the contingency theory[6] that we used to validate the methodology for changing situational aspects and factors. This presented some problems as the contingency theory does not really provide a framework for such dynamic markets and developments. Nonetheless we tried to apply this theory as we were aiming for a comprehensive and valid approach which considered all relevant and existing theories and methods.

Within this phase we also screened all kinds of pragmatic approaches used in the implementation of BPR. Operational models from different consultancy companies were therefore analyzed and evaluated regarding their

[6] Donaldson, L.: "Contingency Theory", Ashgate, Aldershot, March 1994 .

procedures, contents, and tools. This gave us an overview of how BPR projects were realized and underpinned our findings from the internal studies concerning the focus of the dominant process.

As already mentioned, we developed the CCR approach – based on the DIM – alongside verticals and horizontals which provided a framework of dimensions for comprehensive CCR initiatives. In the following section these verticals and horizontals will be described to aid your understanding of the types of topics and issues that should be tackled. Furthermore, this section should provide an overview of the generic approach, and afterward an option for an operationalized CCR approach will be presented. This will give you an understanding of a tangible and pragmatic implementation plan that includes the relevant modules, activities, and checkpoints.

The CCR Horizontals

The horizontals represent areas driving a company and are essential to CCR projects. Horizontals are fixed elements in every CCR project. This means that for successful implementation of a CCR project, comprehensive coverage of all four horizontals is crucial. Why are they called horizontals?

The term arose during the workshops and analyses of the findings, when the DIM was born. Using the DIM to evaluate the dynamic relevance of the four horizontals over the project flow, we measured their impact by validating them against the different phases –called "verticals". Imagine using a pen to draw a line vertically downward starting from a specific phase. By doing that it is possible to identify the specific impact or relevance of the phase.

In running this evaluation we analyzed the important vertical streams. Based on this procedure we finally agreed on the term verticals (and horizontals) and the correlation between the verticals and their impact on the horizontals' relevance. These horizontals as such are not innovative at first sight, but cover a bundle of modules required to ensure understanding of a consistent approach.

Strategy

The "strategy" horizontal covers all strategic and strategy-linked topics and issues and consists of 6 modules and 32 activity packages. Therefore, its impact at the beginning of CCR projects is large and much important information can be gained from this horizontal. Gaps arose in this horizontal, ranging from no strategy at all up to completely diverging opinions of what the strategy was supposed to be. This horizontal is especially important when considering the paradigm shift from BPR to CCR, as most BPR initiatives did not deal enough with strategic issues and did not consider at all strategic internal alignment on both the vertical and horizontal dimensions. Strategy-focused activities were more or less marketable add-ons to the sales process, as otherwise the client would have considered BPR projects as simply IT projects.

Let us take a closer look at the different modules of interest within the strategy to get a much better impression of the issues.

Vision

In this area the initial objectives for the c-commerce solution as well as their alignment are analyzed. We frequently faced different opinions of what the mission and vision were supposed to be. This created top-down problems in communication and acceptance, as official messages from top management were misunderstood and the set actions confused other parts of the organization. Within other projects we figured out, that the initially planned c-commerce solution was supposed to be completely different regarding for example products or service.

The vision module covers the strategic alignment of a c-commerce solution with the company's strategy. Many problems can evolve from these issues, as c-commerce solutions are not an integral part of a company's strategy. This often happens when overall planning and annual goal setting are discussed, and causes confusion and frustration.

Regardless of whether we are talking about c-commerce companies or c-commerce solutions, the strategic alignment, internal integration on the horizontal and vertical levels as well as an in-depth understanding of the originally planned c-commerce solution are important to the success of a c-commerce solution and its reframing. Within CCR this is being considered by focusing especially on strategic aspects at the beginning of a CCR project.

Throughout the project-flow over all six verticals the Vision module covers strategy and change management topics facilitating the entire project work. Especially within the second and third vertical as part of the Vision module the extend of required reframing is defined and agreed upon. Towards the end of the CCR project the Visioning modules loses importance, whereas the other strategy modules finance, market and structure gain relevance.

Finance

This module deals with all the finance-driven aspects of a c-commerce solution. The original business case for the c-commerce solution is validated according to customary business criteria. During one of our projects the original business case was not even available anymore as the CFO deleted the file.

Why are we using the original business case? This helps us to understand the value creation module, the logic behind and the expected cash-flows. Furthermore we can immediately identify inconsistencies within the business case, maybe having had impact on the failure of the c-commerce solution. If we would get to the point, that the business model as such – due to false assumptions – caused the damage, we would then use this know-how for analyzing the remaining part of the initial c-commerce solution.

Initially, the business model(s) as well as the finally implemented value creation model are evaluated and matched to the contingency situation. Furthermore, due diligence[7] is required to get a deeper understanding of the value created or the cash-burn rate realized.

Level of Innovation and Distinction (LID)

The LID module is closely linked with the finance module, as information from the former will be considered when evaluating the solution as such. Within the LID module aspects such as the uniqueness of the solution, technical expertise, and the concept or idea behind the solution will be validated alongside certain criteria such as

- sustainability
- risks
- time-to-market
- type of innovation (Software, Hardware or a combination of both)

---

[7] Bing, G.: "Due Diligence Techniques and Analysis", Quorum Books, August 1996

Based on these issues the financial analyses integrate the intangible assets and also consider those financial aspects and values that are not directly measurable.[8]

In some projects we engaged further externals to enable a more detailed evaluation of the LID parameter as many c-commerce solutions were based on very specific technology components, that required technical experts for evaluation to engage.

Market

As part of the market module, core market segments as well as clients' needs and requirements will be evaluated. This information will be matched to the products or services provided by the specific solution that has to be reframed. The products or services will furthermore be benchmarked[9] against similar products or services already available on the market. Here once more, we sometimes engage external experts for valid investigations.

An inherent part of the market module is the screening of the size of the market, the growth rate, and potential competitors. The market module mainly follows conventional guidelines of strategy or management projects, but correlating them with the results of the business model evaluation as part of the strategy module to assess similarities and tendencies. This allows us to generate a set of parameters we use for analyzing the impact of the market developments on the application of the business model. In essence, we gain an understanding of how the business model would have worked, considering all other drivers of the c-commerce solution would have been aligned and consistent.

Before benchmarking a product or service a more detailed analysis of the core product or service is often useful. Based on our experience we know that an initial analysis provides essential input for the required product/service alignment or adoption and indicates the fit with the client's needs.

---

[8] Lev, B.: "What Value Analysts?", November 1999

[9] Czarnecki, M.: "Managing by Measuring: How to Improve Your Organization's Performance through Effective Benchmarking," Amacom, 1999.

Performance Measurement and Management (PMM)

The PMM module is inherent part of three of the four horizontals and is important for the development of an adequate evaluation system for the reframed solution. The PMM module primarily focuses on the identification of performance indicators, their validation, whether they measure what they are supposed to, and whether the information as such is valid. Here statistical criteria such as objectivity, reliability, and validity come into play to facilitate consistent and value-adding measurement and management.[10] Information and data gained out of the strategy, market and finance modules are being assessed regarding valid and useful performance measures.

Structure

An important part when reframing a c-commerce solution is the structure of the organization delivering a product or service. Therefore, rough screening of the originally defined target-organization has to be done to evolve – similar to the strategy module – if the target-organization would have in alignment with the strategy, and product and service delivery requirements or not, and if the transformation process was set up adequately for establishing the new structure. This also was done to evaluate the competences of the different units and where interfaces between these units exist, potentially causing conflicts. This module is linked with the "people" horizontal as diverging responsibilities and views of the different units' rules and tasks are being considered and discussed.

From an external perspective, the organization is evaluated alongside the existing network of partners, and potential new partners are identified. The existing partners will be analyzed for their input and their value to the specific c-commerce solution. Many times we found that 70 to 80 percent of registered partners do not create any added value or strategic advantage. Based on this screening the network of partners can be optimized and resources allocated more effectively.

During the second and third vertical, the structure module provides the required input for developing the appropriate organization and to establish a successful transition process. Especially in the third vertical close coop-

[10] Chang, R. Y.; Morgan, M. W.: "Performance Scorecards," Jossey-Bass, April 2000

eration with the "people" horizontal happens as during the CCR implementation vertical, the people horizontal has to facilitate and drive the transformation process.

Processes

This horizontal comprises 3 modules that are based upon 13 activity packages. Within this horizontal we tackle conventional process issues focusing on:

1. Potentials
2. Competences
3. PPM

Overall we are using process workflow approach and Zig Zag diagrams to enable efficient identification of processual critical areas such as

- bad ratios between value-adding and non-value-adding activities,
- process flow breaks due to media-changes such as changes from IT to manual, when data have to be entered manually into an IT system even though they would be available digitally out of another system,
- redundancies,
- overall quantity of process, activity packages and activities and their coherence.

The process horizontal, as part of the whole CCR approach, does not play such a dominant role as within the BPR framework, as already indicated earlier. Nonetheless, there are some issues to be addressed to ensure a successful reframing of the specific solution.

Potentials

Based on available process documentation the core processes are defined and analyzed according to the results and information from other verticals. The process analysis focuses on the level of integration with contingency systems in a technical and non-technical dimension; many solutions lack the required integration of processes and IT enabling the use of fully automated processes.[11]

[11] Kalmbach, C.: "Dispelling the Myths of Alliances," Anderson Consulting, June 2000.

Depending upon the industry and the availability, benchmarking analyses can be done alongside the defined core processes to evaluate further potential for improvement. Here specific industry process blueprints can be used to facilitate an efficient screening and analysis process. Based on our experience the interesting potentials are found in the peripheral aspects of processes – not the processes in the sense of workflow or bundle of activities which offer real value-adding potentials. Therefore the interface between technical solutions and the automation of the processes offers huge potentials. This seems to be the result of quick and dirty implementations, and does not really consider the optimized usage and implementation of vertical and horizontal interfaces.

To facilitate the later implementation of an adequate PMM system, following the identification and realization of the potentials, the process and task owner should be defined. This is necessary to identify a specific person in case the process parameters are not within the predefined range of acceptance. We were often confronted with the situation where we had evolved potentials but there was nobody responsible for the "hidden" potentials. Thus, we could not initiate the required changes and had to set up a human resource structure in order to do so.

Competences

Using the output of the "potentials" module, processes, tasks, and activities can be aligned with the new roles and responsibilities. At the outset, core competences have to be defined based on the results of the "strategy" horizontal. This link is necessary to define the right set of core competences for achieving and reaching the defined and reframed targets and goals – strategically as well as operationally. These core competences are analyzed alongside a proven concept with six subcategories and are added to two peripheral groups of competences, namely, the occupational and the behavioral ones.

Within the as-is organization we are evaluating the responsibilities to be in a position to understand whether or not there are competency gaps that have to be closed. In close alignment with the latter module of this vertical, new roles and responsibilities are being identified, selected, and named, as is the individual in charge of these.

As underlying concept or idea we are initiating so called parameter-based skills matrices. These matrices enable us to match individuals' skills pro-

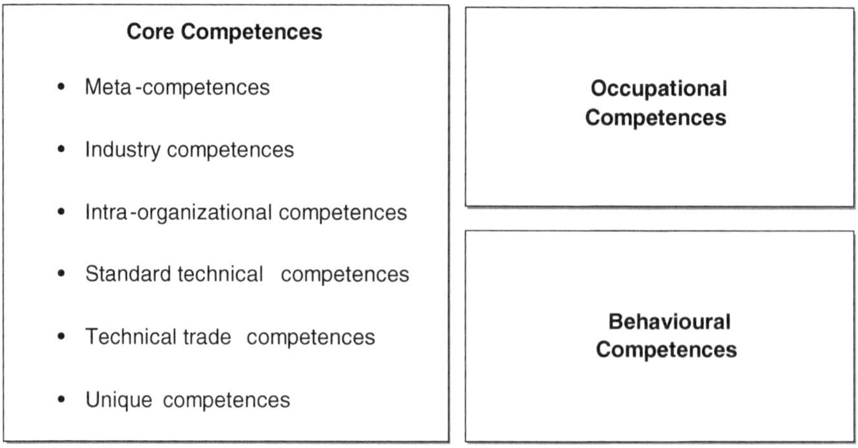

Chart 6.2 Types of competences[12]

files with to-be requirements immediately leading to relevant training and development needs. This happens in close alignment with the "people" horizontal mainly driven by the "people" horizontal.

Performance Measurement and Management (PMM)

In the area of processes the PMM-module focuses on the development of operational key performance indicators (KPI) for the reframed core and supporting processes. Especially in the verticals 3 and 4 the PMM-module plays an essential role as the KPIs for the reframed c-solution or c-company respectively are being developed. To ensure an efficient and functioning PMM system as part of the CCR project, a consistent KPI system or pyramid has to be evolved. More so, for each core process with all linked supporting processes specific process owners have to be identified. After the finalization of the CCR project an e-PMM system will be the IT basis for entering, consolidating and evaluating key performance data. The "e" enables the reframed company to track their data based on a web technology based tool ensuring online and comprehensive information management.

[12] Meta-competences represent basic knowledge and skills that are broadly applicable for work performance in general. Examples are learning ability, ability to tolerate change, cooperative abilities, communication skills, and so forth.

Technology

This horizontal, focusing on the reframing of the inherent IT-oriented issues and infrastructure of the c-commerce solutions, covers 5 modules with 33 activity packages and plays a major role because one key issue is the definition of the performance of the current IT components, the definition of parameters for the reframed c-commerce solution that can be supported by the current IT, and the development of a business case, which has to be invested to gain an understanding both of the initially planned and the as-is IT environment, and of the strengths and weaknesses of the latter. This information is essential to estimate the reframing effort in the "technology" horizontal, considering available, already in place components and those additional ones that are required to enable the support of the reframed c-solution. This horizontal and several other activities depend strongly on the contingency situation, top management, and the financial situation of the company, and whether any further investments in IT are possible or explicitly denied.

The "technology" horizontal consists of the following five modules:

1. Infrastructure
2. Software
3. Hardware
4. PPM
5. Security

Infrastructure

Infrastructure in this environment means components that are key to the c-commerce solution, and necessary and irreplaceable for delivering the product or service. Based on the analyses of these infrastructural components, it is easy to get an understanding about the existing factors of differentiation compared to competitors. Furthermore it becomes obvious how long, if at all, these factors will exist, which means, of course, when the know-how advantage will be gone.

In the next stage the infrastructure is evaluated for its performance and to deliver the core product or service within a possibly existing range of acceptance This leads to the conclusion whether or not, for the on-going delivery of the product or service, alignments in the area of the infrastructure have to be realized. Here as well the contingency situation comes into play, as decisions are required on whether further investments should be made in the current offering. Also important is information from the strategy horizontal providing details on potentials and risks by continuing to sell and to promote the current offering that cannot be as successful as expected, otherwise the CCR project would not have been necessary.

Based on these details the alignments and changes required in the area of the infrastructural components should be documented and implementation initiated.

Software

The software focuses on all kinds of supporting products and solutions that are installed and in use and are somehow linked or connected with the c-commerce solution and delivery of the offering(s). This area inherently deals with all kinds of existing data, be they master data or supporting or peripheral data.[13] Also analyzed are the backbones[14] of the databases available and their links with other infrastructural, software, and hardware components, which will be discussed later.

The outcome of the software part is a set of required activities and changes in this area, evolving and aligning with the reframed strategy and offering, and, if a close link or interface to the delivery of the newly reframed offering exists, it will be considered which parts of the software are to remain as software and which parts will be essential for the delivery and therefore have to be considered as an integral part of the infrastructure. It is clear – when reframing the offering – that some infrastructural components will no longer belong to the group of infrastructures and will be moved to the conventional software area.

Hardware

Hardware is used in the conventional way and deals with the existing hardware components. This is essential when reframing the solution, as thorough screening has to be done on the performance limitations of these components supporting the delivery of the current offering.

---

[13] Master data: data concerning the core business. Supporting or peripheral data: data that support office administration.

[14] Central computer or group of computers with high capacity of data transmission, connected to several smaller computers.

When reframing the c-commerce solution, in our experience, the required IT performance changes. This leads to the stage where the reframed offering and linked systems have to be analyzed for new and adequate levels of performance, in terms of technical performance requirements. Based on these indicators and their range, the existing hardware has to be evaluated against a potential gap arising after the reframing process has been completed.

For the hardware topic it is essential to be clear about the massive investments that have been made in the last few years. Most investments are still not amortized and therefore CFOs in most cases are not willing to extend the budget for further investment in IT. This means that the optimal fit between the existing hardware and the reframed solution is essential for success. Obviously there is a close link between the three topics of infrastructure, software, and hardware. All of them should be aligned with the reframed solution to enable a positive CFROI.[15]

Based on the initial assessment of the existing hardware components and the results from the other verticals, an evaluation of any gap between the hardware and the reframed solution can be carried out. Analysis of this gap leads to the development of a new hardware blueprint and defines the limitations of the reframed solutions as the findings of this activity are fed into the content-driven strategic and financial reframing of the c-commerce solution. These feedback loops[16] are very helpful and form a sound basis for the reframing process as such, because they ensure consistency for the whole solution.

The gap analysis also provides details on how the existing hardware could be extended and establishes a link to the results from other verticals. This means that a company's top management could indeed decide upon possible investment in the hardware if the reframed solution were to require such an investment. The analysis shows that the minimum investment required to assure an efficient performance for delivery of the reframed c-commerce product or service could be defined and calculated quantitatively. This is an important point, when developing the business case for the reframed solution.

---

[15] Madden, B. J.: "CFROI Valuation: A Total System Approach to Valuing the Firm", Butterworth–Heinemann, Oxford, April 1999.

[16] Seebacher, Uwe G.: "Performance Measurement and Evaluation," in: OU Business School MBA Event, Brussels, 1997.

PMM

In alignment with the PMM activity set[17] of the other horizontals, the focus in technological aspects is on the components' performance as such, supporting the delivery of the product or service of the reframed solution. At the beginning, analyses of all three categories – infrastructure, software, and hardware – are done. This evaluation occurs on a process basis measuring the times for the different processes and activities. Depending upon the specific company or part of an organization, whether or not process-based management is in place or at least the relevant indicators, process-based parameters have to be developed for the PMM analysis.

Our experience showed that the concept of process-based management or value management is a useful tool for quickly evolving the set of parameters required to assess the technology. Based on the assessment, the performance is documented and matched to external benchmarks. This allows an understanding of existing potentials or weaknesses to be gained, and leads into the development of reframed indicators or parameters aligned with the new product(s) and/or service(s) to be offered after completion of the CCR project.

Finally, as part of the technology horizontal, the adoption of an existing PMM system or the implementation of a new system can be useful to ensure on-going evaluation and assessment of IT-related components and systems. In the case of large, multinational companies or c-commerce solutions, the implementation of an ePMM[18] system can be of advantage – as indicated already in the "process horizontal" section – because, on an index basis, the evaluation can be realized on time and globally provides a consistent goal hierarchy and information on those processes, areas, products, or regions that are outside their predefined ranges of acceptance.

---

[17] Simons, R.; Davila, A.; Kaplan, R.: "Performance Measurement & Control Systems for Implementing Strategy: Text & Cases", Prentice Hall College, Englewood Cliffs, June 1999

[18] Seebacher, Uwe G.: "Electronic Performance Measurement and Management (E-PMM) zur prozessbasierten Center- aber auch Unternehmenssteuerung," IMC, 3/2001.

Security

The last of the five areas within the technology vertical focuses on security and integrity issues.[19] This area is of growing importance because, as more and more firewalls[20] have to be crossed, more and more information flows from one intranet to another and the cracks[21] become more and more tricky to close in all kinds of security systems.

In most of our CCR projects security was not a very big issue, as the companies either were using up-to-date security systems or had only internal processes and one front-end web page, which does not require a huge security system.

After an initial evaluation and discussion of the requirements for the reframed solution, an assessment of current security standards and technologies is undertaken. Mostly, the support that IT provides is enormous, as the system administrators know their systems' weaknesses and problems. Therefore, not much time has to be invested. What makes the assessment complicated, however, is the fact that the current systems follow other rules and workflows and the reframed systems as such are not in place to provide more detailed information on the important areas and processes concerning security issues.

Based on the assessment, the concept for adoption is evolved and converted into a time matrix dealing with the process of realization and implementation of the reframed solution. Within the fifth vertical, "implementation of CCR-plan," the technological realization along with the discussed sets of activities is carried out to form the backbone of the reframed solution.

People

The people horizontal with its 5 modules and 20 activity packages tackles issues of communication, commitment, identification, and motivation of all personnel involved. The theoretical background lies in disciplines such

[19] Escamilla, T.: "Intrusion Detection: Network Security beyond the Firewall," John Wiley & Sons, September 1998

[20] TechRepublic: "Network Administrator's Security Resource Guide," TechRepublic, August 2000.

[21] Stephenson, P.: "Investigating Computer-Related Crime – A handbook for Corporate Investigators," CRC Press, Boca Raton, FL, September 1999.

as change management or strategic human resource management (see also Chap. 8). During the last few years people have understood and learned more about the need for change management, in order to lead individuals through all the different kinds of change projects and initiatives.

The people vertical refers to the following:

- Improving the quality of information
- Dealing with any personal resistance and political pressures
- Building organizational awareness, understanding, and psychological commitment for effective CCR
- Decreasing the uncertainty surrounding decisions linked to CCR initiatives

The people horizontal comprises five modules:

1. Management
2. Communication
3. Teams
4. Human resources
5. PMM

This horizontal is the most complex one. In many ways the requirements for coherence and consistency arise from the other horizontals, but, in the end, the real implementation of the change is left to the individuals within the reframed company or solution. Most change programs do not work because they are guided by a theory or a model of change that is fundamentally flawed. The common belief is that the place to begin is with the knowledge and attitudes of the individuals concerned. Changes in attitudes, the theory goes, lead to changes in individual behavior, and this kind of change will lead to organizational change.

Such theories have got the change process entirely backward. In fact, individual behavior is powerfully shaped by the organizational roles that people play. The most effective way to change behavior is therefore to start at the top of an organization – with the senior managers and ideally with the most charismatic ones. Having them on board provides one cornerstone for the successful implementation of CCR. Many times I have heard people complaining that yet another project is added by top management to all the other on-going activities and daily business, from the top down as it were. This term "top-down" has a kind of negative connotation, but especially in our case for CCR, the top-down approach for initiating the required internal change is hugely important to ensure acceptance within an organization.

Management

This first area aims to focus the entire management of the organization. That means establishing a common sense of purpose among all the leaders facilitating the smooth implementation of the reframing. My experience is that change for the sake of it is not possible to communicate. Rather, the underlying key message for change needs to be transmitted. Using this core message and understanding the importance and the ways of how to place change in the minds of individuals lead to lasting results.

Management especially is key to this part of the exercise. These leaders are probably the toughest to convince and to win over to the change process. They will probably immediately agree on the change as such, as they have to achieve their business goals. But this is by no means enough. During one of my projects a manager once said: "We do change tomorrow between 8.30 and 9.00am. That's when I'm gonna meet my team leaders. I'll tell them that we have to make change and that's it!" I liked that manager – he was so helpful in deepening my understanding of communicating change to top managers in their forties and fifties, with broad experience, and who were mostly pragmatic, sometimes too pragmatic, when implementing new things such as change.

At the beginning it is essential to achieve alignment of the top management. This alignment has to be developed through off-site sessions using different workshop methods. It is closely linked with a team spirit that has to be evolved by working on:

- A common vision
- A common objective
- A common understanding
- An overall commitment to the CCR initiative

Usually, I run a three-day session with top management and also allow some time for alternative exercises such as sports, reading, etc.

The alignment has one big advantage: achieving a common sense of purpose mostly means that top management as such is well on board. By having a common understanding of what has to be done, managers lose their anxiety and become active promoters and sponsors of the CCR initiative. This is key! Managers normally drive the process forward when they become creative and are motivated to support the CCR and change process. This allows the other horizontals to be conceptualized, defined, developed, and implemented on the basis of all kinds of leadership actions.

These leadership actions are activities that deal openly with the relevant issues and topics of concern. By doing this, all involved individuals will:

- Learn more about what will happen
- Get an understanding of the common goal
- Lose their anxiety
- Recognize their managers as leading the CCR activities, actively driving the initiative forward (the most important aspect)

Once, when I was working on the management module, I developed a deep understanding of the client's corporate culture. By working with the managers all kinds of cultural issues were brought up and discussed openly. This enabled me to identify crucial topics and hotspots within the organization, which proved to be very useful for the other areas of the people horizontal.

Based on this experience, I added another target or area to work on, when tackling top management as a group of individuals: the cultural assessment of the client organization. This was based on some key questions on culture, ethics, policies, and practices. Initially I wanted to run structured interviews for the cultural assessment but ended up gathering information based on the workshops and exercises with the top managers.

The management module is essential for the other modules of the people horizontal, as some of the core messages and issues that are identified and evolved have to be considered when dealing with change in the organization.

Communication

This module as such cannot be examined separately from all the other modules, areas, and activities. Nevertheless, as it is crucial to all CCR engagements, this module within the people horizontal deals with the required communication planning and implementation.

At the beginning of a CCR project, a rough plan of required communication activities has to be drawn up. Such a communication plan includes:

- Media analyses (internal and external)
- Target group analyses
- Key messages and hot topics
- Channel analyses
- The timing of communication activities
- Costs of communication

This is not rocket science, but essential to work through on a prestructured basis. It goes without saying that the communication module affects the other modules of the people horizontal as well as the other horizontals. In most CCR projects the marketing or public relations department of the client was involved as this reduces the need for external consultants and, furthermore, the internal staff know the relevant media and channels better than consultants.

Indirectly this enlarged the project team, but was another way of increasing the number of active communicators and facilitators within the organization.

This leads us into the area of communication implementation. Based on the evolved communication planning the concrete activities have to be realized by individuals, departments, and entire business units. Consistency of the content communicated and the time-driven alignment of the defined activities are key. The implementation is heavily dependent upon the procedure for the realization of the entire CCR activities.

Especially at the beginning, experience showed that general information and updates and the communication of quick wins are useful to establish an on-going process of information and communication. In vertical 2, "as-is assessment," and vertical 3, "definition of gaps evaluation," it was sometimes rather hard to evolve content for communication, as the focus in these verticals is more on identification and evaluation. This information does not appear to be as "sexy" as marketing and public relations departments often ask for, which leads into controversial discussions about what to communicate and to distribute.

In some CCR projects it was essential for the organization that we would communicate the commencing of the CCR initiative as a trust-building activity. Bases on my experience more and more investors and shareholders want to be on the safe side by knowing that a company, seeming to be in some kind of trouble, does start initiatives like a CCR project to reduce loss and ensuring long-term success.

In the area of communication implementation several feedback and alignment loops were specially run to ensure an optimal fit with the CCR activities of the other horizontals.

Teams

The team modules comprise three activity areas:

1. Establishment of team spirit
2. Assessment of change readiness
3. Implementation of team-building activities

Overall, this module focuses all the project teams involved on the CCR project. This is important for consistency of results from the autonomous project teams, which are often working independently and in parallel. This experience originates from projects in BPR or ERP implementations where huge teams were working simultaneously but not always achieving results to a certain level of consistency.

The first activity is similar to the "leadership alignment" task and aims to establish a certain team culture and spirit as one of the building blocks for successful teamwork alongside the whole verticals. In this area, the results of the leadership alignment workshops are used to challenge top management's vision and goals. This task is more one of tackling or facilitating an open discussion as the vision is hardly being changed. Nevertheless, I had projects in which the CEO attended team-building workshops discussing the defined vision with the project teams and in the end he redefined the vision, as he understood that the main agreed version was not the one the project teams would go for. Albeit interesting, and not a little dangerous, this openness in the end increased his acceptance and role as CCR promoter.

The assessment of the readiness to change at a team level deals with cross-checking and adding the information and results of the cultural assessment at top-management level. Furthermore, it helps to identify gaps within the different teams concerning their ability to support the CCR change process. This comes into play especially when talking about new roles and responsibilities and new organizational structures after CCR has been employed. Based at the team level, in addition, "hot" topics can be identified and actively dealt with at this early stage of the CCR project. This helps to avoid irritations and resentments arising later during the project flow.

Based on the information gained, team-building activities have to be defined alongside the overall CCR engagement plan. This task works according to the leadership activities and ensures a consistent and aligned procedure.

Human Resources (HR)

The HR modules focus on the integration of and alignment with the overall HR strategy of the company or the specific unit in which a CCR initiative has to be launched.

In this area we start with a brief assessment of the aims and goals for HR activities. This leads to information on whether the company, from an HR point of view:

- Either tries to fulfill short-term staffing and competency requirements by using external recruitment and training and development services
- Or focuses more on the long term by aiming to gradually build up the required competences and expertise internally and to develop the internal labor market

The second alternative requires a certain degree of company maturity as it is the more cost-intensive one and needs a clear and definite direction of where the organization is heading. In assessing the defined goals of HR we normally use tools such as workshops and interviews with standardized sets of questions. Based on our experience, this activity leads directly to the analysis of the current HR and reward systems. This has been shown to be a difficult part as especially in the HR area much irritation has been caused and mistakes made. In many cases the pay and reward system is far and away from being aligned with the current culture and spirit of a company.

When reframing unsuccessful c-commerce solutions we are in a situation similar to turn-around management projects. This fact forces us to focus on eliminating irritations and problems in the HR area in general and to identify the company's problem areas that have arisen over its existence. Furthermore, the other modules in the people horizontal provide the relevant details which we can use in the next vertical, "gap evaluation," to evolve the aligned HR and – linked with that – payment system. Depending on the predefined culture and understanding of the organizational unit to be re-framed, different mechanisms of strategic HR management will be aligned for the specific contingency situation and integrated into the new HR and payment system.

Most of the challenges presented by the convergence of HR and the cyber-economy and discovered during the different CCR projects to date will be discussed in Chap. 8, where we aim to consolidate the different aspects and issues. Based on the increasing importance of dismantling the barriers to mobility, the HR discussion is relevant to all organizations.

Market

This last module deals with the exchange of experience and expertise in the area of strategic HR management. The market module aims to bench-mark relevant parameters and standards within the same industries as the client's organization but cross-industry as well. This was especially useful when we had to reframe c-commerce solutions in Old Economy companies which did not have in place new and more accurate HR policies and pro-cedures.

Therefore, and for New Economy companies in particular, such as real start-ups, we were often faced with turning down very employee-friendly HR policies and practices because they were very expensive, and were not reasonable when compared to the high cash-burn rate anyway.

For this module we used conventional approaches such as primary and secondary sources, as well as the profound experience and expertise of the different HR institutes in universities.

Conclusion

This chapter was intended to give you an overview of what we did during different CCR engagements. To facilitate ease of reading we structured our activities so that we can now use this kind of approach or business model for further CCR initiatives and of course discussions.

This approach is the first detailed one to be written down and reflects our findings in international CCR projects. The CCR approach as such is located at a high level of aggregation, is down to earth, and concerned with the bottom line.

We are conscious that such an operationalization carries risks, as the door is opened for criticism. As we see this approach and this book as the basis for new discussions on whether or not BPR is overcome and CCR can provide a framework that offers the chance to deal with unsuccessful c-commerce solutions, we want this door symbolically opened to generate an intensive discussion and exchange of ideas.

CHAPTER 7

The New Role of Information Technology

IT has defined for nearly 70 years how businesses should operate in an economy that is increasingly based on providing services (the third sector) rather than on the agricultural or manufacturing sectors.[1] In earlier chapters, we have already seen how various forms of IT and their application have had a major, worldwide impact on organizations' structures, their HR, their strategies, and even their very business models.

In this chapter I shall first present a short overview of the "e-volution" of IT. Then I shall discuss the economic impact of IT, both from a micro- as well as macroeconomic perspective. In the last part of this chapter, I shall go into detail about the roles of IT in the CCR approach.

The "E-volution" of IT

To ponder the beginnings of IT, we have to go back to "Big Blue" in the 1940s,[2] or start even earlier, in the 1930s, with K. Zuse,[3] a German who designed one of the first "calculating machines" by connecting hundreds of ancient switches.

In the 1960s, fragmented IT programs were specially designed for the automation of certain tasks in different areas of a business, particularly accounting, such as preparing a general ledger, a payroll, or an order entry. These programs were mainly self-programmed by the companies' computer experts, using very complicated and time-consuming programming

---

[1] Saultz, K.: "Blue Chip Finds Growth in Service Sector Fueled by High-Tech Industry," Greater Columbus Chamber, 2000

[2] Ifrah, G.: "The Universal History of Computing: From the Abacus to the Quantum Computer", John Wiley & Sons, October 2000

[3] Lee, J.A.N.: "Great Brains – Konrad Zuse: The Machine That Changed the World," http://ei.cs.vt.edu/.

languages like Assembler[4] or FORTRAN.[5] All of these programs were isolated.

During the 1970s and 1980s, suites of customized, integrated applications were in use. The main aim was to integrate functional areas of companies – special solutions were designed for manufacturing, distribution, or finance. Also, programming tools became more and more sophisticated, which simultaneously made the programming work, supporting features like programming modules and the reuse of previously designed modules in more than one program, easier.

In the 1990s, in the larger businesses, enterprise-wide applications started. Companies like Oracle, People Soft, J.D. Edwards, and SAP gained market share in these new business fields and tried to establish standards for the market. The new idea was that one application package should integrate all flows of information and storage and should be able to run a whole business the size of a multinational Fortune-500 company. The development of these applications made the use of sophisticated programming tools and languages like C++ and others necessary.

Development did not stop there, however, and some very early, enterprise-wide applications began to be cross-connected with each other, linking companies.

In the mid 1990s, in the automotive and process industries, many supplier/manufacturer relations were supported by working electronic data interchange (EDI)[6] links, providing information about supply and demand and supporting just-in-time concepts.[7] Unfortunately, EDI could not really succeed. With the start of e-commerce initiatives the idea of integrated business applications grew, integrating business partners by connecting their processes, sharing their data, and automating the supply and demand activities.

---

[4] McQuillen, K.; Prince, A.: "MVS Assembler Language", Mike Murach & Associates, July 1987.

[5] Etzel, M.; Dickinson, K.: "Digital Visual FORTRAN Programmer's Guide," Digital Press, April 1999

[6] Jilovec, N.: "A to Z of EDI," second edition, 29th Street Press, April 1998

[7] Cheng, T.C.E.; Podolsky, S.: "Just-in-Time-Manufacturing – An Introduction," Kluwer AcademicPublishers, 1996

At present, in the year 2002, we have to deal with companies with integrated applications like CRM[8] or supply chain solutions working on top of ERP packages. The companies are linked together with the help of integrated solutions.[9] This means, for instance, that the CRM solution of a supplier is linked directly with the supply chain solution of the customer. The advantage is that these links are no longer one-to-one links like the EDI solutions were, but can be defined anew for each transaction, using virtual markets, platforms, etc. Open standards[10] and standardized interfaces enabled that development.

The Driving Economic Role of IT

Whereas overall spending on IT from the 1930s until the mid 1980s was relatively negligible, the emergence of the World Wide Web in 1989 triggered a boom in IT investment that had been unforeseen.

The relevance of IT for companies soared for several reasons. First, more and more businesses geared themselves up technologically to make the best use of the Internet, which offered useful and cost-cutting services such as e-mail and TELNET. Large investments in the necessary technological infrastructure (computers, software, networks, etc.) had to be made. Second, the World Wide Web changed from a passive medium to an active one, which enabled business transactions to take place within just a few years.[11] As we saw earlier, companies did not want to miss the boat and consequently initiated large-scale, cost-intensive technology projects. Third, as IT started to become more sophisticated as a result of inventions and enhancements, its importance for businesses increased as it shifted from being an enabler toward being a driver. Let us take a closer look at these two terms.

---

[8] "Transforming Customer Relationships with Business Integration," IBM Library, June 2000.

[9] Magretta, J.: "The Power of Virtual Integration: An Interview with Dell Computer's Michael Dell," Harvard Business Review, April 1998

[10] Holstein, W.J.: "Big Blue Wages open Warfare," Business 2.0, April 2001

[11] "Real Numbers 2000," ActiveMedia, June 2000

IT – Driving Microeconomics

Until the mid 1980s, IT only provided a support function in companies. For instance, it *enabled* accounting procedures as well as inventory management to be less cumbersome and facilitated communication between back and front offices. Though IT obviously improved many internal processes, executive directors as well as employees still saw it as a tool that often did not work properly and were skeptical about it as a result of these malfunctions. It was, more or less successfully, integrated into existing structures and intended merely to support them. Technological hurdles as well as people's adversity to change made IT less important. IT was approached in a way where it was literally bent and stretched so that it fitted into existing structures and processes. Naturally, much of its capabilities were lost as a consequence. Investment, though, was very high.

In the New Economy, the role of IT changed drastically. When the "technology boom" started at the beginning of the 1990s, IT still performed most of its enabling functions (and still does). But as it became more diverse and reliable – especially with the advent of ERP systems – the possibilities for its application increased and it started to penetrate companies' core- and value-adding operations and processes, for example procurement, production, and sales. Coupled with the Internet's tremendous networking benefits and the World Wide Web's overall popularity, the communications revolution and globalization, IT became a driver, as whole business models were constructed around this virtuous square and existing processes were remodeled to optimally integrate IT. In comparison to its position as an enabler, IT came to the attention of directors, managers, and employees. The microeconomic relevance of IT had gained weight.

At a microeconomic level, myriad factors come into play and consequently changes may have far-reaching implications. Companies' large investment in IT had itself an overwhelmingly profound effect on their business structures all around the world.

Enormous spending on IT – American companies, for example, increased their annual investment in computers 14-fold in the 1990s in real terms[12] – naturally constituted fertile ground on which new companies specializing either directly in IT, or in providing complementary services such as consultancy or architectural design, could grow. These companies, built from

[12] "The New Economy," The Economist, July 24, 1999

scratch, often had a distinct advantage, for they possessed a flexibility, be it physical, structural, procedural, or human, that could hardly be matched by the older players. They could therefore more easily explore niches and provide tailor-made services.[13,14] An interesting and appropriate example is Juniper Networks Inc.[15] In just three years it captured 35 percent of the market for high-end Internet routers and managed to outpace its rival, Nortel Networks Inc.[16] The key was that Juniper developed its company like a web spun around the Internet, so that it could take advantage of the Net's main benefit: cost saving. Whereas Nortel still handled its sales in the traditional way, Juniper made use exclusively of the online alternative. With an increase in sales of over 17,700 percent[17] within just two years, Juniper's business model has apparently worked. With so many start-ups entering the business world, economies have become more fragmented and the old-style companies' power impaired.

Intensive spending on IT not only made the business landscape more diverse, but, combined with communication and globalization, transformed the way companies did business. Integration of IT helped economies to become more connected and ultimately transparent as more resources were shared and a valuable, though less costly, information exchange on many topics took place. Becoming networked, however, exposed companies more to competition which in turn contributed to an enhancement of processes.

Obviously, the use of new technologies required company staff to acquire novel skills so they could optimally materialize the many opportunities that IT offered them. Furthermore, according to a report by the Department of Commerce,[18] large producers or intensive users of IT will employ almost half the American workforce by 2006. People and change management initiatives were needed to prepare employees for the Information

[13] Reid, R.: "Principles of the New Economy," Business2.0, March 2000

[14] Kelly, K.: "New Rules for the New Economy: 10 Radical Strategies for a Connected World,", Penguin USA, October 1999

[15] Juniper Networks Inc. is a global provider of purpose-built Internet infrastructure solutions.

[16] Nortel Networks Inc. is a global supplier of networking solutions and services that support the Internet and other public and private data, voice, and video networks using wireless and wireline technologies.

[17] 1998: $6 .8 million; 2000: $673 million (Business Week, March 26, 2001)

[18] "The Emerging Digital Economy II", 1999

Revolution.[19] On-the-job-training and seminars made employees (as well as executives) less suspicious of technology and opened their minds to other, more efficient ways of doing certain tasks, like preparing and sending memos and organizing meetings.[20] In general, employees' attitudes toward their jobs changed for the better as they saw that they were essential for the companies' proper working. For those that were not so blessed, there were hundreds of interesting new jobs available at start-up companies specializing in IT, telecommunications, or the Internet. The newly won connectivity made finding the right job even easier. Firms needed to remain progressive if they wanted to retain their employees.[21]

Considering the microeconomic relevance of IT in terms of US companies' spending on it, the number of projects to integrate new soft- and hardware and people–change–management initiatives, as well as networks and their consequential impact on competition, we can see that IT has driven the business world since the early 1990s rather than enabled a few, though crucial, tasks.

Taking a look at the development over time, however, we can observe that since the late 1990s, the relevance of IT – measured by its components' first derivative (relative rate of change) – at a microeconomic level has diminished as US IT investment has plunged by over 30 percent since the beginning of 1998,[22] the number of soft- and hardware integration projects and technological people–change–management initiatives (seminars, on-the-job training, other training, etc.) has drastically fallen, and networks and alliances on an inter-company basis have been established.

This does not mean that IT is no longer relevant for businesses. Rather, the decrease shows that companies are spending less on IT because it has already been integrated and is now fully operational, employees have been equipped with the necessary skills, and large connections and networks to various nodes in the international landscape (suppliers, logistics companies, recruiting agencies, customers, etc.) have been established. This trend is supported by the fact that overall productivity figures have increased (or at least could be measured) since early 1999 and remain steady even dur-

---

[19] Tapscott, D.: "Minds over Matter," Business 2.0, January 1999.

[20] The Department of Commerce's report suggested that value-added per worker in IT-producing industries grew at an annual average of 10.4 percent in the 1990s.

[21] Sailors, F.: "Reduce the Cost of Employee Turnover," FastCompany, March 1999

[22] META; company reports; Thomson Financial Datastream

ing the current downturn. Partly, this is because human resources have been reallocated more productively after an extensive period of training. (And, probably, employees are not using the Internet's many benefits such as e-mail, downloading of files and music, as well as browsing for personal use, that they used to.)

If changes at a microeconomic level occur, a country's macroeconomic situation alters as well and vice versa. This is what happened when companies realized IT's tremendous potential and invested heavily in it. Since we have already discussed some of its microeconomic implications, let us now turn to its relevance to the macro-economy.

IT – Driving Macroeconomics

Many New Economy enthusiasts proclaimed until 2000 that inflation was dead, the business cycle abolished, and economic rules were obsolete. New rules for the New Economy, they believed, needed to be established as the US economy enjoyed buoyant growth, negligible inflation, and, almost by definition, full employment.

The economic impact of IT was indeed profound, but it was far from blowing up old and proven economic rules into bits and bytes.

The New Economy is an established fact, if one refers to the radical change (American) companies are experiencing through the tremendous interaction of IT, communication, and globalization. Neither can it be neglected when easy accessibility of up-to-date information offered by IT is taken into consideration, allowing substantial improvements in corporate efficiency as one factor of production, expertise, is almost perfectly allocated. The New Economy is also firmly in position when one can claim that IT changes the way businesses work and deal with suppliers and customers. In theses aspects, the New Economy is certainly alive and well. The business cycle, however, is not dead and the old rules still apply!

IT has not brought many microeconomic advantages. It has rather been *driving* the longest peacetime expansion in the United States and is currently dragging it down, too. High-tech industry's startling growth has helped to boost the US gross domestic product (GDP). While the IT sector accounts for only about 8 percent of US GDP, it contributed, on average,

35 percent of the country's economic growth between 1995 and 1998.[23] Its impact on GDP is suggested to have been even bigger, since the mushrooming of high-tech companies has helped many complementary "industries" such as consulting and web-design firms as well as banks.

Since 1998, however, US companies' investment in IT has fallen by almost one-third and, naturally, GDP has been adversely affected, too. By the time you read this book, the United States may well be experiencing a recession because two consecutive quarters of contracting national output have occurred. The relevance of IT (spending) on the US economic situation in terms of GDP has thus been overwhelming.

Another issue extensively discussed by some economists, most notably Robert Gordon from Northwestern University, and still disputed, is IT's positive impact on productivity.[24] Though problems with measurement, especially in the predominant service sector,[25], hindered an earlier, statistical proof of IT's productivity-enhancing capabilities, recent figures by various research firms and governmental units have underscored the fact that output per person in industries that invested heavily in IT has grown. IT is therefore macro-economically important as the emergence and expansion of high-tech industries has made the economy more productive as a whole, and has thus raised the prospects for growth and higher living standards.

Yet another essential economic consequence of the widespread employment of IT is that companies could generally raise their efficiency by reducing costs in terms of labor and capital. As a result of globalization, spurred by the rapid spread of IT, international capital markets could be approached and tapped more easily at lower cost. Moreover, general and financial terms (exchange and interest rates) for borrowing money would possibly be more attractive in, say, Japan than in the national market. Capital investment became more attractive and productive, often encouraging firms to substitute capital for (scarce) labor.

---

[23] "The New Economy," The Economist, July 24, 1999

[24] Stamp, D.: "The Invisible Assembly Line: Boosting White-Collar Productivity in the New Economy," American Management Association, 1995

[25] How does one measure productivity in services? Number of phone calls handled without regard for helpfulness, friendliness, and ultimately customer satisfaction?

Combining the factors IT investment and high-tech industry growth (influencing GDP), productivity and efficiency, and expressing them in terms of relative macroeconomic relevance, one can observe that the macroeconomic relevance curve of IT is similar to its microeconomic counterpart (taking the first derivative), though with a time delay of approximately 2½ years. Consequently, IT was transformed from an economic *enabler* to a *driver*. Given this change, it should be no surprise to many New Economy enthusiasts and investors that the business cycle was not dead; on the contrary, it caught them off-guard and wiped out trillions of dollars in wealth. Businesses and ultimately economies cannot grow for ever as demand for their products and services (aggregate demand on a macroeconomic level) naturally decreases. At some points in time, there are limits with which invention, technology, and people cannot keep pace. In the late 1990s, it was, apart from other reasons that I have already discussed in earlier chapters (specifically Chaps. 2 and 3), obvious that market saturation for IT products and solutions had occurred. The economic slowdown, and with it the stock markets' downfall, had to come![26]

Trends and Observations

Today's business is changing very fast. Humans are doubling global knowledge every two years. Every second we make new discoveries and inventions. Every few moments, someone decides to integrate some of these inventions into a business idea. These things demonstrate the speed of change in the markets. Some of the trends are really significant and strongly influence the business world and our technologies, as follows.

Application Clustering

Applications are clustered together within the company's value chain and the core processes but as well cross-company such as in manufacturing industry. Examples are: supply chain, customer relationship management, or business intelligence applications.

Customer-Centric Systems

Customer orientation was the main focus according to BPR. Today's business models focus even more on customers, demanding automation of systems and operation by multiple, and mainly unknown, users across the

[26] Reuters: "FTSE Bounces Back Helped by U.S. Data," November 29, 2000

globe, being 24/7 available and reliable (cf. the front page news about Hotmail when the Microsoft servers were down for 3 days).[27]

Integration and Outsourcing

Today, the possibilities for outsourcing are even more enhanced. Not only can HR or payroll information and organization be outsourced, but also more and more other IT needs can be realized as an outsourcing solution.[28] One example is application service provider (ASP)-based applications provided by an external service provider. But outsourcing also means that whole business processes or areas are outsourced: for example, Federal Express conducts all shipping activities for National Semiconductor in California.

Special, Technological Requirements for CCR

The funny thing about the Internet is that most of the concepts, technologies, and systems have been around for years. HTML or relational databases are not really new concepts invented for the Internet or e-commerce – but the existence of these concepts did make the Internet and e-business possible.

CCR does not require any specific technologies. CCR helps you to analyze existing systems and concepts and decide on how to improve their use, which would ultimately translate into higher earnings.

The technologies CCR mainly dealt with in completed assignments were the common Internet and enterprise technologies. To deal with different systems and solutions within projects, it is important for the success of a solution and its quick implementation to use the following technologies and platforms:

- Standardized
- Open
- Tested/known
- Secure

[27] Delmater, R.; Hancock, M.: "Data Mining Explained. A Manager's Guide to Customer-Centric Business Intelligence," Digital Press, January 2001

[28] Senge, P.: "Through the Eye of the Needle," CIO Magazine, June 2000

Additionally, IT development should be centralized to avoid different decisions on systems and platforms, to align the decisions, and to improve the speed of processes.

CCR – Understanding of Application Architecture in Iterated Markets

C-business enterprise applications in the age of the Internet and integrated markets and solutions can best be seen as being positioned among the business partners, stakeholders, customers, and employees of a certain company:

- The business partners of one company are interacting with each other's functions such as logistics, purchase, production, and distribution. The information needed in these systems has to be clustered and integrated in a supply chain management system. The foundation for all of this information is an ERP system, providing the functional information systems, for example in production or for the whole supply chain management system with information about production schedules, delivery issues, etc.
- Customers of a company are in contact with a customer relationship management system that integrates information from sales, marketing, and customer services. Each customer has to be treated individually, according to their sales track records, the selling aims, etc.
- Stakeholders like investors, government, or responsible authorities need access to enterprise information like legacy systems, auditing data, or management control information. This information has to be provided, based on all company processes and data.
- Finally, as the employees of a company interact with all the company's systems, they have great influence on those systems. In particular, systems related with HR management or administrative control are in permanent interaction with employees.

All these systems closely interact with each other, exchanging information and data. The imagination of a multinational company with hundreds of production facilities and thousands of storage and seal sites may support an understanding of the complexity of all these processes and data flows. Additionally, in the face of fierce competition, all of these processes should happen in real time and should also allow data transfers over the Internet.

CCR Framework for Analysis of IT System Components

The analysis of IT system components in a certain company considering the CCR concept is very important, as is the analysis of the company's situation, in order to spot pressing issues and necessary tasks.

Practical experiences showed that the diversity of existing systems, a large number of initiatives in the IT area, split competences, and political thinking are all big issues in the area of IT systems of a company. It is amazing how many IT initiatives are going on at the same time in a large international company (SAP implementation, migration and customizing, ABAP developments,[29] web initiatives, CRM projects, and so on). After years of little activity in the IT area of Fortune-500 companies, today IT staff have to deal with a variety of projects, new technologies, and both internal as well as external demands. But the main point is that the role of the staff within IT departments is also changing. IT is no longer required just to develop and run the systems – it is becoming one of the main competitive factors in the business world. IT staff have to think in terms of visions and cost/value relations. The evolution of IT managers and intrapreneurship[30] is presenting many challenges along the way.

The CCR approach provides a technological framework for understanding and monitoring complex IT systems (cf. Chap. 6). Delivering CCR projects, it was useful working with a three dimensional approach:

- the platform,
- the solution, and
- the architecture perspective

which describes for each component of the IT system, or, simpler, for each solution, the platform the solution is running on and the architecture the solution is based on. Every system and its parts can be seen as a

[29] Bruyn, G.; Lyfareff, R.: "Introduction to ABAP/4 Programming for SAP, Revised and Expanded Edition," Prima Publishing, July 1998

[30] Oden, H.: "Managing Corporate Culture, Innovation and Intrapreneurship", Greenwood Publishing Group, June 1997

three-dimensional cube. The platform view allows us to define for each of the objects of a complex IT system the platform on which the solution is based. Platforms can be desktops, servers, or host/legacy platforms. Each one needs different tools, so it is important to organize each architecture platform by platform.

From a solution-oriented perspective, enterprise systems can be organized among application clusters or groups describing main applications like HR systems and components like client/server components etc. The applications perform specific business functions and are built from reusable, portable, and scaleable components.

The architectural view helps us to group necessary concepts and tools among the three basic stages of a solution. We defined design, test, and run-time architectures, tools, products, services, standards, templates, and utilities.

Analyzing the IT Side of Web Solutions Using the Framework

This simple framework can be used as part of the Technology horizontal and its modules as described in Chap. 6 to analyze, describe, and develop IT systems and solutions. As already discussed, the first step of CCR is to monitor the as-is status and the initially defined as-is-status – this to understand, what was planned and what was finally realized. Then, differences between this status quo and the planned status are analyzed and interpreted. At all stages, IT is taken into consideration as it is the enabler for all new business models and solutions. And in all cases, the defined framework can be used.

The example of an analysis of web-related systems should help you to understand this framework in detail. Furthermore, it clearly addresses the issues involved and explains, what we are doing in the verticals 1, 2, and 3 of the CCR methodology.

Regarding the web applications (solution view), there are many possible solutions. In this example we concentrate on an "enterprise e-business platform" for external Internet use. Looking closer at the architecture of the platform, we concentrate at first on the development of the architecture. Five areas of interest define this development and need to be analyzed (vertical 1 "Focus and Objectives" and 2 "As-Is Assessment") and described (vertical 3 "Definition of Gaps"):

1. Standards, procedures, and policies define the general instructions and frames for the development
2. Design tools describe the design techniques, concepts, and products used, such as templates and layouts
3. Development tools describe the products and concepts used for the development, such as HTML etc.
4. Testing tools describe the procedures and standards for testing the developed sites
5. Version management helps to coordinate the development of huge web sites

The analysis and description of the run-time architecture is much more sophisticated, as a large number of services need to be analyzed:

- Presentation services define the interface to the user
- Application-enabling services describe services like e-mail management, advertising engine, etc.
- Collaboration services provide the basic services for use of the site, such as search engine, chat lines, audio, etc.
- Business massaging services support the use of XML[31] or EDI
- Payment services help the use of secure payment services
- Security services cluster all the methods and components which deal with safe information transfer, access, and firewalls
- System services provide the basic applications such as directory servers, web servers, etc.
- Communication services organize and manage the interface to the internal systems, such as middleware communication, data access interface, etc.

Finally, the analysis of the system architecture is completed by examining the production architecture. In this area, four main components have to be considered:

[31] Harold, E.; Means, W.: "XML in a Nutshell: A Desktop Quick Reference," O'Reilly & Associates, January 2001

- General standards and policies define the overall procedures for management of the implemented system
- Component monitoring describes the services needed for the permanent control and monitoring of all online components
- Infrastructure management involves permanent management of content, advertising, access, keys, and certificates
- Usage analysis contains all the services needed to monitor usage on a regular basis. The tools used are statistical applications, log file analysis, etc.

This framework has to be programmed with data from the analysis of a given web application and can be integrated in and maintained based on an e-PMM as explained in Chap. 6.

In fact, the process of data collection gives the collecting team an excellent understanding of the solutions implemented and their current status. Moreover, the people involved are required to give a resume of their actions. This creates an understanding of the key issues and change needs to be considered as part of the vertical 4 "Development of CCR-Plan" and 5 "Implementation of CCR-Plan".

Cluster Computing as Enabler for CCR

As indicated already in earlier chapters, in the B2B as well as in the B2C area, c-commerce business applications have to face increasing requirements regarding performance and availability. Based on the fact that CCR focuses on the best-fit reusability, especially in the "technology" horizontal, the emerging field of cluster computing is a welcome development facilitating successful CCR projects.

Within CCR projects we are more and more using cluster computing technologies provided by companies such Scarasoft, IBM, Grey and Compaq, as these technologies enable us, as part of CCR engagements, to even increase the extent to which we can re-use already existing IT-components.

"Cluster" means linking and integrating of the shelf computer systems for increasing the cumulative performance of the entire system. These linked computers, then called "knots", are being connected using a high-performance network. All the computational jobs are then executed and delivered by the in parallel working knots of the machine – the cluster.

Ideally a load-balancing takes place within the entire cluster and its knots, which positively impacts the availability as well as the reliability.

Our experience shows that as part of CCR engagements, with cluster technology it becomes easier to reuse different hardware, software or infrastructural components of existing and unsuccessful c-commerce solutions. Since we first made use of this technological approach, within vertical 4 "Development of CCR Plan" we started to consider cluster technology as inherent part for reframing a solution. In one project cluster technology tremendously reduced the required time for doing the reframing in the "technology" horizontal as we could raise the system's performance only by setting up a cluster delivering the required transactions. Initially we intended to exchange parts of the system, as they would not have delivered the required performance for the reframed m-commerce solution of our client. Through the use of cluster technology we could furthermore reduce the required investment, too.

In this chapter we have seen IT's important role for both businesses and economies around the world as well as its specific role for CCR. IT has profoundly altered the way businesses work because a more vivid flow of information can take place. Economies have become more connected and consequently more dependent on each other, a fact that lets them work more efficiently, but at the same time makes them more vulnerable to financial shocks.

CHAPTER 8

The Human Resource Challenge

One of the major challenges for organizations in the *cyber-economy* and therefore as well within CCR engagements is to cope with myriad factors that are directly or indirectly influencing and changing their most valuable asset – their human resources.

In earlier chapters, I have already discussed to some extent many of the HR-related changes brought by the networked economy. In this chapter, however, I shall deal in depth with one of the most pressing issues that companies are facing and will do so even more in the not-so-distant future.

Setting the Agenda

The speed with which the *cyber-economy* is moving is breathtaking. Sure, we have already seen enormous booms in the 1920s and 1960s, but the previous decade outpaced both these "golden times" in terms of accumulation of wealth, organizational changes, and probably even innovation. Naturally, the transformations brought by the new way of conducting business did not stop at altering the very demands that organizations made upon their employees and the workforce in general.

In the field of HR, there are many different contingency factors, be they of demographic, geographic, social, or economic nature, which determine what types of *human capital* are at a company's disposal.

Changing Demographics

The media often cover the so-called "age bomb,"[1] referring to the demographic development of industrialized countries whose populations contain increasing numbers of older people (50 years of age and above). The consequences of this structural shift are versatile. Its main economic implications, however, are that organizations have a great deal less human resources to refill slots that have become vacant as more and more people

---

[1] McGovern, G.: "The Truths and Myths of the New Digital Age," Chapter 5, Nua Inc., 2000

reach the age of retirement. In addition, these new employees, reduced in size, need to support a virtually exploding number of senior citizens. These two results of the on-going demographic changes mean that organizations have to

- Select
- Recruit
- Develop
- Maintain

people that are more productive in order to guarantee the future existence and well-being of their systems and the general economy. For companies, the only solution to this issue is recourse to a new brood of human capital – the *Net generation*.[2]

The term Net generation refers to 3- to 23-year-olds who have grown up in the digital age and have no fear of using technology as they are constantly surrounded by it. For them, the distinction between work, learning, and playing is blurred. Their creative approach toward issues, their immense ability to adapt quickly, and their global orientation make them the theoretically perfect substitute for a diminishing, older workforce. In practice, however, these young players are less experienced, less reliable, and less loyal, display a great deal of greed and arrogance, but by the same token need to show more responsibility and cooperativeness. The efforts involved in molding them into the company are therefore often exhausting.

Blurred Geography

Topographically, the world has not changed much in the last 2,000 years. Allowing for some natural changes and human interference, moving borders, and the emergence of a couple of metropolises, the world looks pretty much the same. What has changed, however, is the role geography plays for companies and, necessarily, the general workforce.

With the economic shift of most industrialized nations from the first (agriculture, forestry) and second sectors (manufacturing) toward the third sector (services), the importance of geography has drastically diminished as providing services has become a universal task, independent of geographic

[2] Tapscott, D.: "Growing up Digital: The Rise of the Net Generation," McGraw-Hill Professional Publishing, New York, June 1999

factors, though certainly not of culture and differing national attitudes. The issues that mostly influence geographic decisions are image, taxes, and government.

As organizations have become more universal, their need for flexible labor has risen accordingly.[3] The Net generation constitutes the optimal resource because it is international in spirit and subsequently exceptionally mobile. Moreover, young people in their early twenties are well equipped with major business skills and familiar with the language of business so do not shy away from going to strange places. Mobility barriers are already quite low and will increasingly become so. In Europe, for instance, the introduction of the Euro, along with further harmonization of the education and tax systems, will provide fertile ground for a new international business community to grow.

Social Shifts

When the enthusiasm about the New Economy first emerged, many people were afraid of losing their jobs as an emphasis was suddenly put on technological skills and Internet literacy. Even though some people certainly were no longer of use to their companies, most retained their jobs as HR managers realized that experienced and loyal employees who could be trained in technological skills would be more valuable than young and sloppy technical whiz-kids – at least at that time. In addition, the Internet proved to be creating more jobs than destroying them.[4] This fact is supported by a study conducted by Andersen Consulting, which suggests that by 2002, the New Economy will have directly created 5.8 million jobs in the United States and 3 million in Europe.

Even though these numbers look rosy, the *cyber-economy* inherently lacks skilled workers as a result of inadequate or insufficient education.[5] The main problem for the *cyber-economy* is that there are many job vacancies but not enough people to fulfill the requirements. For entry-level posts, most would be overqualified, whereas for landing premium-rate jobs, applicants lack the necessary skills. As a result, many people have jobs that do not match their expectations and competence.

---

[3] Grensing-Pophal, L.: "Job Applicants and Perks: What Is Offered, What to Ask for – and When!" HR.COM, 2000.

[4] "The Internet as Job Creator," InternetNews, August 2000.

[5] Moran, S.: "New Visa Plan," Business2.0, August 2000.

Since skilled workers have become a scarce resource, there has been a shift in the power structure of labor markets. Whereas in the Old Economy an applicant might have been asked "Why should we hire you?", in the *cyber-economy* the applicant is more likely to ask "What can you offer me so that I join you?" People with the right know-how and ambition can thus afford to keep companies on hold and search extensively for the job that is most attractive. Potential employees have thus gained weight in negotiating contracts.[6]

Amending Economic Factors

Having discussed the most important determinants of the *cyber-economy* in all the previous chapters, it is necessary for the presentation in this chapter to monitor three of them and their respective management. They are:

- Intellectual capital[7] (or intangible assets)
- Change
- Innovation

Managing Intellectual Capital

Until recently, competitive advantage depended on the degree to which an organization was able to gain privileged access to natural resources or new technologies, or secure leverage through economies of scale or control over the supply chain. In a global marketplace, however, these ways of creating value are no longer sufficient, because they are easily replicated and have become measures which simply qualify for entry to a given market, rather than features which differentiate an organization from its competitors. *Intellectual capital* is now widely believed to give a company sustained competitive advantage. Intellectual capital refers to *intelligence* [that] *becomes an asset when some useful order is created out of free-floating brainpower – that is, when it is given coherent form (a mailing list, a database, an agenda for a meeting, a description of a process); when it is captured in a way that allows it to be described, shared, and exploited; and when it can be deployed to do something that could not be*

[6] Seaberg, J.: "Talent Crunch – IT Workers Benefit from a Tight Labor Market," Business 2.0, September 2000.

[7] Steward, A.T.: "Intellectual Capital: The New Wealth of Organizations," Bantam Books, New York, December 1998

done if it remained scattered around like so many coins in a gutter. Intellectual capital is packaged useful knowledge.[8]

As intellectual capital is the most precious asset a company can possess, it requires professional management. The problem with managing it, however, lies in its intangibility and its high dependence on particular ways of working, or "routines," and how the organization operates. Once it is properly managed, intellectual capital becomes the source of competitive advantage since such an asset is difficult to imitate.[9] Neither can it be purchased, poached, or transferred to a different corporate setting.

Discussing knowledge management in satisfactory detail would go beyond the scope of this book. There are other excellent sources, such as *Intellectual Capital* by Thomas A. Stewart or *Working Knowledge* by Thomas H. Davenport and Laurence Prusak, which I recommend if you would like to know more about this fascinating topic. In this chapter, however, I shall frequently discuss managing intangible assets in other contexts.

Managing Change

Small, cohesive organizations present few difficulties for experienced managers to direct. Organizational growth, however, contributes to the increasing complexity of many factors. Managing change in these environments thus becomes more of a challenge.

Organizations have never been exempt from change, but the rapidity and unpredictability of change puts a special onus on managing HR in organizations today. Change requires the frequent and constant transformation of attitudes about and relationships with the internal and the external environment.[10] Moreover, streamlined processes and working practices have to be reframed in "new times."

As we will see in a later section of this chapter, change therefore requires not only technological reframing of the company, but also effective cul-

---

[8] Stewart, Thomas A.: "Intellectual Capital – The New Wealth of Organizations," Currency Doubleday 1997

[9] Sullivan, P.H.: "Value Driven Intellectual Capital: How to Convert Intangible Corporate Assets into Market Value", John Wiley & Sons, February 2000

[10] Conner, D.R.: "Managing at the Speed of Change: How Resilient Managers Succeed and Prosper when Others Fail," Villard books, January 1993

tural transformation and harmonization with the new environmental factors.

Managing Innovation

Innovation is essential for the success of an organization because it determines the organization's advantage relative to its competitors. Without continuous innovation, an organization is in danger of losing its flexibility and its attractiveness to potential employees, eventually leading to stagnation. For this reason, it is vital to build an organizational environment that is open to new ways of thinking. This, for instance, could be obtained by encouraging newcomers as part of a CCR project to challenge the *status quo* rather than assimilate it. New employees must also be introduced to the company from a variety of angles. Thus it helps when they have separate as well as joint meetings with the directors of the company's departments. This may help the newcomer to spot and communicate eventual problem areas.

The *cyber-economy* radically alters the HR structure, company requirements as well as employee expectations, and necessitates a new approach to managing HR.[11] In correlation with this HR shift, organizational structures have changed as well.

Modified Organizational Structures

The *cyber-economy* has required organizations around the world to conduct restructuring in the light of this new rhythm with which the business world is forging ahead. This rhythm cam be characterized as presto, risqué, and incessant. It has made typical organizational structures obsolete, as they were hostile to quick decision making and action as well as to creativity. Today, organizations cannot afford to have any of these last two characteristics. Such a hierarchy slows down the time-to-market of goods, services and solutions. Moreover, it impedes workers' drive to think creatively and to communicate new ideas. The knowledge-based *cyber-economy* demands more intellectually stimulating, flexible, and agile organizational forms which shun rigidity and monolithic behavior.

[11] McLagan, P.: "Competencies: The Next Generation," HR.COM, May 1997

Many companies – especially those located in Silicon Valley – have experimented with an array of organizational forms to find the one that would best meet the demands set by their respective products, competitors, and general environment. Some of these developments have turned out to be transient fads. Others, however, have resulted in the emergence of a decent spectrum of effective organizational structures. These new structures are built on the basis of augmented use of new technologies, teams that are intrinsically flexible as they can be formed, re-formed, and disbanded with relative ease, and shrunken hierarchical layers.

Lean and Process-Based Organizations

Lean and process-based organizations were the first to emerge to fulfill the requirements that would give them a distinctive competitive advantage.

Lean management[12] is based on:

- Eliminating unnecessary steps
- Aligning all steps in an activity in a continuous flow
- Recombining labor into cross-functional teams dedicated to a given product or activity
- Continuously striving for improvement

Its stated objective is to support every employee's disconnection from hierarchical barriers in order to facilitate the free flow of knowledge and thus to optimally interlink the employee's intellectual capital with and within the organization. The lean organization concept thus necessitates a phased journey of emphasizing value-adding activities and downsizing the organization to a reformed state – essential aspects when reframing an organization.

By steering toward a lean organization, a company automatically becomes multi-polar. Whereas in the past the business landscape was dominated by organizations possessing an all-powerful center formulating the strategic direction, drafting plans, and monitoring performance, the new phenotype is that of organizations inhabiting a "federation" or a "constellation" of strategic business units that are usually interdependent, relying on one another for critical expertise. As a consequence, the historical and traditional division of organizational roles and departmental activities into line and staff

[12] Henderson, B.A.; Larco, J.L.: "Lean Transformation: How to Change Your Business into a Lean Enterprise," Oaklea Press, Richmond, May 1999.

positions has become archaic as well. Every part of the company has become more involved as competitive pressures commanded the merger of competences in order to reduce costs.[13] This in turn has contributed to companies' flexibility because employees can be and are placed multi-dimensionally. In this latter regard, however, it is important not to permanently assign individuals to cross-functional teams, as this would adversely affect their functional career path. Rather the solution is a career path that alternates between concentration on a specific value stream and dedicated, intense knowledge building within functions.

Network and Virtual Organizations

A *network organization* has been defined as an "economic entity that operates through a cluster of compact business units, driven by the market, with few levels of decision making and a willingness to outsource whatever can be better done elsewhere."[14] This free flow across organizational boundaries can reach a level when the organization as such becomes obscure and unrecognizable, a *virtual organization.*

The main characteristics of a dynamic network organization as conceptual components of CCR, according to Snow, Miles, and Coleman, are:

- Vertical desegregation – a great number of business functions such as product design and development, manufacturing, and market distribution are increasingly performed by independent organizations within a network
- Brokers – intermediaries perform the linking function between sets of organizations and their activities
- Market mechanisms – the market holds together organizational control mechanisms
- Full disclosure information systems – broad access computerized information systems dislodge prolong trust-building processes based on organizational experience

Network and ultimately virtual organizations turn their attention away from formal structures and policies and toward the importance of patterns

[13] Storfer, P.: "Merging Competencies and Technologies," Speech given at the IHRIM, Boston, 2000.

[14] Snow, 1992

of social relationships within the respective organization. They came into being as a consequence of many factors, in particular the requirement for flexibility and learning, joint production management,[15] and dominating high-tech and cultural diversity.

Requirement for Flexibility and Learning

Many products or services are now intended for more specialist markets and may show short product life cycles. In this situation, companies need to develop more flexible modes of production. Moreover, acceleration of the pace of internal change as well of the rate of organizational learning is almost obligatory. A network-based organization – or at least some elements of it as result of a CCR project – can open up access to more numerous sources of information and as a result offer a richer set of interactive and mutual learning opportunities.

Managing Joint Production

Throughout the recent past, one could observe a move within industrial organizations from a model of large, vertically integrated companies to a new form of *value-adding partnerships*, where a set of independent companies work closely together to manage a flow of goods and services along an entire value chain.

Joint ventures[16] and strategic alliances[17] are the most prominent forms of value-adding partnerships and have already become a common feature of the business world. Through joint ventures, organizations are able to achieve a number of objectives such as diversifying their product portfolio by marketing smaller companies' goods and services. Furthermore, by working closely together with other companies, an organization can rapidly acquire new expertise and reduce its costs by pooling resources.[18] An-

[15] Stenzel, J.P.: "PTIIF Electronic Commerce Statement," Telecommunications & Information Industries Forum, 1998.

[16] Lynch, R.P.: "The Practical Guide to Joint Ventures and Corporate Alliances: How to Form, How to Organize, How to Operate", John Wiley & Sons,New York, July 1989.

[17] Dent, S.M.: "Partnering Intelligence: Creating Value for Your Business by Building Smart Alliances," Davies-Black Publications, Palo Alto, October 1999.

[18] Tennessen, D.J.: "Pooling Resources in the Information Age," Journal of Extension, October 1997.

other essential factor, in particular for cross-border trade, is that setting up a joint venture may circumvent national restrictions.

From an HR management perspective, joint ventures and strategic alliances pose several challenges. The relevant cultures have to be blended, staff problems need to be addressed, and compensation schemes must be drafted.[19]

The basis for every joint venture and alliance is the establishment of an honest partnership that itself necessitates a lot of hard work on both sides.

The High-Tech Base

New organizations operating in knowledge-based industries such as biotechnology, which employ highly educated, young, and mobile professionals, are increasingly the targets for partnerships with large corporations because they are a great source for learning how to produce innovative products and how to manage novelty and continuous change. Additionally, they usually draw on the latest technologies with whose operation older companies are anxious to become familiar.

Cultural Diversity

International business demands knowledge of other cultures and tactfulness in dealing with them. As a consequence of the internationalization of many organizations, both large and small alike, networks have evolved that allow subsidiaries to play an important, directing role in harmony with the center.[20]

Rather than overriding differing cultures and beliefs, employees' training toward becoming *corporate diplomats* is crucial.

The HR management considerations of network and virtual organizations are numerous. One critical factor, for instance, is that expertise and resource capability are widely available throughout the network, but at the same time are as difficult to locate as they are dispersed. The HR challenge in this regard lies in identifying, retaining, developing, and appropriating such scarce resources.

---

[19] Rafter, M.V.: "Keeping the Peace," TheStandard.com, January 1999.
[20] Lee, K.: "The Diversity Training Group," HR.COM, 2000.

Another critical feature is that the dissolution or drastic reduction of boundaries may cause customers and suppliers to be treated as joint partners. This, however, is of no benefit to the company. The goal instead is to loosen external boundaries so as to create a win–win situation along the whole value chain.

Network organizations also require managers and staff to change their assumptions and behavior. Instead of developing plans and strategies independently, planning needs to be coordinated and even shared with other participants in the network. This means that participants must be willing to share information without fear of losing their power within the network. The general tendency to hoard expertise and information is one of the most articulated threats to the functioning of network and virtual organizations. The key to solving this problem is that management should strive to involve as many employees as possible in decision-making processes for which the disclosure and application of individual expertise is essential. Furthermore, when such a contribution to a solution is rewarded, then there is a good chance of disbanding any barriers to the free flow of information.

One of the critical components of network and virtual organizations is their outsourcing activities. Therefore, let us take a closer look at them.

Strategic Outsourcing

Outsourcing entails the externalization of production and services. This practice has been a major global trend affecting companies of all sizes. In the past, the phenomenon found little recognition as it did little to challenge the nature of the classic formal organization. In recent years, however, the extensive conduct of outsourcing as a popular way to cut costs and to refocus on core competences has contributed to the dismemberment of many organizations.[21]

There are many different types of outsourcing that take place on various levels within an organization. Sub-contracting, for instance, has been an age-old practice. Subcontracting[22] office cleaning, however, may not give an organization strategic competitive advantage. Debating which profes-

[21] Chatham, B.: "Mergers, Acquisitions and Saving IT Dollars," CIO Magazine, March 1998.

[22] Wangemann, M.: "2001: Subcontract Management Manual," Harcourt Brace Professional Publishing, San Diego, CA, January 2000.

sional and managerial tasks can be outsourced, however, radically alters the structural integrity of organizations and has indeed an impact on an organization's position among its competitors.

In a complex, fast-moving market, outsourcing is a quick way to gain access to specialist services. Moreover, outsourcing may significantly be of lower cost than producing in-house. Advances in information and communication technology have helped outsourcing to grow in importance, as services such as billing can be subcontracted to a "supplier" almost anywhere in the world at a lower cost. Moreover, defective components or mediocre services can be more easily rejected.

In addition to the commonly outsourced services such as catering, security, and IT services, various HR functions can themselves be outsourced. Recruitment, training, retirement planning, outplacement services, relocation, counseling, etc. are just the most prominent ones. The reason for subcontracting on a large scale as one outcome of a CCR project in numerous business areas is that organizations can then again refocus on their core competences and let other specialists concentrate on the things that they are themselves best at doing.

Though the benefits of outsourcing are many, there are considerable disadvantages, such as issues of confidentiality, trust and risk sharing – to name just a few. A serious strategic HR management issue as well is the potential loss of expertise in certain areas that may be difficult to recover. In contrast to strategic partnerships, organizations are not in direct contact with the outsourcing company. Therefore, they do not have the opportunity to gain expertise. Rather, they risk their company's loss of culture, shared vision, and unity. Outsourcing thus poses a tremendous challenge to HR management.[23]

The modified organizational structures generate new managerial problems. A central problem is that in place of rules and procedures the new organizational form is meant to be built on commitment from all staff and is supposed to rest on shared values. A feeling of unity and partnership, however, is hard to attain if a company is constantly thinking about how to become even leaner (i.e., downsizing), and an employee's position within a company that probably outsources as much as 60 percent of its business activities is not clearly defined. In their pursuit of flexibility, companies have largely forgotten that their employees are searching for some degree

[23] Harris, B.: "Installing the Virtual Workforce," Government Technology.

of certainty at least. Cross-functional and interdepartmental teams may be most effective for companies, but their excessive use leads to employee estrangement and dissatisfaction. Still, most envision the classic "American dream." And in this regard, a symbiosis of hierarchical, lean, and network organization may be best.

Developing and Maintaining Human Capital in the Cyber-Economy

After having discussed some organizational issues, we considered to be of growing importance, when talking about reframing c-commerce solutions and entire companies, the *cyber-economy* is obviously and rapidly changing job requirements. New skills on a managerial, communicatory, personal as well as technological basis have to be acquired. This leads to one of the most burning concerns of organizations: should new people with the necessary knowledge be recruited, or should current employees be developed?

The answer to this question is not found easily in any company. Neither should a decision be made haphazardly. By all means, organizations must not forget that individuals with lives and families rather than "valuables" are involved. It is very important to keep this in mind when referring to "human capital" or "strategic assets."

Before we return to the issue of how to develop and maintain human capital in the *cyber-economy*, I would like to briefly explore the reasons why *strategic human resource management* (SHRM) is so important for companies operating in the *cyber-economy.*

"Old" vs. "New"

It all boils down to deciding whether to fire and hire or to train and develop is not so much a cost, but rather a strategic, long-term approach toward HR management. This does not mean that costs are not a decisive factor. But, again, a proactive perspective is needed in this regard as well. It is necessary to consider the question whether the initially large costs, incurred in finding, selecting, recruiting, and integrating new, expensive employees, in the long run outweigh the benefits of the lesser costs of maintaining and developing existing employees. The emphasis, however, should be put on the HR strategy.

Organizations wish to retain their youthfulness, agility, and flexibility. Therefore, they constantly strive to attract talented, motivated, and young people. A modicum of arrogance and creativity coupled with vigor and curiosity are the characteristics that will ensure the future existence of any company.

Undisputedly, organizations have to have a constant inflow of fresh human capital in order to stay in business. The issues, however, are to what degree, how fast, and where exactly should HR flow into a specific company and replace its current HR base? The constant threat is that employees who have been working for the company for a long time may become disillusioned and inaccessible. They may decide to keep their expertise to themselves. They may also be unwilling to help novices establish formal as well as informal contacts within the company and with customers. This may be because they perceive their younger colleagues as adversaries whose ultimate goal is to take their place in the not-so-distant future.

Organizations have to be careful not to take on too many new people within a short period of time. Preferably, the in- and outflow of HR should follow a natural and harmonized cycle that bodes well for a company's culture. Long-term, intra-corporate partnerships with a dual flow of information between older employees and the new hands should emerge. Experienced staff should see themselves as the mentors of the younger generation. The latter should in turn contribute to this partnership by bringing in knowledge about new technologies, novel managerial concepts, etc. By facilitating these partnerships, an organization can approach the HR challenge in a natural and strategic way. Moreover, it can get the best of both worlds: senior employees' managerial competences and young employees creativity and flexibility.

HR as Strategic Asset

Resources have been defined by Wernerfelt as "those tangible and intangible assets which are tied semi-permanently to the firm." Resources thus include office space, machinery, trade contacts, skilled labor, reputation, brand image, managers' ability to engage in teamwork, technological expertise and know-how as well as efficient working practices. By examining this list, incomplete though it is, one can observe that companies possess overlapping as well as unique resources. Resources that are identical, for example geographic location, office space, machinery, and the like, are easily imitated. Unique resources that are non-tradable, non-imitable, and non-substitutable, however, can provide competitive advantage. To make it hard for resources to be imitated, so-called *resource mobility barriers* have to be high.[24] This means that a given resource must be elusive to either copy or even transfer. It must be sustainable and heterogeneous. An example of this type of resource is a corporation's culture because it is valuable, rare, imperfectly imitable, and cannot result from a planned process of change by imitating a firm.

One of the most unique resources within an organization is its employees. This is because people cannot be copied or imitated. They are the drivers that add value to an organization's activities by using their very specific knowledge and personality. Especially in the highly competitive service sector, it is above all *how* a certain service is provided. And how a service is provided depends on the individual's personality. Employees are thus a strategic asset that largely determines an organization's competitive advantage.

Since the *cyber-economy* is especially driven by creativity, innovation, and know-how[25] – all of which are unique HR attributes and hard to copy – competitors in consequence have to attempt to steal away, to *head-hunt*, employees from other firms.[26] Therefore, it must be in the major interests of any organization to ensure that its HR base is not violated.

We will now return to the main issue of how to develop and maintain human capital in the *cyber-economy*.

The HR Imperative

Human capital is, by its nature, very different from other, traditional forms of capital. Capital goods, securities, and bank deposits are all forms of capital that are freely acquirable and disposable at will. Human capital, in contrast, is none of these. Its acquisition involves a long and costly procedure of finding, selecting, and recruiting individuals. Its disposition requires the negotiation of compensation and can mean direct and unwelcome contact with trade unions. Moreover, human capital "possesses" free will and can leave a company at any time.

---

[24] Spak, J.: "Strategies for Keeping Good People," HR.COM, 2000.

[25] Reid, H.R.: "Principles of the New Economy," Business 2.0, March 2000.

[26] Henningsen, L.: "Effects of E-Business on Human Resource Functions," HR.COM 2000.

Human capital is in one sense very similar to capital goods. To reach its potential, new machinery, for instance, has to be modeled, programmed, and integrated according to the organization's individual needs. The machine already has a specific design and architecture, but it must also allow for tailor-made components. It is essentially the same with potential employees.

HR departments recruit a person because her or she is closest to the job profile. That very person, however, will certainly have areas in which he or she excels as well as ones in which his or her competences may be incomplete or edgy. Therefore, training and development are needed, both for the organization's as well as the individual's benefit.

Training and Development as Corporate Strategies

Training refers to the "process of attaining specific, detailed, and routine job skills and techniques" whereas development refers to the "broad scope of improvement and growth of abilities, attitudes, and personality traits."[27] Training and development are important for an organization that wants to grow and develop, for it must have people who want to grow and develop.

A wide spectrum of training and development methods is at the disposal of companies. The most important ones are *on-the-job training*, which includes coaching, planned progression, job rotation as well as temporary or anticipatory assignments, and *off-the-job development*, which usually takes place on executive development programs at universities or other educational institutions, as laboratory training, or in organization development. The critical point for companies is to identify the features that elevate training and development approaches from the tactical and *ad hoc* to the concerted and strategic.

While the actual training and development activities as experienced by trainees are central, they represent only one part of a cyclical process incorporating several other key players in the organization. For training and development to be strategic, both have to be closely tied to and harmonized with the organization's core values and beliefs, its *mission*. From this focal point, training and development can have a tremendous impact on both business and HR strategy. A strategic approach to training and devel-

[27] Mosley, Pietri, Megginson: "Management – Leadership in Action," 5th Edition, Harper Collins.

opment can be described as one where all the people involved are engaged in a connected, unambiguous, and developmental purpose which assists in simultaneously fulfilling an individual's learning goals and the organization's mission.

The strategic purpose of training and development is multi-dimensional. The most strategic function of training and development is to give the organization a competitive edge, both through the content of such activities and the way in which they are delivered. The quality of training and development initiatives naturally determines the result, that is the degree to which employees have skills. Furthermore, the more an organization gains a reputation for progressive training and development, the greater its chances of attracting high-caliber candidates when recruiting. Another strategic aspect of training and development is that it functions as a catalyst for change. Training and development introduce employees to and confront them with new ideas, new approaches, and the urge to challenge conventional wisdom. In this way, the organization constantly keeps in motion, as do its employees. Yet another strategic purpose of training and development is to assess and address any skills deficiencies in the organization and to introduce remedial measures. One of the most essential strategic aspects is that training and development encourage a *learning climate* in the organization. The focus here is on the learning needs of individuals, guided by organizational goals and supported by the belief that each member of staff has a latent talent waiting to be tapped.

Learning as Corporate Strategy

Learning constitutes one of the most important HR processes within a company. It can occur on an individual as well as an organizational basis. There is a discrepancy between the potential for individuals to learn within an organization through training and development and the ability of organizations to encourage learning, innovation, and change. While it is of course true that organizations consist of people, and that learning can only be an attribute of a thinking organism, it is also true and important that organizations differ significantly in the extent to which their structures and systems encourage collective learning.

Individual and Organizational Learning

As we have seen above, individual and organizational learning are essential for keeping a company and its employees flexible and in turn competitive.[28] On an individual and organizational basis, the stakeholders in the organization – senior and line managers, HR management staff, employees, clients, and customers as well as training specialists – need to have a concerted interest in continual learning activities. They need to promote learning facilities and training programs as well as flexible learning opportunities. Learning is not a process that can be repeated at any time. The ability to learn and thus to acquire knowledge has to be constantly trained in order to obtain the desired results. As the Red Queen admonished Alice in *Through the Looking Glass*, "It takes all the running you can do, to keep in the same place." And since organizations do not want to keep in the same place but want to advance, it takes even more running.

The Learning Organization

The idea of the learning organization emerged around 1988 in the United States and the United Kingdom, but many of the ideas inherent in the concept were developed much earlier in systems theory and in work during the 1950s and 1960s on the importance and nature of, and barriers to, learning within organizations. Nowadays, the common definition of a learning organization is that of a company where people continually expand their capacity to create the results they desire, where new and expansive patterns of thinking are nurtured, where collective aspiration is set free, and where people are continually learning how to learn.

The learning organization concept demands:

- *Transformation* in the form of structural changes
- New systems and new policies
- *Transfiguration* of organizational values

The problem with the learning organization concept, however, is that it requires managers to have a large repertoire of leadership skills, which are difficult to attain. In the learning organization the manager is defined as a teacher, therapist, coach, developer, and mentor.[29] Moreover, managers should guide their staff, improve their performance, and offer feedback skillfully. One can easily see that the human capabilities are largely overstretched.

---

[28] Garvin, D.A.: "Learning in Action: A Guide to Putting the Learning Organization to Work," Harvard Business School, April 2000.

[29] "Effective Managers, Happy Employees," Small Business Reports, May 1994.

One remedy for this problem is partly based on a shift toward extensive *individual learning*. Training and development initiatives, which were discussed above, are the most effective forms of individual learning because of the cross-functional and departmental activities as well as the involvement of external consultants. In this way, the overriding burden caused by the concept of the learning organization is taken off the shoulders of many managers.

Human capital in the *cyber-economy* is very mobile and volatile. Learning, training, and development are by no means sufficient to retain organizations' most important asset. Neither is monetary compensation. In order not only to retain its human resources, but also to encourage potential employees to join the organization and to stimulate present employees to produce or perform more effectively, an organization has to constantly search for new means of how to induce individuals or groups to achieve the its objectives while also working to achieve their own goals. In short, they have to be *motivated*.

In the contemporary management literature, there are whole chapters dedicated to motivating employees. Usually, these deal with *content* and *process theories* and their most prominent representatives.[30] For the purpose of CCR, I shall concentrate on two very important content theories: Abraham Maslow's *hierarchy of needs* and Frederick Herzberg's *motivation-maintenance theory*.

Motivation in the Cyber-Economy

Content theories refer to theories of motivation that are concerned with the question of what causes behavior. In contrast, process theories deal with how behavior originates and is performed.

Maslow's hierarchy of needs is a concept that implies that human needs may be arranged in a hierarchy of importance progressing from a lower to a higher order, and that a satisfied need no longer serves as a primary motivator of behavior. The basis of all needs constitutes physiological needs such as the need for air, water, rest, and exercise. Then come safety needs (the need for shelter and security), social needs (the need for acceptance and association as well as giving and receiving friendship and love), and

[30] Jones, G.R.; George, J.M.; Hill, C.W.: "Contemporary Management," Irwin McGraw-Hill, New York, July 1999.

esteem needs (the need for self-esteem and reputation). On the top of Maslow's pyramid rest self-actualization needs, which refer to needs for self-fulfillment, realizing one's own potential, and for continuing self-development.[31]

Based on Herzberg's findings, *motivating factors* and *maintenance factors* were isolated in his research efforts. Motivating factors create satisfaction because they are directly concerning work *content* issues, whereas maintenance factors, referring exclusively to work *context* issues, are only preventing dissatisfaction.

In the *cyber-economy*, motivating employees is very difficult because people, especially highly educated ones, have become very idealistic. Money as a primary motivator for young individuals entering the job market is simply no longer enough. Rather, they seek a combination of challenging, meaningful, and creative work, relative freedom both in business as well as in private affairs, and monetary compensation that reflects their skills and ability to learn. By the end of the day, these *high-flyers* want to look back on their achievements and say "Well, I materialized on my potentials… I contributed to the world."

Learning is one form of self-actualization and thus has a motivating effect on individuals. First, continual learning is expected to result in higher pay.[32] Second, it is also perceived as an intellectual challenge that keeps a job interesting, which in turn largely contributes to an employee's satisfaction. By learning, employees are offered the chance to build a career as they grow into new responsibilities. In the *cyber-economy*, many a start-up firm offers its employees this possibility because its size allows for internal job flexibility. Moreover, such firms know that education and training programs are essential to develop employees and the organization in harmony with the pace of the *cyber-economy*.

One very effective way of motivating employees is to network them within and outside the company. Through a set of formal as well as informal ties with other departments, groups, and individuals, an employee can actively observe his or her important role not only with colleagues but also for the company as a whole. Moreover, people can learn a lot more with less en-

---

[31] Maslow, A.H.: "Dominance, Self-Esteem, Self-Actualization: Germinal Papers of A. H. Maslow," Wadsworth Publishing, Wokingham, January 1973.

[32] Tapscott, D.: "Minds over Matter," Business 2.0, January 1999

ergy when they share their knowledge with other people through various channels of communication.

A very significant motivator for people is to be affiliated with an organization that feeds their sense of pride. A "hip" start-up company that is buoyed by both the media and the stock market and possesses a great image may fulfill this need, as may an organization with a long history of excellence. The problem with "hip" companies, however, is that once they lose their popularity, employees may feel inclined to leave and move on to the next gig. Companies that attract young talent mainly because of their image may see a harmful outflow of human capital once things turn sour.[33] Just recall *boo.com*: once it could no longer pay for extravagant cars, apartments, and parties, its employees as well as potential ones lost interest in it. It is therefore vital at some early stage to transcend the superficial tie that binds employees and start-ups and to start working on loyalty.

According to Herzberg, money is not a primary motivator. As a maintenance factor, it rather has the function of keeping employees satisfied. Though already extensively disputed in the Old Economy, Herzberg's conception has become all too wrong for the *cyber-economy*. Young people, as we have seen above, do indeed put an emphasis on other factors. Money, however, is naturally on top of the list since young people are searching for fame and fortune and wish to build up the foundation for their lives as they have spent, on average, up to six years in college. Young firms, starved of cash, needed to react to this trend and extended the use of relatively new incentive systems such as stock options for employees, and performance-related as well as skill-based pay. Whereas the former may be familiar, the latter is quite new and needs some explanation.[34]

Skill-based pay systems compensate employees on the level of their skills and proficiency. The idea is that employees who know more are more valuable to the company and should be paid accordingly. Though this is very logical, Old Economy companies compensated employees on the basis of seniority rather than skills. The *cyber-economy* turns this approach inside out and thus helps to dissolve hierarchical barriers based on age.

Developing and maintaining human capital in the *cyber-economy* is essential in order to avoid high employee turnover rates. The *cyber-economy* is

---

[33] Tapscott, D.: "Minds over Matter," Business 2.0, January 1999

[34] Leonard, B.: "New Ways to Pay Employees," HR.COM, September 2000.

in an age of intellectual property and skilled individuals have gained a lot of power in negotiating job contracts. In order to avoid depreciation of their most valuable asset, organizations have to approach their HR management activities – learning, training, and development as well as motivation – from a strategic perspective.

Cyber Competences and Capabilities

In the *cyber-economy* an individual's knowledge is not just essential. Rather, it has to be embedded in a variety of competences and capabilities (cf. Chap. 6 on our approach in the area of the people horizontal) that make that individual distinct and ultimately translate into an organization's spectrum of competences and capabilities.

Core Competences

Core competences on a firm basis are defined by Hamel and Prahalad as "a bundle of skills and technologies rather than a single discrete skill or technology ... It is this integration that is the hallmark of a core competence. A core competence represents the sum of learning across individual skill sets and individual organizational units."

The dividing line between particular skills such as design disciplines or flexible manufacturing and the related core competence, for instance, fast cycle-time production, is hard to define. It is, however, relatively obvious that any core competence must have a set of underlying, mostly HR-based skills. Therefore, we will now move away from competences as attributes of organizations and consider them as attributes of people.

On an individual level, competences refer to a person's knowledge, aptitude, and skills. One of the most important differentiating factors is how competences are at industry, firm and task level. This is because the organization wants specific skills geared to the requirements of its task and role structure.

An individual's competences may be categorized as *meta-*, *industry*, *intra-organizational*, *standard technical*, *technical trade*, and *unique competences*. Whereas meta-competences, namely, analytical capability, ability to communicate, ability to cooperate, etc., as well as industry and standard technical competences are required a priori, intra-organizational, technical trade, and unique competences constitute the human valuables to a company, because they are organization or industry-specific. These competences build the strategic basis for a firm's competitive advantage and they thus have to be learned, trained, and developed.

In addition to these core competences, the *cyber-economy* demands and articulates other, more sophisticated competences that serve the purpose of positively differentiating a company in the marketplace because they cannot be replicated. The most important ones are behavioral competences.

Behavioral Competences

Competences based on behavior and psychology rather than job-based, functional ones distinguish the high performer from the rest because it is his or her very attitude toward work, the capability to integrate him- or herself as well as self-motivation, that makes him or her unique. It is an employee's distinctive personality traits that make them valuable to a company. The possession of:

- A drive for achieving objectives, for example concern for improvement, risk taking or initiative, and ownership or accountability
- Problem-solving abilities
- Capability of interacting with others
- Readiness to work in teams, for example building consensus, coaching and development, and focusing on development

makes up the four main employee competences that are required, because in the *cyber-economy* interpersonal networks as well as partnerships are strategically imperative. Therefore, it is important that employees display that they are competent in establishing, developing, maintaining, and sometimes even diplomatically breaking ties with their colleagues as well as clients.

Behavioral competences are the one distinctive HR advantage that companies in the *cyber-economy* need to build on and develop.

Evaluating HR Initiatives and People in the Cyber-Economy

HR practices as well as people have to be evaluated in order to take appropriate measures. Especially in the area of HR the definition and deployment of valid key performance indicators (KPIs) is essential as building the basis for strategic human resource management. A consistent set of HR KPIs can – as part of the PMM-module of the CCR methodology – easily be integrated in an e-PMM solution enabling a reframed organization keeping up with the changes in the HR area playing an ever growing role for competitive advantage.

Based on our experience we can say, that organizations that succeeded in integrating operationally measurable HR KPIs in their e-PMM tool ended up with the development and establishment of an strategic human resource management.

Evaluation can be considered at two main levels, namely, the strategic and operational levels, which in turn comprise outcomes and processes.

Strategic Evaluation

Strategic evaluation is concerned with the fit between HR policies and practices and the strategic goals of the organization. This means that any organization's HR system should be oriented so it pays attention to the issue of whether it is accorded strategic importance in the organization. Moreover, it must be examined to what extent the principles of HR management reflect the current state of knowledge about best practice. Furthermore, the system should support the organization's strategic goals and smooth out differences between policies and practices. Thus, management checks to see if what actually happens is consistent with expectations.[35]

Strategic evaluation is essential in the *cyber-economy* because it considers satisfaction from four main perspectives that are of increasing importance. First, the financial perspective and the creation of shareholder value is taken into account. This is critical because a strategically oriented company must constantly strive to retain shareholder support for its actions. Second, due regard is paid to customers and their satisfaction plus their retention in order to keep market share in an ever more fragmented and competitive business environment. The third perspective is the internal one, involving quality, response time, cost, and new product introductions, and dealing with the fundamental financial aspects of every business. The fourth perspective refers to learning and growth, for instance employee skills, motivation, and information systems, already discussed earlier.

[35] Bernthal, P.: "Evaluation That Goes the Distance," HR.COM, 2000

Evaluating HR initiatives four-dimensionally allows a company in the *cyber-economy* to constantly check that its overall strategic advantage is not impaired in any way regarding the three principal stakeholder groups: employees, customers, and shareholders.

Operational Evaluation

Operational evaluation concerns how well HR practices are designed and delivered and focuses on outcomes and processes.

Outcome evaluation measures the goals achieved by HR practices. The goals of an HR initiative may be very diverse. Building employee commitment, achieving given skill levels for employees, recruitment targets as well as reducing labor turnover may all be goals of an HR management. In order to evaluate the outcomes of HR programs one can consider the reactions to them, check whether people have learned something or display different types of behavior, and one can refer to hard outcome measures in terms of effectiveness or efficiency.

Process evaluation is concerned with the processes by which goals are achieved. In this case, continuous monitoring as well as diagnosis are conducted in order spot the weak points of HR initiatives. Process evaluation can help to identify, for instance, why low morale among employees has occurred and thus impeded expected results.

The *cyber-economy* poses many challenges to the classic concept of HR management. As the *cyber-economy* puts a tremendous emphasis on intellectual or human capital, and new competences are required but provided by too few people, recruiting candidates have more leverage in getting the job conditions they desire. Moreover, many start-ups often offer more interesting jobs in terms of money as well as fulfillment of esteem and self-actualization needs. All of this means that organizations have to keep pace with the new imperatives incessantly. Changing external as well as internal factors also mean that organizations have to constantly realign their HR strategies in order to build or maintain competitive advantage.

HR management has changed from the tactical to the strategic. Thus, it poses one of the most overwhelming challenges to companies in the *cyber-economy* and implicitly for CCR projects.

CHAPTER 9

CCR: For Which Companies?

After explaining the value of CCR in today's world of highly dynamic competitive markets, that is, after explaining the "why" of CCR, in this book we have also provided insights into the "how" of the method. But now we have to talk about the "who and where" or, in other words, about areas where the implementation and use of CCR can make sense.

As a first step we will describe which companies and departments can use the CCR methodology successfully. We will then continue to explain how CCR can be used in reframing existing e-business initiatives like e-procurement, e-selling, e-CRM, etc. The question we will answer is: "Can CCR cause a turn-around of all initiatives?" Explanations on that topic will be supported by using a special developed "CCR galaxy," which allows us to understand the correlations between different e-initiatives.

Successful CCR Implementations of the Past Leading the Way

In dealing with the main question within this chapter, "Which companies could implement CCR successfully?", we can use another question to help us: "Which companies have already implemented CCR successfully?"

The projects we remember best are those with large multinational clients. This is because of the enormous amount of time and effort we had to invest in internal and external communications and building awareness around the projects. Of course, these projects lasted much longer than those for small companies. And our large clients had an enormous need for reframing, as discussed next.

It took some time for large multinational companies of the Old Economy to obtain proof of the market for Internet technology and in general of e-business.[1] But soon some of these, being recognized in these markets as

---

[1] Kirsner, S.: "Collision Course," Fastcompany, February 2000, page 119.

innovative leaders,[2] decided to initiate the first efforts in the area. The media reported on them enthusiastically and with growing intensity. This drove whole industries almost to panic stations (the AOL and Time Warner merger was often interpreted as the final call for Old Economy companies before being swallowed by the New Economy[3]).

Often the procurement and marketing departments were the first to start activities within companies. Mostly these activities were uncoordinated and were pushed only by the well-known commercial slogan: "Just do it!"[4] The result is clear: these efforts created an immense need for reframing and CCR after the planned results were not reached.

The discussion above may have given the impression that only CCR could help such large companies. This impression is wrong! In this age of fast, upcoming, and even struggling business ideas in the area of the New Economy, for instance biotechnology etc., CCR can be used in many different segments where e-business projects are conducted.[5] One of these is in scalability and flexibility: each start-up company can use CCR and should use CCR. Our experience with a few small companies using CCR was excellent, because the flow of information and communications within such a company are much easier. Moreover, the pressure for success is much higher, because the substance of such a company is much lower.

Often the investment involved comes from venture capital seeking a short-term and high reward, demanding the best results from a company's performance. These expectations leave no room for any underperforming aspects, which puts great pressure on management. Nevertheless, this pressure is very supportive of the staff's and management's commitment and motivation to change.

The following example describes one of our most successful engagements. A company providing information and services on the Internet on marriage asked us to help with their business model: the expected returns could not be reached, after one year of business online. We conducted a c-

---

[2] Andersen Consulting: "Thought Leadership: A Key Contributor to Engaging Employees and Clients at Andersen Consulting," October 1999

[3] Hurt, E.: "AOL/Time Warner Merger Approved," Business2.0, January 2001

[4] Mougayar, W.: "New Rules. New Metrics. Keeping Score in the New Economy," Business 2.0, September 1998

[5] Reid, R.H.: "Principles of the New Economy," Business 2.0, March 2000

assessment (cf. Chap. 10) as the first step in CCR, analyzing the company in all the relevant areas: technology as well as strategy, process, and people. We discovered very quickly that, due to the small size of this type of Internet start-up company, all the highly motivated staff were not really coordinated and focused on their business objectives by management.

The technology as well as the processes, however, were well implemented. Our findings were not really a surprise to the staff but very revealing to investors. Management did not deploy the best people adequately with regard to their personal profiles and skills. There was a strong need for a profit and operation-oriented type of management. Instead, the company was led by a visionary person oriented on the long term. Our findings had a deep impact on management, as you can imagine.

Different Departments: One CCR Approach Used

But who were the clients within the companies we were helping? In working for large companies we usually started by checking and rethinking some specific c-business-related projects in the areas of conventional forms of c-commerce such as e-procurement and e-billing. These types of projects were undertaken in different departments mainly involving IT, procurement, or sales. These departments were the owners of the project, responsible for the budgets, and also being blamed for missed targets. Reframing such projects, we concluded very early during the first phase of our analysis, meant that e-business solutions could not be regarded as isolated solutions like early IT solutions. On the contrary, these solutions must fit within the strategic e-business concept, the e-concept of the company, although at first sight an e-procurement solution seemed to be clearly located as the responsibility of the procurement department.

We were often confronted by our customers with the question "What is an e-concept or e-strategy?"[6] And our reply to this question was that only an e-business solution can be lasting and of value, if it fits seamlessly into the rest of a company's activities.

[6] Robert, M.; Racine, B.; Michel, R.: "E-Strategy, Pure & Simple: Connecting Your Internet Strategy to Your Business Strategy," McGraw-Hill Professional Publishing, December 2000

It often turned out that we had to expand the focus of our activities to derive the solutions that would fit into the rest of the company's operations concerning overall strategy, IT infrastructure, etc. So the projects we started initially as CCR projects to reframe an "e-" related initiative in a specific department soon turned into company-wide CCR projects. Our experience showed that CCR projects to reframe a special "e"-enabling initiative of a department had to start with a clear definition of the organizational boundaries. Nevertheless, in most cases issues arose that could only be solved by refocusing the projects onto the entire company and leveraging the CCR project to one at company level. For this a good example was our work for a major client in the travel industry, who called us in to help some IT staff with an underperforming portal for consumer travel. We ended up by changing the understanding of responsibilities for marketing and branding within the whole company. This project helped our client to become clearer about the relevant tasks and roles. And it also helped the IT staff to obtain a common understanding about their role.

The discussion above focuses on the scope of the entire CCR project. In talking about the success of such a project we have to distinguish between the responsibility for the project and the responsibility for the contribution of the project. Of course, all relevant departments have to make joint efforts during the project. Therefore the following delivery responsibilities of CCR projects can be defined:

- Within the vertical "focus and objectives":
  - For the strategy horizontal, the business planning and development department is crucial, supplying all the required information on vision, strategy, organization, etc.
  - For the process analysis, the project is heavily dependent upon the departments involved and the business process department, if it exists (we often found such a department at several clients)
  - The IT department has to support the project with information on data, IT processes, software, and hardware
  - Finally, the work within the people horizontal can only be delivered with help of the HR department
- All following verticals:
  - The conclusions and tasks within the strategy horizontal can only be developed in close cooperation with the business development and business planning departments

- Results within the process and people horizontal can only be achieved if departments and the staff already involved in the "focus and objective" vertical also contribute during the subsequent project verticals
- The situation for related tasks within the technology horizontal is similar: only close cooperation with the IT department will lead to and ensure improvement of the solution to be reframed

In discussing the organizational responsibility for CCR initiatives we should add some comments on the relevant regional aspects. We found that it is not relevant where (in regional terms) the responsibility for the reframing of an e-initiative lies. But, similar to the points made above on the organizational aspects of responsibility for a CCR project, in most cases we discovered that CCR projects concern senior management questions, at least sales or procurement senior management. So the CCR initiative is soon located in the same place as the senior management, often at the headquarters.

Are CCR Projects Suitable for All Industries?

In discussing the different aspects of CCR we have been talking mainly about multinational and Internet start-ups. The use of CCR was not related to company size or department. But what about whole industries? We all know that the very special needs and requests vary greatly between different industries.

According the NACE Industry Code,[7] we differentiate the following industries:

- Fish industry
- Farm and forestry industry
- Mining
- Process industry
- Utilities
- Construction industry
- Consumer business

[7] "NACE Book of Standards/21805," National Association of Corrosion Engineers, January 1994

- Accommodation and restaurants
- Travel and transportation
- Financial services
- Real estate
- Government and defense
- Education
- Healthcare
- Services
- Private households
- Foreign organizations and institutions

Having a closer look at these industrial areas we can discover that c-initiatives or c-business-related efforts have been made across all of them: we remember in particular e-marketplaces for consumer goods and services. We can also recall information on organizations or governmental interaction channels on the Internet or various services that can be booked over the Internet, etc. The Internet touched all these sectors and in trying to make their efforts profitable we are dealing in CCR projects with all of them.

Of course some of these industries made much more effort than others, trying to quickly obtain a competitive advantage. Typically, these industries are heavily involved with the use and development of new IT technologies and the definition of new business models for such technologies: namely, media/entertainment, computer (hardware, software), telecommunication, and financial services. The CCR framework was used in various cases in these industries, because they felt the pressure of changing markets and falling stock prices most, being heavily involved in Internet business. But almost all industries were touched by New Economy thinking, to a different extent of course, in trying to implement Internet-related solutions. Even industries such as chemicals and insurance started their own initiatives.

Concerning this fact, we cannot conceive of industries that could not use or apply and take advantage of the CCR methodology. It is also not important whether a company deals with an end customer in the B2C market or if it deals with other business customers in the B2B market.

We can now answer the question we started with: CCR is suitable for all c-enabling initiatives which missed their objectives. In implementing CCR it does not matter if the company is a large multinational or a start-up company, whether it is a known player in the market or a newcomer, or if it operates in standard industries or as an active New Economy player. CCR is suitable for all kinds of companies in all the different industries.

CCR: Helping all C-Business Initiatives to Be Successful?

In this section we will take a closer look at typical c-business initiatives that were conducted. These initiatives often do not meet the objectives that were expected and soon become a topic for a CCR project. But can CCR be used for all types of such initiatives? What are the experiences in this field?

We should start this discussion by providing an overview of the common types of Internet-related initiatives in the market, bringing all the known buzz-words into a sound relation, using a picture we have called the "CCR galaxy." The most important initiatives in terms of the number of projects conducted in the area will be highlighted and typical CCR projects in each field will be briefly described.

"The CCR galaxy"[8] is based on the following well-known concept: using Porter's classical picture of a value chain[9] we can strongly simplify the view of a typical company in the markets by defining the buy (buy basic materials), sell (sell end products), and managerial/administrative (plan and control all activities) sides of a company. An e-procurement solution enables the procurement activities of a company and is clearly related to the buying side of the company. Due to the high focus on security matters within Internet business and Internet-based solutions, an additional dimension is added, called "security."

This distinction of internal activities is a result of practical experience: security issues are considered to be of essential importance for several applications and business ideas in the e-commerce area. The "galaxy" provided is a result of our work: we learned that it helps to arrange the c-initiatives into the main areas they are focusing on: internal or external,

---

[8] Summit: "Making the e-transformation," Worldwide Information Systems, October 2000

[9] Porter, M.E.: "Competitive Strategy: Techniques for Analyzing Industries and Competitors," Free Press, 1998

which means focusing on the company or on the markets. An exception to that rule occurs at the initial stage of CCR engagements where our experience showed that the structure described later is not required. Therefore, at stage 1 (cf. CCR galaxy chart) we do not differentiate between buying or selling, the managerial or security dimension, or internal or external. In this initial phase two main approaches are key and shared by all initiatives:

1. C-assessment (cf. chap. 10)
2. Development of a c-strategy (cf. chap. 6, horizontal "strategy")

Based on this initial picture of what we call the CCR galaxy, we can now take a closer look at some of its initiatives to give you an impression of some of our experiences from different studies and engagements related to its different areas.

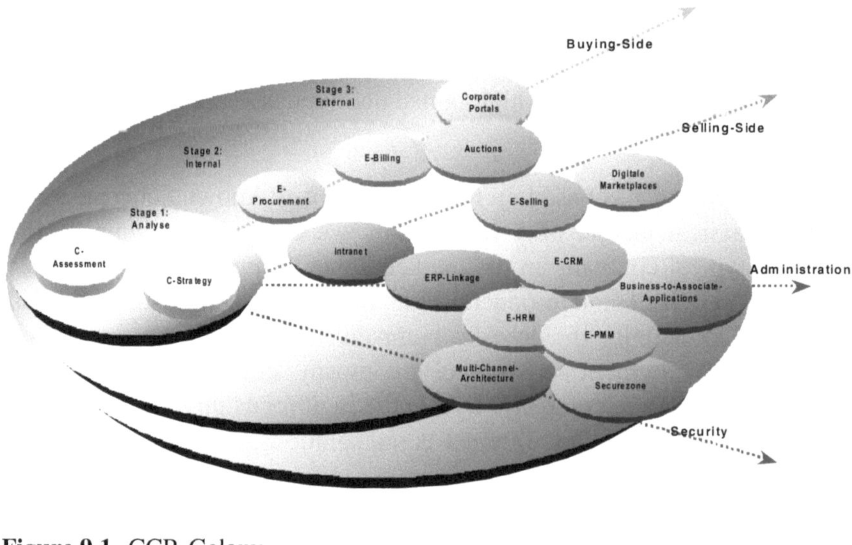

Figure 9.1 CCR-Galaxy

CCR in the Area of E-Procurement

The term "e-procurement" describes Internet-enabled procurement activities: the Internet allows processes and data flows to be accelerated. This makes things much smoother and cheaper within the procurement area. The future procurement process could possibly look as follows: overnight the intelligent Internet-based procurement software checks the price, process, and transition terms for several articles specified by the procurement department, based on the requirements of the production sites. Lists of these articles are provided and take several things into consideration, such as existing contracts, critical resource lists, etc. During the day employees can order the articles required and the system automatically checks the orders for consistency, gets approval from those persons responsible, consolidates orders, orders the materials, and tracks the delivery and billing.[10] Today this process is still a vision, although several efforts have been attempted. In most cases only so-called "c-articles" (small, low-priced goods like minor office supplies)[11] can be handled in this way. But these first solutions have already achieved a significant reduction in cost[12], and development is still going on.

E-procurement was one of the first e-enabled areas of the market. We recall one serious solution provider talking about cost reductions of about 30 percent of process costs in that area when using e-procurement tools in the late 1990s. And we all know how much consultants and salespeople like such numbers! Soon executives started to love these numbers, because stakeholders were convinced by these dramatic cost reductions. Companies started to buy and implement e-procurement solutions and soon important cost optimization was realized: the companies saved money ordering a pencil case! But this did not apply to ordering a complete production site in Europe or elsewhere. The markets then realized that statements predicting cost reduction can only be valid for particular areas and specific groups of articles – and of course only for some markets. Imagine the situation at a company which is using highly sophisticated tools for procurement but has no one to load the prices and catalogs into the system because they do not need to make these investments – due to sales that may be generated without virtual catalogs.

What is the situation today? In the area of e-procurement we often find quick and dirty solutions without any kind of logical interface to an exist-

---

[10] Szuprovicz, B.O.: "Supply Chain Management for E-Business Infrastructures," Computer Technology Research, September 2000.

[11] Business Open Learning Archive: "Pareto ABC Analysis", http://sol.brunel.ac.uk/~jarvis/bola/operations/stock/pareto.html.

[12] Abbott, J.C.: "Optimize Your Operation: Stories, Tools and Lessons for Using the Principles of Process Management to Improve Your Quality," Robert Houston Smith Publishing, March 2001

ing market or company strategy.[13] In this area it is very important to watch and analyze the markets. The truth is: "You should not have the fastest solution in the market, but you should have a good and working one!" CCR can help to streamline and reframe the implemented solutions resulting in a good and working solution. The existing solutions were the first implementations of e-business solutions, which often today

- Are not used by the staff (missed communication, awareness, and training)
- Do not work promptly (missed seamless connection to back-end systems[14])
- Do not provide the needed information (not really adapted process chains)
- Cannot compete with existing personal contacts between seller and buyer (missed acceptance)

We have often encountered the issue of non-acceptance in the companies we worked for. And after all that experience we are convinced that it is an important cultural issue which CCR does have to deal with. The changes can be influenced by a better business plan, an improved fit with company strategy, or improved prioritization of the projects. The culture has to be an c-enabled culture.

This problem of non-acceptance of an existing e-procurement solution that led to serious problem after implementation was experienced most in one engagement we conducted for a large supplier within the automotive industry. This industry is extremely cost oriented, having already provided for years highly integrated production value chains – as can be seen by different ongoing initiatives dealing with c-synchronization of cross-companies' value chains. The suppliers deliver entire system solutions to the automotive companies, providing joint research and development. Due to the extreme cost orientation, cost reduction within the supply chain is a highly important topic. Years ago this industry established EDI connec-

---

[13] Grappa, M.: "Promises, Promises," Business 2.0, November 2000

[14] Hodges, J.; Bulik, B.S.: "Dot-Com Hits and Bombs," Business 2.0, January 2001

tions on different layers and was one of the first to establish Internet technologies for its businesses.[15]

Our client established an Internet-based e-procurement solution for all types of products, participating in different e-marketplaces and integrating several EDI connections. But the expected cost savings did not occur.

We started an in-depth analysis which was intended to take about two months. Our team of business consultants could not find any issues among the systems, process, or the technology. The contracts were well negotiated and the e-procurement solution fitted in very well with the company's strategy. After several weeks of interviews, workshops, and interface as well as process evaluation, we came to the opinion that the staff working within the procurement area were the main issue for that solution: The procurement team felt personally affected when a part of their decision-making process was transferred to a computer system. I remember the senior procurement manager approaching me after one session and asking, "Uwe, how come you never give up looking for problems? Our e-proc system is working perfectly! We use the system – what more do you want? We don't like it – but we try to take advantage of it." At that moment I realized what was really behind these questions: the team was afraid of something. These were the words of somebody who was afraid of what the next step of automation would be. Most of all, they were disappointed that in the new situation they had to give up some of the privileges they enjoyed when negotiating with the sales staff of their suppliers.

Our solution to that issue was simple as such, but hard to communicate to the steering committee of the project. How do we tell someone that they are not communicating correctly and also not providing enough training – especially in the area of procurement? In general this is a pretty "soft" issue – but, frankly speaking, such issues are really the hardest ones!

We had to motivate the staff by training them and focusing them on the new objectives. They had to share the success with the systems – only a joint effort was rewarded.

Our solution was clear. We set up a meeting with the steering committee and agreed on developing a communication and training plan – what today

---

[15] Laabs, J.J.: "Expert Advice on How to Move forward with Change," HR.Com, July 1996

is part of the "people " horizontal of our CCR methodology. The week after, we were given the "go" by the board of directors and six weeks later we jointly ran the first session of the developed plan. After one month the client's HR team was put in the driving seat and enabled to run the sessions. Today the procurement team has installed a quality circle for continuous improvement of their e-procurement system.

CCR and E-Selling

Similar reframing potential can be seen in the area of e-selling solutions. After the Internet was recognized as the future turnover generator at the beginning of all early e-commerce activities, a race began among companies to establish rather slow working but expensive e-selling tools. Some of these companies visualized incredible profits, but finally most of them ended with severe headaches and sunk costs. Most costs gave rise to

- The non-existent alignment of solutions with the companies' global strategy
- Ill-defined roles and responsibilities
- The wrong tools
- Missed hardware investments

The first CCR projects we conducted dealt with the improvement of such issues – by then, we frankly did not know, where we would be ending up – and turned into CCR projects for whole companies, often reframing the whole business strategy and influencing the IT strategy.

Today many of the larger companies do have a kind of "e-selling" solution in place. They prefer not to talk about it and not to get into discussions on this relic of the once "beloved" Internet business solution.[16] The support for and maintenance of existing solutions are minimized. Only a few players act against the mainstream, players of course like Amazon or Yahoo. It is salutary to remember times when large multinational players were thinking about giving up their core business areas while focusing on e-business. But only few tried to match the e-selling ideas and solutions with the "old" business. That is where all the potential for CCR solutions is still to be

[16] Webber, A.M.: "New Math for a New Economy," Fastcompany, September 1998

found. Our experience shows that we are again wasting opportunities and losing the speed resulting from innovations in our businesses. And one main area of interest is sales, an area where most of the business ideas were and still are developed.

In helping our clients with their struggling e-selling solutions we discovered that one major problem was the following. Often our clients had to deal with the problem of undefined responsibility for sales efforts. Everyone was responsible for something: sales was responsible for the contribution, IT was responsible for systems, marketing was responsible for branding and for content (or was it IT who were responsible for content?). As long as these activities were not clearly correlated with individuals and roles and clear process ownership is established, nothing will work the way it should. This "responsibility-issue" impacts as well the last vertical "e-PMM" as only clear defined process and indicator owner enable successful performance management.

I would like to bring up here another client engagement that should facilitate the understanding of CCR in the area of e-selling. One of our clients asked us to help streamline the company's Internet-based sales[17] of its products. The market in which the client was acting was extremely competitive – the market for semiconductors – and our client provided these electronic components to business customers. This market is shared by only a few global players and is driven by technology and price. Product life cycles are extremely short and thus new products achieve superiority for only a few weeks. After that, prices dramatically turn down and the product becomes a mass product within months.

Our client faced the problem that some of the company's clients had established Internet-based sales possibilities for end consumers. This meant that delivery had to be extremely fast and flexible. The preferred solution was to integrate the Internet-based end consumer order process at the clients' site with our client's own sales process by linking these processes using some kind of interface. "Unfortunately all our efforts failed – the delivery times got worse than those of the competition!" the CEO got back to me and awaited some kind of advice.

We initiated the "focus and objective" vertical, analyzed the implemented solution and soon ended up analyzing the whole company, discovering

[17] Tischler, L.: "Recipe for Success," Fastcompany, May 2001

complete confusion about roles, responsibilities and processes within the organization. They were not clearly defined: no one knew who was responsible for the Internet solution as such – marketing, sales, or IT? Each department tried to do its best but missed rules, which made it even harder to establish standard processes. Employees ended up spending the whole day chasing after decisions and decision makers, but these roles were not clearly assigned to anyone.

As part of the second vertical "as-is-assment" we – besides this confusion – discovered further issues in the area of IT. What happened was that the product departments, being in charge of selling, had individually defined IT subject matter experts: "We had to do this as otherwise we would have never been able to get our products linked onto our clients e-selling solutions! Forget our IT disaster!" – pretty amazing stuff which I was told during a workshop. The fact was that all the different product departments had developed different kinds of infrastructure and functionalities, which led to a completely inconsistent environment. And here's the winning factor: By running the first two verticals at the beginning of each CCR project, it is possible to gain an understanding, what the initial goal was and what finally all involved ended up doing. Only with this explicit know-how, it becomes possible to identify areas, where problems could have had emerged leading to a c-commerce solution not realizing the pre-defined business objectives.

After having defined the gaps as part of the third vertical "definition of gaps", we were clear with what to start the "development of CCR plan". We ran focused interviews and brown paper sessions and managed to define core processes such as Internet site-related processes (content management, coding, etc.), sales-related processes (order delivery, order fulfillment, etc.), and marketing (branding, commercial messages, etc.). These processes were quickly implemented and we achieved an important improvement in operational speed and quality, meeting the benchmarks based on the internal acceptance of a shared service department called IT Service and the awareness of the huge benefits from using common and agreed procedures and policies.

CCR and Customer Relationship Management

Another area of c-enabled solutions where CCR can add essential value is customer relationship management (CRM) solutions. These solutions support all staff who are in contact with the consumer, such as sales or call center staff. CRM systems collect, provide, and maintain all necessary consumer information such as:

- Sales
- Deal details
- Consumer needs
- Contact history
- Comments on consumer contact etc.

This information allows the sales or service staff to deal with every consumer on an individual basis, providing personalized services and therefore improving customer care. The overall aim is to improve customer profitability. Furthermore, internal reports can be defined, providing the company with an excellent opportunity for real-time information and evaluation. But often these sophisticated software solutions do not have the required quality data or staff acceptance is low. Another crucial factor of why CRM solutions are not fulfilling their expectations is that companies do not succeed in getting their clients to provide the information required for the value-adding process.

The latter issue can be very relevant if the customer is an important contributor to sales income. Considering the high number of CRM implementations on the market, it is not surprising that some significant CCR experiences were made in that area. Based on our experience in the CRM area we often encountered the situation where isolated call center solutions for one business area had to work on a wrong database. Based on such contingency factors our approach for reframing the CRM solution was to

- get an understanding alongside all four horizontals of the CCR methodology, why the CRM solution was initially implemented (vertical 1) and
- define on the one hand what kind of added value the existing solution contributed in essence and on the other hand to what extent the solution was integrated in the workflows as well as the organizational structure (vertical 2)

Mostly we got to the point that as part of the CCR we would have to improve the quality of the primary data and then to enable a broader use of the CRM solutions by the other business areas. This reflected the fact that companies were investing millions of dollars for CRM software not considering that their data base was by then not that far developed in qualitative perspective allowing maximum usage of the acquired CRM tool.

The interesting think about CRM is that it is still a product that can be sold in "post-e-commerce" times. The reason is that CRM was never really connected to the e-commerce hype by the markets. This is as such quite interesting, as the origin of CRM is the idea of networking between market players in a highly connected economy – and obviously the Internet is a network of connected individual computers and networks exchanging information. But somehow CRM is still an area that companies have yet to enter, while e-commerce and Internet are words that should not be used in any investors' meeting.

In one of our projects we had to deal with a CRM solution for a medium-sized company in the insurance industry which asked us to check its efforts within the CRM area. This client had about 3,000 employees working at eight different locations and selling very specialized insurance products to end consumers. The market is getting more and more competitive after years of shared profits and almost no competition. On a global as well as European level, some full service providers tried to dominate the market, also providing niche products like those of our client. During the last few months the competition had grown to a new level after several alliances and mergers between insurance companies and financial institutions. Our client was providing very cheap solutions and decided to improve customer handling by implementing a huge customer care center that could be reached by telephone, e-mail, or by one-to-one direct personal contact. After months of preparation the company started to implement the system but soon came to a point where our help was needed. Lukas was called by their CRM manager, urgently asking for a meeting to discuss their CRM issues.

We then jump-started the CCR project. After finalizing the "focus and objective" vertical we discovered that the initially planned CRM solution was on its way to be implemented – no reframing need in the strategic, process and technology horizontals at that early stage of the project. But as finalizing the first vertical delivery we evolved that strong management skills within the project management area were missing: the different sub-projects were working on their own, but had only a moderate exchange of information. Another problem was the really strong resistance of some departments to define and implement the new solution: staff were fearful of losing their skills if they had to provide only simple information about contracts and payments to the customer and let the systems work out the details and calculations.

During the second vertical "as-is-assessment" we realized that there were also some issues in the area of the technology vertical because the client had invested in some new IT hardware to provide the required performance. Nevertheless, the idea was to use the existing database which was full with client data. Not surprisingly, the performance of the newly installed CRM system led to long waiting times and consequently frustrated clients. The key reframing aspect was either to increase the capacity of call center staff or to find a way of increasing the performance of the database using new hardware. After we had defined the missed information and managerial issues as the main challenges, we started by establishing training and information events for the staff and uninvolved management, exchanging important parts of the project management and initially the technical reframing process.

This example demonstrates how CCR can help as well projects, that are on their way of being delivered. This means that harm can be minimized, if managers are aware of drifting away from the initially planned c-commerce solution.

CCR and the E-Marketplace

Changing our focus now from the company to the external perspective, we can take a look at the interfaces between different market players in the network economy and spend some time discussing the e-marketplace, the place where the interaction between companies takes place.[18] Some time ago the e-marketplace was regarded as the key business of the Internet future. Consultancies such as Anderson Consulting (now Accenture) proclaimed the building of hundreds of e-marketplaces during the following years. Very quickly, many small providers of e-marketplaces had to turn down their business as big players in the computer industry or from the Old Economy entered the area with high expectations of profit. Soon also, these marketplaces were consolidated and this process is still going on.

E-marketplaces are portals in the Internet where different buyers and sellers try to find a match, a process which in reality takes place in physical

[18] McAffee, A.: "Economic Impact of the Internet Revolution," amcafee@hbs.edu

marketplaces. Different technical and logical solutions for the trading process are possible, such as auction or price line concepts. Different access possibilities also can be implemented, such as closed communities or "public access" providing access to everyone who wants to enter a specific marketplace. In the area of e-marketplaces it is essential to analyze whether a company has really to assign to one or more marketplaces, as well as evaluate the real need for and outcome of such a decision. CCR can support that decision.

More strategic components have also to be analyzed: Has the market changed since we decided to join it? Do we still need to participate? Does it generate profit? Will it bring any value? Again, the aspect of cost saving is another strong win that CCR can provide by considering the best-fit re-usage of existing parts and components, may they be technical or processual, as part of the reframed solution. As marketplaces continue to be consolidated on one hand, and big players in the market decide to build and run new marketplaces on the other, the need for CCR-based considerations will increase tremendously.

One project we handled in the area of e-marketplaces was located in the chemical industry and was typical of all the questions that must be posed before becoming involved with and investing in e-marketplaces. Our client was a small supplier of basic chemical products for different industries like the automotive and oil industries. Other market players like BASF, Dow, and Atochem became involved in e-marketplaces at that time, joining existing ones or establishing their own (e.g., ChemConnect). Our client was not really aware of the Internet and all the possibilities such solutions could provide to the business, although some initiatives were under way, managed separately by each of the existing business units.

After our initial analysis as part of the "focus and objective" and the "as-is-assessment" vertical, we realized in the third vertical that in divergence to the initial e-strategy of the client, by far too many projects had been started. For being able to develop an efficient CCR plan, we ran a cyber (c-)assessment (cf. chap. 10) delivering a matrix clustering the projects according to the project-specific

- business impact
- involved risk and
- required investment volume

We produced a portfolio of currently running projects for the client, providing for the first time an overview of all existing Internet-related activities. The involvement in e-marketplaces was not an established project at the time. Due to the importance of the e-marketplace for the whole company, management decided to establish one explicit project in the area. This was a strategic type of project to analyze all existing marketplaces and those of the future. Not only was the reframing focusing on company strategy and content issues, but also we had to validate technical issues such as an interface and linkability to the different marketplaces. Based on this information we reframed both the content-driven aspects and the technical-driven perspectives of the client to ensure an optimal fit in both dimensions.

After that work was completed, we decided with our client to join two of the existing marketplaces. Due to the efficient reframing, this involvement had a CFROI of below one year and therefore can be seen as a positive and long-lasting investment.

CCR and E-Billing

E-billing solutions deal with the idea of smart billing processes enabled by the Internet.[19] The main goal is to:

- Simplify and consolidate billing
- Track bills
- Improve money transfer processes in the B2C and B2B areas

This means that in future the consumer or business user will have the possibility of "smart payment" of bills by using handheld devices like cell phones. E-billing also supports sophisticated credit card or transfer solutions allowing payment over the Internet. Finally, solutions that support the user with bill management also belong to the area of e-billing.

This entire area is of immense interest for financial service companies. Existing e-billing solutions are supporting other solutions like e-selling or e-procurement but are often not of crucial importance for companies. The exceptions are, of course, financial service companies who see their core

[19] White, Z.: "1999 Fee & Billing Survey of A/E/P & Environmental Consulting Firms," Zweig White & Associates, June 1999

business based on the Internet. CCR in that case can help to improve the seamless fit of established solutions with a company's solution set. CCR can even help to answer the question: "Do we really need that expensive e-solution?"

An example of a sophisticated Internet-based solution of the future, involving a leading-edge e-billing solution, is a company providing condominium chalet holidays in the Midwest United States. These chalets are rented by people for holidays. But most of them are owned by people who also spend their spare time there. The company provides a unique service to the owners: in the chalets there are a large number of sensors. The owner can check the sensors over the Internet to get information about supplies in the chalets. This makes it possible to buy and replace needed supplies – to some extent a p-commerce approach.

Only one issue arose in this process: ordering had to be done by a fax that was sent by the owner of a chalet to the supplier. This disrupted the whole process. We helped the client to implement the following seamless solution: the owner of a chalet could check the supplies at the chalet over the Internet and order any supplies needed by simply pushing an ordering button. Besides that reframing of the solution from an fax-based to a real p-commerce solution, we also reframed processual components, and slightly reframed the initial solution by adding e-billing functionality. The client could therefore use the infrastructure already in place, because, based on the CCR methodology and our experience, we ensured that the solution requirements and IT functionality and performance were adequate. From the results of a later customer survey, the additional functionality provided by e-billing created a huge added value to the customer for a relatively small investment needed to optimize the technical as well as content fits.

The topic of e-billing solutions can also be used to demonstrate one of the core truths about the Internet – how important it is to analyze the regional markets and market characteristics before implementing a solution. Despite the fact that the Internet is a global network, users prefer regional orientations and we all live in our own regional contexts. The same thing happens on the Internet: e-billing solutions are quite successful in the B2C business in the United States but not so in Europe. The reason is simple: in Europe the consumer is not used to paying bills every month, because the bank payment process is more sophisticated.

CCR Mythology for All Companies – for All Purposes?

In summary it has to be pointed out that CCR can contribute important wins by reframing all kinds of cyber-business solutions as well as their inherent components and focusing them on profits and on reducing costs. The main contribution is making one aware of previously made investments. One of the basic features is a sound strategic analysis which helps to fit the c-business initiative in the company's contingency situation.

Moreover, CCR helps to develop realistic business plans and objectives, supporting the implementation of these plans, and eventually reframing the existing unsuccessful c-business solutions. The approach is based on a fundamental analysis undertaken in all the relevant fields of an entrepreneurial action represented by the four horizontals of CCR. The approach is valid for companies of all sizes in all business areas.

CHAPTER 10

Cyber-Assessment as a Starting Point

Just a short time ago, everything in business was about the vocal “e”. Business processes such as procurement and trading were extended with the prefix *e*, not only to indicate the intrinsic change of these activities toward more use of web-based technologies, but also to display a great deal of novelty and thought leadership.

In the very first chapters of this book, I have already introduced you to the main problems that arose as a consequence of companies hastily designing and implementing projects to materialize on cyber-commerce applications. This was all too natural, because fierce competitive pressure demanded that organizations follow up and commit virtual clients and customers very quickly[1].What could be observed was that the quantity of Internet initiatives was indirectly proportional to the realization of expected results. The more companies invested in and spent time on e-commerce projects, the less they achieved their objectives.

Because of my personal experience with companies that tried to enter the cyber-commerce world too fast, i.e., without much prior planning, and ended up with by far too many so called “e”-initiatives, I began to think about a standardized approach that would enable companies to focus and prioritize their cyber-solutions without necessarily losing much of their investments. I developed a methodology that I called, once completed, *cyber-assessment.*[2]

Cyber-assessment can be a useful starting point or tool for CCR projects. It describes the procedure of analyzing and evaluating current and planned cyber-commerce activities. It is your aid in identifying whether a project is leading or will lead to desired results. Based on this methodology, you can make more informed decisions on what to do with various projects.

---

[1] Lea, W.: “CyberStaking: Why Partnerships Matter”, Silicon Alley Reporter, September 2000

[2] Seebacher, U.G.: “Optimierung der E-Business-Aktivitäten durch E-Assessment”, Information Management & Consulting, April 2000

Cyber-Assessment: The Methodology

The term cyber-assessment originated in the course of developing various cyber-strategies and as a consequence of thorough analysis and evaluation of cyber-commerce solutions. The methodology is based on four modules; the modules themselves comprise various activities on which I will expand in detail throughout this chapter.

The c-assessment methodology enables businesses to:

- Analyze the c-commerce dynamics of their respective industry as well as of their main competitors
- Identify the crucial value- and cost-drivers from the perspective of c-commerce solutions along the company-specific value chain
- Spot the core processes of c-commerce activities
- Define new projects
- Analyze the coherence of parallel Internet projects within the company
- Evaluate and prioritize current and newly defined c-projects and derive strategic recommendations for action

By studying the methodology of c-assessment, one can summarize and allot its various parts to four modules that constitute the main activities of every c-assessment.

Module One: Industry Analysis

The basis of every successful c-assessment is an analysis of the particular industry in which an organization is doing business to determine the industry-specific status quo regarding development as well as potential of c-commerce solutions.

Knowing about one's competitors has been crucial to business from the start. In the c-economy, nevertheless, it takes on even more importance.[3] This is because the globalized, networked economy exposes you to compe-

[3] "Trends and Outlook – Digital Commerce Strategies", Jupiter Research, February 2000

tition from every corner of the world.[4] Software solutions can be provided to a corporation from, say, Nevada by a small firm located somewhere in mainland China. Information is even more global: An information provider from Norway may suddenly find a competitor operating in Malaysia. The consistent competitive infiltration and fragmentation of every industry requires organizations to constantly conduct thorough studies in order to take actions that allow them to preserve their valuable share of the market.

At the beginning of module one, the organization has to sketch the industry-specific value chain, which is then broadened in scope with information and experiences foreign to the individual industry. The integration of this precise knowledge, acquired through a system of co-operation and partnerships with other companies coming from different fields of business, as well as with consultants, is essential, for it allows a cross-industry comparison that can aid in identifying possible shortcomings and deficiencies, the solution for which may be found in other industries.

On the basis of the defined value chain, critical value- and cost-drivers are spotted, resulting in a so-called value-driver analysis. It is vital to incorporate the value-driver analysis in module two for conducting a comprehensive company study along with an evaluation of the company's core processes.

In step two of module one, the value chain is subjected to an examination of transaction costs.[5] Generally, transaction costs are organized into

- (Internal) process costs
- Inventory costs
- Transportation costs

To receive optimal information about transaction costs, it is advisable to team up with experts of a company's operative units, because these specialists must have access to the pertinent data.

Taking into consideration the planned project duration, the transaction costs analysis can be carried out on various levels of detail – from an activity-based costing perspective right up to a qualitative analysis. Because

---

[4] Reid, R.H.: "Principles of the New Economy", Business2.0, March 2000

[5] Menard, C.: "Transaction Cost Economics: Recent Developments", Edward Elgar Publishing, March 1997

time is an important aspect within CCR projects, we mostly go for a high-level transaction costs analysis that is sufficient to identify the main industry-specific cost factors and the potentials for cost reduction.

Throughout the third step, an estimation of the possible reduction in costs serves, along with benchmark data, as the starting point for teams to identify sources and leverage points for reframing transaction processes. Our experience shows that ideally these teams have to be made up of individuals from various departments and sections within the company, as well as of external consultants, in order to reach their full problem-solving potential.

Parallel to the steps described above, a systematic screening of dot-com start-ups and of c-strategies set up in businesses is performed. Thus, industry-specific trends plus competition are qualitatively analyzed to guarantee up-to-date information on the market. This is important, because it ensures that within the c-assessment process the goals can be continuously reframed according to changing environmental factors.

Module Two: Internal Analysis

A substantial aspect within the framework of every c-assessment is the conception of long-term, value-adding decision alternatives[6] coupled with the analysis of current and planned c-commerce projects. For this purpose, a company's core processes are examined by gathering information through surveys and interviews, as well as by sifting through any existing documentation. The results are then discussed with managers and team leaders.

This first step is very essential. First, it forces companies to study their ongoing projects critically. Not seldom, organizations discover that various projects are no longer up-to-date, in terms of both technology and their actual goals. Second, projects planned for the future can be better designed in harmony with current ones.

The second step within module two concerns the documentation of all c-commerce projects – past, present, and future – in a universal format, e.g., template. Its objective is to describe all projects according to certain criteria:

---

[6] Caudron, S.: "Consumers' Revenge", Business2.0, November 1999

- Responsible people
- Sponsors
- Content
- Time frame
- Finances

This task is tightly connected with step number one of the next c-assessment module. Module two, however, is rather directed towards a primary documentation of the project landscape, which in module three then constitutes the basis for project evaluation.

The information gathered may be assembled in a so-called project master plan that can be installed as a database to facilitate the management of multiple projects in the future. This master plan has to be fine-tuned from time to time to meet revised company standards.

The next phase deals with an analysis of the core processes' value drivers[7]. For this purpose, the company-specific core processes are categorized into subprocesses and single activities. On the level of the single activities, these are differentiated according to the following criteria:

- Value creation
- Logistics
- Security
- Inventory

On a subprocess level, the value-adding activities can be identified and aggregated regarding value creation. Furthermore, the combination of the project master plan and the value-driver analysis[8] identifies value-adding activities or subprocesses that could be optimized with the help of a CCR project.

Along the value chain, potential c-commerce solutions are identified[9] which support processes and make them more efficient. Exact knowledge

[7] Libert, B.D.; Boulton, R.E.S.; Samek, S.M.: "Learning To Juggle", Business2.0, June 2000

[8] Scott, M.: "Value Drivers", John Wiley & Sons, 1998

[9] Knight, J.: "Value Based Management", McGraw Hill Professional Book Group, 1998

about the marketplace, creativity, and constructive teamwork are the critical factors. Moreover, it is important to extract decisive information through internal and external interactions in order to spot whether a c-commerce option is value-enhancing or –reducing. The results are a qualitative analysis and evaluation of the impact that an option may have on an organization's core processes. Finally, all value-adding options are sketched.

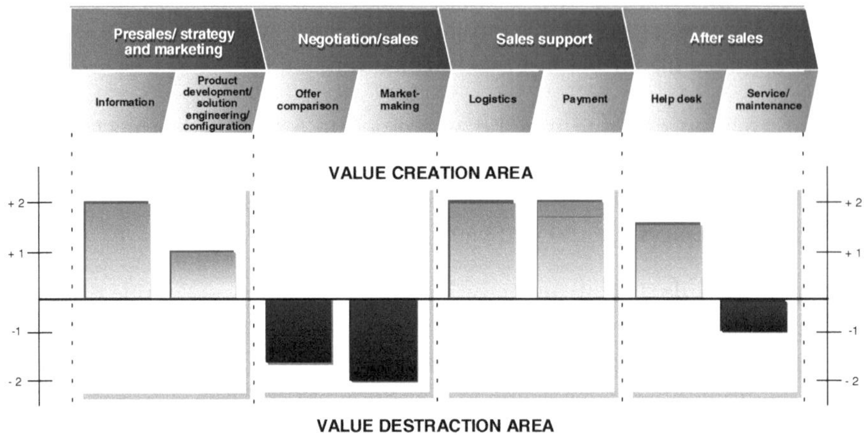

Fig. 10.1 Impact analysis of c-commerce project

Module Three: Analysis and Evaluation of Cyber-Commerce Projects and Options

Following modules one and two, module three copes with the central question of how existing c-commerce options can be prioritized in order to help an organization achieve maximum benefit. When a company is engaged in multiple projects, then those with similar content as well as those with differing content should be coordinated so as to prevent large overlaps. Overlapping projects unnecessarily consume many human, physical, and monetary resources that could be allocated more effectively. Avoiding them is one of the first steps towards saving a lot of money.

C-commerce alters the sustainability of processes. Sometimes existing projects cannot generate the value they were originally designed to deliver. Only an unambiguous and straightforward evaluation can lead to a rational basis for making decisions about which projects to continue and which ones to reframe or stop all together. This is a very hard task for companies, because evaluation of projects may cause various feuds among project leaders as they struggle to convince managers of the advantages of their project over others. Diplomatic skills are required. But one should not get stuck in extensive negotiations. Time is essential in the c-economy.

The evaluation of projects and options follows certain criteria. The first level exclusively involves monetary indicators. Typically, the total internal and external project costs are compared with the expected growth in turnover and the decrease of costs. Once calculated, the absolute figures have to be scaled to make them comparable to non-monetary measures. A Likert Scale may be best for this purpose. The second level contains non-quantifiable indicators such as:

- Process quality
- Customer satisfaction
- Customer commitment

The third level involves determining whether the projects fit into the general strategic concept of the organization. This task should be carried out exclusively by executive managers, because they know best about where the company is heading. All indicators of levels two and three are again evaluated according to a Likert Scale.

Aggregation of the individual criteria produces a result that goes beyond the usual calculation of a project's net present value (NPV)[1]; it articulates the overall value or use for the company. Thus, the emphasis is not only on money but also on factors such as potential for customer satisfaction and retention, market share and power, and impact on image and brand.

Risk[2] is another factor taken into consideration in module three. Usually, the risks entailed in a project are determined by the following criteria:

- Responsible people
- Definition of task separation
- Communication channels

[1] Emigh, J.: "Net Present Value (NPV) and Cost of Capital", Computerworld, July 1999

[2] Young, I.D.: "Introduction to Risk Calculation in Genetic Counselling", Oxford University Press, September 1999

- Requirements and capabilities of the project and the participants
- Knowledge about the degree of standardization of planned information technology solutions
- Ongoing requirements for change
- Duration of implementation
- Number of employees involved
- Dependence on other projects

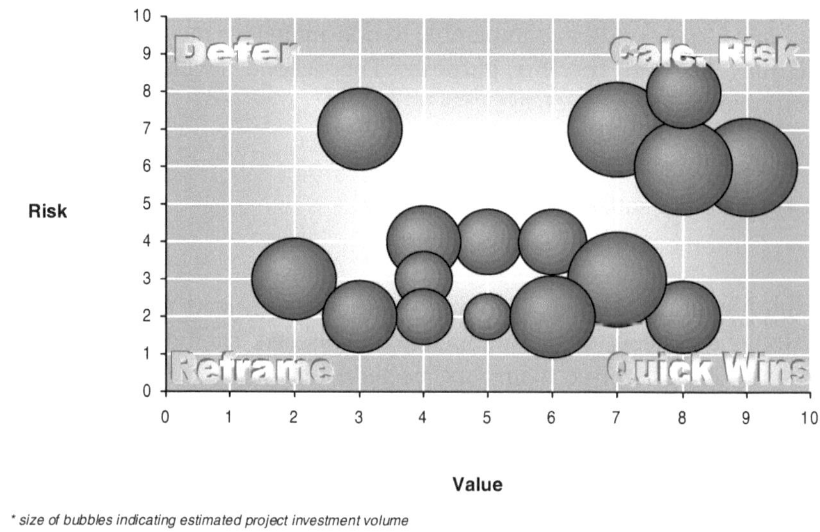

Fig. 10.2 Project-Risk-Value-(PRV-)Matrix

Based on selected key figures, an overall indicator of a project's degree of risk (low, middle, high) can be determined. Naturally, the classification of risk into low, middle, and high is rather subjective, and results may be distorted if this is undertaken by mostly internal personnel. Therefore, it is of utmost importance to call in external consultants who can evaluate the risk involved critically.

Once the value impact, the involved risk and the estimated required project investment volume of all projects are evaluated, each can be positioned in a three-dimensional matrix – x-axis: value impact; y-axis: involved risk; size of bubble: required project investment volume – to make a comparison relatively easy. Based on the findings consolidated in a so called Project-Risk-Value (PRV-)Matrix (cf. fig. 10.2), companies and we, when initiating a CCR project, can decide whether to continue a project, reframe it, freeze it, or stop it right away.

Module Four: Strategic Recommendation for Decision-Making

The future of all projects with high value and low or bearable risk can be reflected on. At this early stage, it is already advisable to think about the implementation strategy. The fundamental question has to be: To make or to partner?[1]

Especially in the implementation of CCR projects, partners play a vital role. Software solutions, the mobilization of critical mass, and the formation of communities are tasks that a company often cannot cope with on its own. Therefore, at the very beginning of module four the methods for achieving the success of a project must be scrutinized. Note that every project is different, and so are the roads to success.[2]

For every project, the critical success factors are defined, and it is determined whether the organization possesses the competitive advantages and the competence that enable it to realize the project with its own resources. Success factors are, for instance:

- Company size
- Market power
- Market share
- Financial strength
- Leverage in negotiations to win "launch partners"
- Image

If the preconditions for the realization of a project are met by the company, then the recommendation may be that the company should implement the project without partners. This recommendation, however, does not exclude the possibility of outsourcing. The more complex and cost- and time-

[1] Chatham, B.: "Mergers, Acquisitions and Saving IT Dollars", CIO Magazine, March 1998

[2] Bendor-Samuel, P.; Staedke, J.: "Turning Lead into Gold: The Demystification of Outsourcing", Executive Excellence, October 2000

intensive a project is, the more sensible it will be to outsource the development, integration, and implementation of software.

If the preconditions are not met, a company can use existing c-commerce solutions such as digital marketplaces or can search for a partner as part of the reframing process. In searching for a partner, a company has to consider strategic fit – could the partner also be of use in the future? – and coherence of attitudes and cultures, as well as possible negative aspects such as high costs.

The effect of module four is that a company can be strategically positioned within the c-economy, because the questions of which projects should be implemented and how this should be done are answered. Module four orients projects according to a company's long-term objectives being an inherent issue of successful CCR projects.

C-assessment is a valuable starting point for CCR, because it shows that careful selection of relevant Internet- or c-commerce projects has a positive impact on their success. Especially for bigger companies, c-assessment is helpful in opting for projects and solutions that create the highest value and in implementing them efficiently and in conformance to the company's overall strategy.

Case Study: eZoka Group

SupplierLinx: CCR in the Area of Collaborative e-Procurement

As mentioned in a previous chapter, some companies already intuitively apply fragments of the CCR methodology without having read about it before. Such companies are aware of the changed metrics of the New Economy and have, at least partly, adapted to it.

One such company is eZoka Group. I first learned about the company a few weeks ago when I read a *Newsweek* article. What caught my interest was the many ideas of the CCR approach reflected in it. The article mentioned eZoka as an example of a company adapting to today's changed business contingency factors. I decided to contact this company to see how far they had pushed their "self-made reframing" approach. I arranged a meeting with Ben Evetts, head of public relations of eZoka Group. He explained in detail how the company had reframed its business strategy. I quickly realized that the company would be the perfect illustration of such an "unaware and intuitive" CCR approach.

eZoka Group is a managed technology provider, offering purchasing and supply solutions to companies operating across Europe. It was founded in November 1999 in recognition of the lack of procurement efficiencies offered to small and mid-sized businesses. They developed eZoka's "Group Buying Service" in line with the market expectations of that time, which predicted that small and medium-sized enterprises (SMEs) would be keen to purchase from Group Buying Services as news spread of the price benefits offered by aggregated purchasing. Shares of ventures focusing on e-business collaboration such as Ventro were riding high, and analysts predicted massive short-term growth potential.

The eZoka MarketPlace was launched in August 2000, with 30,000 products and services available. Through careful market research on the buying habits of SMEs in the UK, the MarketPlace exceeded its initial targets month by month, and interest from organizations wishing to launch the service remained strong.

However, while the outlook remained good for eZoka Group, some worrying trends began to appear in analyst and media reports. The word "e-procurement" became synonymous with failed return on investments, huge barriers to entry, and little or no supplier integration. Indeed, Forrester estimated that the average level of supplier integration was only 30%, and according to AMR Research, purchasers of e-procurement systems had received only 30% of the total potential return on investment. It was obvious that there was a clear market requirement for supplier integration, and this was needed rapidly in order to retain credibility for the industry as a whole.

The Strategy

Aware of these problems, eZoka decided to take a different path. Thanks to its early research and the experience of its management team, the company decided from the outset to reject the "buy-side" model used in competitor offerings. eZoka reframed the widespread strategy of e-procurement vendors and developed a cross buy-and-sell side model as its overall strategy.

> *"Everyone was trying to implement buy-side models. If we wanted to succeed in the long term we had to position ourselves differently. There is no challenge and no future in saying "me-too". The key to success was ultimately a cross buy-and-sell side model."*
>
> *Sonia Lo, Chief Executive Officer*

This realization was and is the cornerstone of eZoka's success. eZoka effectively allows suppliers to participate in a market place without competing directly on product lines. This removes the need to aggressively mark down prices. In return, however, eZoka insisted that suppliers execute orders of all sizes. It is this unique methodology that has allowed eZoka to provide a comprehensive supplier database, which delivers prompt fulfillment service to its customers.

The Process

As previously mentioned, from its inception eZoka had rejected the supplier integration methodology of its competitors, who outsourced the function to manual content factories in Southern Asia. eZoka Group had always believed that this outsourcing approach was unsatisfactory, since it remained costly and gave companies little or no control over their database. Another problem was the fact that suppliers did not want to hand over control of their catalogue to a third party. Lack of trust in such third parties resulted in reticence from the supplier community. Not surprisingly, suppliers were not prepared to play, especially when hefty fees were often demanded of them in order to participate in an unproven channel.

This resulted in a massive lack of supplier liquidity in the e-procurement industry, a problem which needed to be addressed rapidly in order to ensure long-term growth for the sector. In particular, the issue for eZoka was effectively twofold:

3. The poor reports could potentially slow growth in its current (SME) market.
4. Even more critically, its plans to launch a mid-sector product which combined the eZoka MarketPlace methodology and workflow functionality could be severely damaged without rapidly addressing the industry-wide lack of supplier liquidity.

> *"We had to expand our strategy of supplier integration, in order to stimulate market growth. This required us to take an industry leadership position in order to prepare the market for the next generation."*
>
> *Sonia Lo, Chief Executive*

A timely opportunity for eZoka appeared: The issue of sustainability for a single-product company had been discussed, and the industry's failure to integrate full supplier bases into workflow systems allowed the deployment of the SupplierLinx technology into new markets, as part of the reframing in the "process-focused" area.

Therefore, in the summer of 2001, eZoka Group launched SupplierLinx, making it available to its competitors and to purchasers of competitors' workflow technology. The goal was to advance supplier liquidity throughout the market in the long term, while sowing the seeds of customer satisfaction in preparation for the launch of its mid-sector product (TradeLinx) in the autumn of 2001.

The SupplierLinx rollout also resulted in a reframing of the revenue stream. Customers and suppliers alike were quick to see the benefits of integrating suppliers at no cost to themselves (the supplier), while allowing suppliers to retain ownership of their catalogue content and enabling operators to take a long-term view of generated returns through trade margins. As a result of this, eZoka Group can guarantee supplier liquidity to its customers, and to date it remains the only full-service offering within the UK market, as well as attracting interest from the manufacturing industries of Southern Europe.

The Technology

Due to eZoka Group's initial technical infrastructure, which included the supplier 'on-ramping' functionality, the only change in technology strategy was to make the export of data totally application agnostic. Prior to the rollout of SupplierLinx, the eZoka Group (XML-based) database needed only to export into the co-buying platform format that had been developed for the MarketPlace. Therefore, in order to allow the export of data to any application, eZoka Group developed and integrated an IO server that allows compatibility with all major e-procurement infrastructures.

> *"The technical infrastructure was already in place but to really open up this new revenue stream, myself and our technical team had to develop the IO Server to open up our database to any application."*
>
> *Simon Warrick, Chief Technical Officer*

The People

When plans were set to extend the product offering of eZoka Group, the skills of its personnel were crucial. eZoka Group carefully planned its recruitment to attract highly experienced people and, as a result, the overwhelming majority of staff members have many years' experience in the Old Economy. This experience ensured that eZoka has been realistic in the projections and targets it has proposed.

The skills of the eZoka purchasing team have been crucial to the success of the new direction. In addition to their role of ensuring full service, best prices, and advice to users of the UK MarketPlace, the team has now been leveraged in order to provide high-level advice to all new clients – ensuring best practice in every new offering.

> *"To ensure that clients maximize the value of the eZoka Group services, an early consultancy process is required. The eZoka Purchasing team has over 50 years of experience in this area and the deployment of their skills is imperative to our success."*
>
> *Dale Heathcote, Chief Operating Officer*

Conclusion

Although not recognized by eZoka Group as a reframing methodology, the process which they undertook clearly relates to the management of CCR. This as well was confirmed in the meetings with Ben Evetts, when I described CCR to him. The results have been positive for eZoka Group: an expanded revenue stream that has opened up new markets both in the UK and Europe and continued strong support by its investors.

Case Study: Multi-national IT Company

CCR in the Area of Procurement

One of our first and probably one of our most interesting and challenging CCR projects was with an international IT product and service company in the US. From the very beginning we were aware that a successful project with this client, one of the godfathers of the New Economy, would give us enormous momentum for the future evolution of our methodology.

One day, the head of the Procurement unit (PU) called me at my office. He had read an article I had published several weeks earlier in a well-known business magazine. This article addressed some of the issues of CCR. Although CCR was at that time still in its infancy, he liked the idea of our approach and wanted to know more about it. We met a few days later and he bombarded me with questions. Some of them were really challenging. I guess this was one of the moments when I realized the full importance and the extent of the methodology we were evolving – clients come to us, asking for advice!

The head of the Procurement business unit, I just call him George, and I were speaking exactly the same language, and we quickly became friends. In the course of the discussion he became increasingly clear about his problem:

Unlike many other New-Economy companies, George's company has never shown the cash-burn mentality so often cited, and believe me, the company would never have gotten so far if it had. George told me about the hurdles he was facing every day in his department. His plan was to reframe the entire procurement process with the help of a CCR project.

The Strategy

The moment he told me about his intentions, I knew that his problem presented the perfect case for testing our methodology on an international level. Besides, I was convinced that I could help him. We signed a deal for a first strategic assessment. Normally, it takes several weeks, sometimes even months, before we start with strategic assessments. Especially in large corporations such as George's, administrative and political processes sometimes last very long before you can get started. George wanted the strategic assessment to start only a few days later. The time pressure he put on me and my team showed me how keen he was on the topic.

The findings of the strategic assessment were astonishing, even for me. The PU had to handle thousands of requests weekly for purchases under $1000 each, also referred to as MROs, such as books, business cards, or catering, but also IT hard- and software. High-volume, low-dollar transactions represented 75% of the corporate procurement but only 3% of the total dollars flowing through the accounts payable department. The lack of automated and standardized procedures made the process of creating and tracking payables highly complicated. As a result, the PU had to dedicate several resources to processing requisitions into purchase orders (POs), resolving problems, and trying to clearly articulate business rules and processes for an increasingly complex and growing business. The company relied on dozens of paper forms and a diversity of custom applications for procuring goods and services, a process which was not only slow, manually intensive, and costly, but also prone to human data-entry errors. When we presented our results, George totally agreed:

> *"You see, the entire purchasing process is manually intensive, inefficient, and confusing for both end users and vendors. It is honestly hard for us to keep up in such an environment. Our employees are wasting their time on the procurement process instead of getting their job done."*

We decided the best way to deal with this was to apply the existing CCR methodology – at least what at this time was already some kind of structured and usable of the later CCR methodology – for reframing what was essentially the procurement problem. The reframed tool should encompass all the control and validation functionalities that the requisition personnel were dealing with and push them onto the Intranet. After completion of the CCR, the employees should be empowered to order needed MROs online in a simple and short process, still using the existing IT infrastructure components as effectively as possible.

The Process

As already described in the section on strategy, the existing procurement process was slow, manually intensive, and prone to human data-entry errors. Our concept was to implement an easy-to-use system which would be widely accepted and which would take care of as many tasks as possible automatically.

Based on the existing procurement process, we identified the high level of transport activities within the process flow, on the one hand, and the non-existing integration with other processes, on the other, as the key levers within the CCR. The reframed solution was to provide easy-to-use online forms for ordering office supplies but also validate information such as pricing and availability. The reframed application was also to ensure that orders were linked to the appropriate accounting code and automatically routed to managers for notification or approval. A very tricky part of the CCR was the idea of integrating billing functionalities into the reframed solution. This was to be realized by linking the solution directly to the corporate accounting system, so that requisitions would automatically be uploaded as purchase orders.

We already knew from previous CCR projects in the area of e-procurement that the key to success was the reframing of the available front-end to an intuitive one, allowing employees to easily order items in a controlled fashion without going through a complicated process. Therefore, the reframed tool automatically detects user and cost group when logging in. Products are listed according to predefined categories. Self-explanatory order forms tailored for specific kinds of requisitions make it possible to complete the ordering process in less than 3 minutes. Upon submission of the order, the e-procurement application generates an order-tracking number for future reference. Financial controls protect the company from fraud so that unauthorized people cannot order goods. Orders are automatically routed for management approval within minutes. Once orders are approved, purchase orders are automatically generated by the accounting system and sent to the supplier via electronic data interchange (EDI).

The Technology

Included in our strategic assessment was a state-of-the-art analysis of hard- and software available. One reason why George liked CCR was the fact that our methodology seeks to best integrate existing technology and thus keep costs under control. This fit perfectly with his organization's concept of aiming not for a fancy "nice-to-have" application but for a highly functional, widely accepted, and financially reasonable application which would reduce procurement cost and not create new expenses.

As expected, as one of the godfathers of the New Economy, the client was pretty well equipped not only with soft- but also with hardware. Thus we faced few restrictions in this dimension. In cooperation with George programmers, we reframed the procurement application based on the existing Intranet. It took three programmers, some consultants, and 4 months to run the CCR project and finally release the reframed procurement tool. George had his quick win and enough visibility in the entire company.

Within this CCR project we could reuse more than 70 % of existing components having been parts of the old procurement solution. All these components already existed and did not add to the costs. Previous optimization approaches would have neglected the cost-saving potential of implementing such existing software. What is more, we would never have been able to reframe the procurement process within such a short time period without integrating existing components.

The People

Anyone who has already experienced project work knows about the importance of politics. Consultants are pretty expensive, and the last thing you want from them is bad news.

To a large extent, people confronted with the procurement process at the client organization were aware of the existing problems and they were also aware of the need for a change. The reframed procurement solution was the way out of the misery, and it was easy for us to illustrate the benefits of the new, reframed solution. The important thing, when working with these people, was to integrate them during the entire process. Providing turnkey solutions without integrating the people who have to deal with the problem is a more or less 100% guarantee of failure. Thus we created a working group in which the workers could express their concerns and their ideas for improvement. The information we got out of this working group was highly valuable for us and was constantly integrated in the project work. The good thing about this approach was that we did not need any internal marketing for a turnkey solution. People were not surprised when the tool went live – they had already known about the solution long before. They knew about its benefits and – even more important – they accepted it on a broad scale since e-procurement reflected their own ideas brought in via the working group.

The complicated thing was to communicate properly to the people working in the PU. They, too, saw the benefits for their organization, but at the same time the solution was, for understandable reasons, a potential threat to them. The reframed solution would take over much of the administrative procurement tasks and thus gave them the impression that their jobs would become obsolete. One of the comments I remember pretty well went something like this:

> *"Such a system is complete nonsense. First it costs you a fortune, then it kills our job and at the end of the day nobody uses it – we've had that a thousand times before!"*

The person who made this statement pretty much reflected all of the thoughts we had when we were developing CCR. We knew from the very beginning that the reframed procurement solution could never take off without the support and buy-in of the PU. Thus, one of our central tasks was to communicate to those people that the new system would not kill their jobs but would only free them from administrative tasks that prevented them from doing real value-adding tasks such as strategic sourcing.

The Results

To date, the reframed e-procurement solution has been deployed in more than 40 countries, supporting most of the organization's locations. In the USA, employees use it to complete 100% of their requisitions. The reframing has had a dramatic impact on the way employees deal with requisitions and on the company's resource allocations. This is reflected by the number of people working in the PU who have been reassigned to more strategic tasks. Within the first year of operation, 80 % of the people reassigned who had been responsible for processing POs, allowing them to focus on more leveraged procurement functions, such as analyzing procurement data and negotiating volume discounts with vendors. Additionally, further people of the PU have been reassigned, as the e-procurement has been rolled out to subsidiaries around the world.

Not only people working in the PU but also employees overall were freed for more strategic tasks. On average, it takes about 3 minutes to place an order. When George presented the results of the project at the board meeting, he was obviously quite proud of the results of our joint effort. I remember one statement he made which really brought the message to the point:

> *"The biggest boon from our reframed application is that it removes the rules, paperwork, hidden procedures, and other obstacles that keep employees from doing their jobs. Instead of dealing with this process, they can focus on making and selling our products."*

Another benefit is increased power: Today, this solution handles well over 250.000 transactions a year and more than $3.0 billion a year in orders. The organization uses this volume of transactions to negotiate unbeatable prices with selected suppliers. In return for a consistent flow of orders, these suppliers offer steep discounts on goods and services.

Within the first years of operation the reframed solution has saved the company more than $6 million in head-count costs, improved volume discounts on supplies by streamlining the supplier base, and reduced administrative costs from $70 to just $6 per order. Apart from these quantitative benefits there are a considerable number of qualitative benefits, such as simplified administration and billing, easy and time-efficient ordering of supplies and services, and streamlined workflow by transactions directly uploading into the company's ERP system as well as directly with suppliers.

The Future

All these figures illustrate the enormous success of our project. I personally, and I guess all the other people involved in the project, were and still are pretty proud of the results, but praising oneself for previous achievements is, from my point of view, the most lethal thing you can do. As in so many other areas, constant evolution is an absolute need for survival. Thus we created a team of three developers, three testers, two program managers, and one product manager who are responsible for taking user feedback and improving the site on a quarterly basis. This activity was initiated based on the last horizontal of the CCR methodology, described in Chap. 6.

I take this opportunity to thank the entire project team for their effort and contribution to running the CCR for the reframing that e-procurement solution. The work was driven by an open and friendly atmosphere but was heavily focused, nonetheless, on achieving the predefined targets. This underlines the success of both the joint project team and the CCR methodology.

Case Study: US-Based Internet Start-up

CCR Helping Internet Start-ups to Grow up

The following case describes CCR at a US-based Internet start-up company. Like so many other New Economy initiatives, this company started to struggle seriously following the shift of the market at the beginning of 2000. After several challenging months, the management of the organization decided to reframe its business ideas and approaches in order to adapt to the changed business environment and its changed contingency factors. The case also illustrates the implications of our reframing project on the company's processes and technologies. We decided to include this case at this point for two reasons:

1. It reflects the typical Internet start-up situation in 2001, which suddenly was forced to become more cost-driven.
2. It illustrates the adaptability of CCR for small and medium-sized enterprises.

The company was found in June 1999. The vision of the management team was convincing:

> *"The idle computer screen is untapped real estate that could become a space for personalization, escape, inspiration, and information, and thus become a potent marketing medium."*

Their business model was based on an end-to-end Internet platform for displaying high-quality media and entertainment content that would replace the traditional screensaver and turn the computer screen into a new media channel. The first version was successfully launched in August 2000. Today, the company partners with international institutions such in IT and media industries as well as a number of top university athletic programs.

In the spring of 2001, the founders sat down to discuss the latest problems with generating revenue in the volatile Internet business. Many Internet companies were struggling with declining advertising revenues caused by a range of issues:

- Market predictions were bad – the fear of a recession and increasing cost-cutting pressure forced companies to cut down on advertising spending.
- Increasing competition and declining transparency on the web forced online marketers to lower prices.
- The failure of the Internet economy created a negative image of online advertising.

Advertising revenue represented a major part of their revenue stream. Like many other start-ups with similar revenue models, our client struggled seriously after the market shifted. Even big players with business models based on the generation of marketing revenue such as Excite@home lost out. Many companies with such a model were struggling.

During the preceding year, a number of important deals were closed in the entertainment and sports industries. The total number of subscribers continued to increase. Nevertheless, with the drop in advertising spending it became clear that a simple marketing-based revenue stream would not allow the company to meet set targets in terms of a break-even point. The CEO was frustrated:

> *"This is no good! We've already got an enormous pool of users, about 1.5 million, and our product is continuing to attract hundreds of thousands of users each month. There has to be a way to monetize this demand!"*

I had met the CEO of the client organization at a business conference several weeks earlier. Being a salesman, I explained what I was working on and he became interested in CCR. When the management reached this crossroads, he recalled our discussion and gave me a call. We met a few days later in my office.

The Assessment

That first meeting gave us a solid impression of the challenges the company was facing. We decided to have some of our consultants perform the realization of the first vertical "focus and objectives" and the second one "as-is assessment," which included reviewing the business plans, the markets, the competitive situation, and the advantages of our client.

The analysis revealed that a real challenge was facing the client organization, since some of the company's technologies were highly innovative. Therefore, as part of the second vertical of the CCR methodology, we contacted a number of key customers, key business partners, industry experts, and innovative newcomers, as well as analysts and business angels in order to generate a consistent valuation of the company's available technology and offerings.

As part of the "process" horizontal we then conducted a process analysis combined with a closer look at the organization, including a thorough check of the entire team and their skills. As mentioned in previous chapters, human know-how and expertise represent one of the most valuable assets of the New Economy. Our client was well-armed as far as human capital was concerned; individually and together, the team possessed superior business experience and proven skills.

Four weeks after our first meeting we presented the results of the first and second vertical and our suggestions regarding a solution:

- Reframing of the client focus
- Reframing of the existing business model towards a transaction-based one
- Reframing of alliances by involving additional external partners
- Reframing of organizational structures according to the overall changes
- Reframing of the underlying systems

Above all, we recommended that the initial business idea remain unchanged, since continuity represents a high asset, internally as well as externally. The client's management team was pleased with our findings and recommendations. We thus proceeded with the operational conversion of our CCR approach.

The Strategy

Our recommendation was to reframe the business model by expanding it. Reframing activities in the area of strategy addressed the following topics:

The end-consumer targeted was the individual and anonymous Internet user who was committed to using the product. First, we targeted communities consisting of committed users. People fascinated by sport clubs were offered the client's screensaver, which provided them with photos and information about their favorite sport clubs. Our suggestion was to expand that proven model.

The next group addressed in our strategy reframing was business users. The available platform could become a communication tool between companies and their employees. A company could use the screensaver to provide permanent information on stocks, the menu in the canteen, highway traffic reports, new rumors, etc.

Discussion about reframing the existing strategy and the underlying business model also required a reframing of the revenue model. Breaking even with a purely advertising revenue-based business model had become unrealistic. Also, Internet users had become increasingly prepared to pay for premium services offered via the Internet. According to our experience, a transaction-based revenue model would be adaptable and adequate.

The Process

The proposed strategy reframing had an impact on the internal sales and marketing processes. Some of the in-house sales and marketing activities were outsourced based on a profit-sharing model.

Therefore, we needed to redefine interfaces and responsibilities. Our task was to support the client organization and those in charge of negotiating contracts during the process of screening adequate outsourcing partners.

Finally, we facilitated the reframing of new process responsibilities, ownership, and interfaces. We identified all of the tasks that needed to be performed in the analyzed fields of sales and marketing. Additionally, we identified all roles and responsibilities in that process. We decided to avoid heavy cuts in this dimension in order to keep the business running and to maintain reframing costs at a minimum level.

Adding our client's product to their partners' existing products resulted in additional reframing efforts in the programming and developing processes. The client organization had to consider and improve its screensaver's compatibility with partner software. This task complicated the development processes by creating additional loops, as each new component of the screensaver had to be double-checked with partner software to ensure such compatibility.

The Technology

When engaging in CCR projects with small start-ups we repeatedly experience financial restrictions as a major challenge. The head of operations, expressed this problem exactly:

> *"The idea sounds promising but we just cannot afford to dump all of our existing technology. I don't think that we will be able to raise the money needed for changing it."*

Nevertheless, we realized that the need for additional financial resources would be unavoidable in order to adapt the existing technology to the reframed solution.

The management team was concerned about these additional investments, but after illustrating our approach in detail and discussing the ways to reuse their existing technology, we got the final "*Go.*"

A check of the existing back office systems showed that we needed some time to adapt the existing systems to the reframed business ideas. New customer tracking and payment functionalities were needed for the new revenue model, and sophisticated and confidential sales data had to be exchanged with the sales partners in the markets. It took us about 8 weeks to reframe the systems, and after this project phase was completed we started the marketing campaign. Eight weeks later we switched to the new system.

The People

Based on the decision to reframe the strategy towards B2B business, we recommended that they hire additional sales and marketing staff. In order to keep costs and overhead low, we decided to work with marketing and sales professionals from an external professional sales organization.

A great deal of work was generated as a result of the creation, acceptance, and awareness of the reframing project. Our work would not have been possible without the support and the commitment of all employees. All along, we knew that it was important to create awareness concerning the potential outcome of such a reframing engagement. We wanted all employees to perceive the project as a win-win situation.

This buy-in also required a lot of work by the top management team. They had to communicate the importance of the project for the future survival of their struggling business.

Unlike our experiences in large companies, the cooperation with the staff was phenomenal. These people were motivated, bright, and extremely skilled. They all were committed to their company. I guess they were aware of how a prospering business can disappear in a very short period of time.

The Future

Several months have passed since we first met our client. We all enjoyed working with this organization and we will remember especially the evenings in the vineyards of Napa. In recent months, more and more Internet companies have struggled and given up. Even companies offering excellent services on the Internet, with best-of-breed products, sound marketing and branding, and solid leadership teams are struggling and failing. Today, this company still exists, whereas others in the same segment offering similar products failed. Their own success underlines the success of our CCR project and the added value created through our approach. This is one of the earliest cases proving our concept and its applicability to small and medium-sized companies.

Epilogue

By the time this book is in your hands and you have gone through our new ideas, many more things will have happened.

Many more companies in the New Economy will have failed and many new ideas will have been turned down. The ever-increasing pace of innovation and development is forcing all of us to adapt our behavior and, more importantly, our way of thinking to enable us to cope with the convergence of the Old and New Economy into the Cyber Economy.

Right now, I have just completed a business trip, and read an article on the plane home. In this article Alan Greenspan thought that the US economy was on the edge of a recession. We all know that recession implicitly means decreasing purchasing power and decreasing volumes of investment. Even more so, these developments are strengthened by increasing uncertainty and aversion to risk, leading to smaller budgets for future technologies. Companies cutting costs in this area will unavoidably lose out since new applications and their underlying technologies will be essential for future evolution of the companies.

Here, once again, the core messages of the CCR approach sprang to mind. Based on this contingency situation, the combination of smart reusability of existing technologies together with the creative and innovative reframing of

- Visions
- Objectives
- Strategies
- Business models and
- Processes

will enable companies to realize unknown synergies. These synergies will impact heavily on the success of companies in the ever-changing cyber-economy, driven by sustainable competitive advantage. In addition, these companies will become capable of developing the competences and expertise required to deploy new applications based on "innovative" technologies.

The establishment of such new competencies and expertise increases the importance of a company's human capital so much that the reframing of existing HR policies and procedures becomes a must.

When you have read this book the author and his team will have realized further CCR engagements, broadening their experience within this new management approach and its closely linked success factors. Furthermore, we are well on the way to consolidating further findings for you by preparing the next publication on CCR case studies – to insure an on-going discussion and evolution of the CCR methodology. We encourage you to participate in this discussion by contributing

- a CCR case study for the new book,
- your experience maybe as you just finished a CCR project or just starting a reframing initiative, or
- by just forwarding any comments or questions you may have using our e-mail address info@c-cr.net.

Any kind of experience you have gained with CCR will be dynamically integrated into the further evolution of the CCR methodology.

Further Reading

Abbott, J.C.: “Optimize Your Operation: Stories, Tools and Lessons for Using the Principles of Process Management to Improve Your Quality”, Robert Houston Smith Publishing, March 2001

Active Media: “Real Numbers 2000”, June 2000, http://www.activmediaresearch.com/real_numbers_2000.html

Adams, M.; Smoak, B.: “Managing Manufacturing Improvement Using Computer Integrated Manufacturing Methods," Proceedings of the IEEE/SEMI International Semiconductor Manufacturing Science Symposium – ISMSS ‘90, 1990.

Ahlberg, C: “Visual Information Seeking: Tight Coupling of Dynamic Query Filters with Starfield Displays”, Boston, USA: Association for Computing Machinery

Aikat, D.: “Adventure in Cyberspace: Exploring the Information Content of the World Wide Web Pages on the Internet” Doctoral Thesis, Athens: Ohio University

Akella, R.; Choong, Y.; Gershwin, S.B.: “Performance of Hierarchical Production Scheduling Policy”, IEEE Transactions of Components, Hybrids, Manufacturing Technology, No. 3, 1984.

Albrecht, K.: “Total Quality Service: Das einzige, was zählt.”, Econ, 1993

Allen, B.: “Information Tasks: Toward a User-Centered Approach to Information Systems”, Academic Press, 1996

Amor, D.; “Internet Future Strategies: How Pervasive Computing Will Change the World”, Prentice Hall Computer Books, August 2000

Amor, D.: “The E-Business Revolution: Living and Working in an Interconnected World.”, Upper Saddle River, 1999

Andersen Consulting: “Thought Leadership: A Key Contributor to Engaging Employees and Clients at Andersen Consulting”, October 1999

Anderson, J.C.; Narus, J.A.: “Business Marketing: Understand What Customers Value”, Harvard Business Review, 1998

Andrews, K.: "Visualizing Cyberspace: Information Visualization in the Harmony Internet Browser", 1st IEEE Symposium on Information Visualization, IEEE Computer Society, 1995

Apter, M.J.: "Models of Development", Survey of Cybernetics: A Tribute to Dr. Norbert Wiener" Ed.J. Rose, 1969

Armbruster, B.: "Handbook of Nasdaq Stocks Fall 2000", Financial Information Services, November 2000

Ashbrook, J.: "Cookie Dough", Business 2.0, November 1999, http://www.business2.com/content/magazine/marketing/1999/11/01/11442

Bakker, C.P.; Seebacher, U.G.: "Konzeptionelle Entwicklung von Internet-Portalen, Information Management & Consulting" February 2000

Bakos, Y.: "A Strategic Analysis of Electronic Marketplaces", MIS Quarterly, 1991

Baldwin, C.Y.; Clark, K.B.: "Managing in an Age of Modularity", Harvard Business Review, September 1997

Bardini, T.: "Bridging the Gulfs: From Hypertext to Cyberspace", Journal of Computer-Mediated Communication, 1997

Barman, S.: "Simple Priority Rule Combinations: An Approach to Improve Both Flow Time and Tardiness," International Journal of Production Research, Vol. 35, No. 10, 2857-2870, 1997.

Barnard, C. I.: "The Functions of Executive", Cambridge, 1938

Batstone, D.: "Just Say No to IPO", Business 2.0, March 1999

Batstone, D.: "The 25 Most Intriguing Minds of the New Economy", Business 2.0, August 1998

Bauer, C.; Glasson, B.: "Extending the Concept of a Reference Model across Industries", Joint Working Conference on Information Systems, Helsinki 1998

Bauer, C.; Sharl, A.: "A Classification Framework and Assessment Model for Automated Web Site Evaluation", 7th European Conference on Information Systems, Copenhagen Business School, 1999

Bauer, C.; Sharl, A.: "Acquisition and Symbolic Visualization of Aggregated Customer Information for Analyzing Web Information Systems", 32nd Hawaii International Conference on System Sciences", IEEE Computer Society Press, 1999

Bauer, C.: "Using Reference Models to Develop WWW-Based Applications", 9th Annual Australasian Conference on Information Systems, 1998

Beam, C.; Segev, A.: "Automated Negotiations: A Survey of the State of the Art", Wirtschaftsinformatik, 1997

Beam, C.; Segev, A.: "The Rise of Electronic Commerce: Contributions from Three Factors", Fisher Center for Management and Information Technology University of California, 1996

Beard, D.V.; Walker, J.Q.: "Navigational Techniques Prove the Display of Large Two-Dimensional Spaces", Beha Information Technology, 1990

Becker, W.: "Strategisches Management", 2nd Edition, Bamberg, 1995

Belz, C.: "Strategisches Direct Marketing: Vom sporadischen Direct Mail zum professionellen Database Management", Vienna, 1997

Bendor-Samuel, P.; Staedke, J.: "Turning Lead into Gold: The Demystification of Outsourcing", Executive Excellence, October 2000

Bezos, J., CEO of Amazon.com, Interview on CNN, April 2000

Bichler, M.; Scharl, A.: "Multi-dimensional Approaches to Automating Resource Allocation", 1st International Workshop for Transaction-Based Electronic Commerce", Perth, Australia, 1999

Bieber, M.: "Enhancing Information Comprehension through Hypertext", Springer, 1999

Bing, G.: "Due Diligence Techniques and Analysis", Quorum Books, August 1996

Bitran, G.R.; Tirupati, D.: "Development and Implementation of a Scheduling System for a Wafer Fabrication Facility," Operations Research, Vol. 36, No. 3, 377-395, 1988.

Blasius, J.: "Correspondence Analysis in Social Science Research", Academic Press, 1994

Bolisani, E.: "Communication Processes and Electronic Communication: A Framework for the Assessment", 7th European Conference on Information Systems, Copenhagen, 1999

Booz-Allen & Hamilton: "Corporate Internet Banking: A Global Study of Potential", 1999

Bordewijk, J.L.; van Kaam, B.: "Towards a New Classification of Teleinformation Services", InterMedia, 1986

Boston Consulting Group: "B2C report", November 1999, http://www.bcg.com/publications

Brauer, J.: "Die EN ISO 9000 – 9004 umsetzen", Hanser Wissenschaft, München, 1997

Bridges, W. P.: "Managing Transitions: Making the Most of Change", Perseus Publishing, September 1991

Brown, S. A.: "Customer Relationship Management: A Strategic Imperative in the World of E-Business", John Wiley & Sons, May 2000

Bruns, W.J.; Kaplan, R.S.; Cooper, R.; Schleifer, A.; Rapier, D.M.: "Understanding Costs, Business Fundamentals Series" Harvard Business Review, December 1998

Bruyn, G.; Lyfareff, R.: "Introduction to ABAP/4 Programming for SAP, Revised and Expanded Edition", Prima Publishing, July 1998

Burgelman, R.: "High Technology and Strategy", California Management Review, 1996

Business Open Learning Archive: "Pareto ABC Analysis", http://sol.brunel.ac.uk/~jarvis/bola/operations/stock/pareto.html

Business 2.0: "Alley Chat", January 2000, http://www.business2.com/content/magazine/filter/2000/01/01/14925

Buyer, L.: "Do Profits Matter?", Business 2.0, April 2000, http://www.business2.com/content/magazine/filter/2000/01/04/11324

Buzzel, R.D.; Bradley, T.G.: "The PIMS Principles: Linking Strategy to Performance", Free Press, August 1987

Carter, L., CFO of Cisco Systems, Interview on CNN, August 2000

Caudron, S.: “Consumers’ Revenge”, Business Finance, June 2000

Chakrabarti, S.; Dom, B.E.: “Mining the Web’s link structure”, IEEE Computer, 1999

Chandrasekaran, B.; Josephson, J.R.; Benjamins, R.: “What Are Ontologies and Why Do We Need Them?” IEEE Intelligent Systems, 1999

Chang, R. Y.; Morgan, M. W.: ”Performance Scorecards”, Jossey-Bass, April 2000

Chatham, B.: “Mergers, Acquisitions and Saving IT dollars”, CIO Magazine, March 1998, http://www.cio.com/archive/031598_forrester_content.html

Chatham, B.: “Mergers, Acquisitions and Saving IT Dollars”, CIO Magazine, March 1998

Chen, H.; Yao, D.D.: “Dynamic Scheduling of a Multi-class Fluid Network," Operations Research, Vol. 41, 1993.

Cheng, T.C.E, Podolsky, S.: “Just-in-Time-Manufacturing – An Introduction”, Kluwer Academic Publishers, 1996

Chu, W.; Chin, L.; Le, V.; Weicher, M.; Yu, D.; “Business Process Reengineering Analysis and Recommendations”, University of New York

Chuah, M.C.; Roth, S.F.; Mattis, J.; Kolojejchick, J.: “SDM: Selective Dynamic Manipulation of Visualizations”, 8th Annual Symposium on User Interface Software and Technology, Pittsburgh, 1995

Clark, K.B.; Weelwright, S.C.: “Product Development Challenge: Competing Through Speed, Quality, and Creativity (Hardcover)”, Harvard Business Review, February 1995

Clay, J.: “Evaluating the Sticky Factor of E-Commerce Sites”, Business 2.0, June 1999, http://www.business2.com/content/research/numbers/1999/06/14/12447

Collins, A.M.; Loftus, E.F.: “A Spreading Activation Theory of Semantic Processing”, Psychological Review, 1975

Collins, J.: “Built to last”, Harpercollins, 1996

Conger, J. A.; Karungo, R. N.: “Towards a Behavioral Theory of Charismatic Leadership in Organizational Settings”, Academy of Management Review, 1987

Conner, D.R.: “Managing at the Speed of Change: How Resilient Managers Succeed and Prosper when Others Fail”, Villard books, January 1993

Coppel, J.: “E-Commerce: Impacts and Policy Changes” October 2000, http://www.as400.ibm.com/developer/ebiz/documents/ecommerce.html

Cordes, J.: “What You Should Know about Knowledge Management”, CIO Magazine, August 2000, http://www.cio.com/analyst/080700_rfgonline_content.html

Coveney, P.: “Business Angels: Securing Startup Finance”, John Wiley & Sons, June 1998

Creech, B.: “The 5 Pillars of TQM: How to Make Total Quality Management Work for You”, Plume, December 1995

Crell, E.: “Four Lessons for Finance”, Business Finance, July 2000,

Crimmins, F.; Smeaton, A.F.: “TetraFusion: Information Discovery on the Internet”, IEEE Intelligent Systems, 1999

Cristofari, M.; Tronci, M.; Caron, F.; McDuffie, E.: “Interaction of Control Policies In A Flexible Manufacturing system,” Proceedings of the 8th European Simulation Symposium (ESS ‘96), Genoa, Italy, 1996.

Crowston, K.; Williams, M.: “The Effects on Linking on Genres of Web Documents”, 32nd Hawaii International Conference on System Sciences, 1999

Czarnecki, M.: “Managing by Measuring: How to Improve Your Organization’s performance through Effective Benchmarking”, Amacom, 1999

Daly, J.: “Daily Insight”, Business 2.0, June 2000, http://www.business2.com/content/insights/opinion/2000/06/12/15281

Damsgaard, J.; Scheepers, R.: “A Stage Model of Intranet Technology Implementation and Management”, 7th European Conference on Information Systems, Copenhagen, 1999

Daniel-Falk, L.: "Merchandising Strategies for the Competitive Nineties 2: Creating the Total Shopping Experience for the Savvy Nineties Shopper", RTW review, June 1997

Davis, J.: "Marketing's New Trip Successful Marketing Isn't Dead. It's... the Grateful Dead", Business 2.0, Mai 1999,

Davis, S.: "Future of Wealth", Harvard Business School, 1997,

Deighton, J.: "Cyber Marketing", Harvard Business School, June 2000, http://www.hbs.edu/knowledge/cyber-market.html

Delmater, R.; Hancock, M.: "Data Mining Explained. A Manager's Guide to Customer-Centric Business Intelligence", Digital Press, January 2001

Deming, W.; E.: "Some Theory of Sampling", Dover Pubns, July 1984

Dennis, S.: "E-Commerce to Push Int'l Trade Sky-High", Infowar, November 2000, http://www.infowar.com

Dent, S.M.: "Partnering Intelligence: Creating Value for Your Business by Building Smart Alliances", Davies-Black Publications, October 1999

Derosa, D. F.: "Currency Derivatives: Pricing Theory, Exotic Options, and Hedging Applications", John Wiley & Sons, October 1998

Domasch, H.: "Show Me the Cash Flow", Business 2.0, July 2000, http://www.business2.com/content/magazine/investing/2000/06/28/13611

Donaldson, L.: "Contingency Theory", Ashgate Publishing Company, March 1994

Downes, L.: "Unleashing the Killer App: Digital Strategies for Market Dominance", Harvard Business School, 1998

Draig, D.: "Surviving in the Aftermath of the B2C Crash", Business Finance, April 2000

Drucker, P.: "Knowledge-Worker Productivity: The Biggest Challenge", HR.Com, August 2000, http://www.hr.com/HRcom/index.cfm/2/8CA6E6ED-26AC-11D4-8DE3009027E0248F

Drucker, P.: "Sage Advice", Business 2.0, August 2000, http://www.business2.com/content/magazine/indepth/2000/08/08/15450

Earman, J.: "Carnap, Kuhn, and the Philosophy of Scientific Methodology", World Changes: Thomas Kuhn and the Nature of Science, Cambridge: MIT Press, 1993

Emarketer: "E-Commerce 2000 Report", August 2000, http://www.emarketer.com/ereports

Emarketer: "Emarketer's eBusiness Report", June 1999, http://www.emarketer.com/ereports/ebiz

Emarketer: "Emarketer's eConsumer Report", September 1999, http://www.emarketer.com/ereports/econsumer

Emarketer: "Emarketer's Report on B2B", October 1999, http://www.emarketer.com/ereports/ecommerce_b2b

Emarketer: "Emarketer's Report on B2C", June 1999, http://www.emarketer.com/ereports

Emarketer: "Online Shopping Worries: UK Style", December 2000

Emarketer: "Path to Website Profitability", Business 2.0, June 2000

Emigh, J.: "Net Present Value (NPV) and Cost of Capital", Computerworld, July 1999

Encyclopaedia Britannica, 2001

Engelbar, D.C.; English, W.K.: "A Research Center for Augmenting Human Intellect", Fall Joint Computer Conference, San Francisco, 1968

Escamilla, T.: "Intrusion Detection: Network Security beyond the Fire-Wall", John Wiley & Sons, September 1998

Etzel, M.; Dickinson, K.: "Digital Visual FORTRAN Programmer's Guide", Digital Press, April 1999

Fabian, A.C.: "Introduction", Evolution: Society, Science and the Universe, Cambridge University Press, 1998

Falchuk, B.; Karmouch, A.: "Visual Modeling for Agent Based Applications, Computer, 1999

Fayol, H.: "Administration Industrielle et Générale", Paris, 1916

Ferstl, O.K.; Sinz E. J.: "Grundlagen der Wirtschaftsinformatik, Band 1, 2. Auflage", München, 1994

Fickel, L.: "Bid Business", CIO Magazine, June 1999, http://www.cio.com/archive/webbusiness/060199_auct_content.html

Fickel, L.: "Know Your Customer", CIO Magazine, August 1999, http://www.cio.com/archive/081599_customer_content.html

Fidler, R.: "Mediamorphosis: Understanding New Media" Thousand Oaks: Pine Forge Press, 1997

Fiedler, F. E.; Chiemmers, M.M.: "Improving Leadership Effectiveness, 2. Auflage", New York 1984

Fisher, K.: "Surviving in the Aftermath of the b2C crash", ePerformance, Mai 2000,

Fishman, C.: "Way to Enough", FastCompany, July 1999, http://www.fastcompany.com/online/26/norskhydro.html

Fogel, D.B.: "Evolutionary Computation: An introduction, Some Current Applications and Future Sirections", Brain-like Computing and Intelligent Information Systems", Amari and N. Kasabov, 1997

Forrester Research: "Forrester's Research on B2B and Forrester Research: Telecommunication, 9-10/2000.

Forsa Studie: ComputerPartner, 20/2000.

Forsa Studie: Werben und Verkaufen, 16/2000.

Fortin, D.R.: "Defining Targets in Cyberspace Is No Easy Task", Marketing News, November 1996,

Freisler, S.; Kesseler, M.: "Document Engineering, Schema GmbH, http://www.schema.de/doku/html-deu/schemappu/vortrag/document.htm

Froomking, M.: "Flood Control on the Information Ocean: Living with Anonymity, Digital cash and Distributed Databases", University of Pittsburgh Journal of Law and Commerce, 1996

Frost & Sullivan Report 3887 (09/00), Press Release September 2000

Fudenberg, D.; Tirole, J.: "Game Theory", MIT Press, October 1991

Fulk, J.; DeSanctis, G.: "Electronic Communication and Changing Organizational Forms", Organization Science, 1995

Furnas, G.W.: "The Fisheye View: A New Look at Structured Files", Technical Memorandum, New Jersey, 1981

Garvin, D.A.: "Learning in Action: A Guide to Putting the Learning Organization to Work", Harvard Business School, April 2000

Global Equity Markets: "Valuation Waltz", The Economist, May, 2001

Global Equity Markets: "When Capital Markets Rule", The Economist, May 2001

Goldsman, T.: "Web's Great Order Disorder" Business 2.0, September 2000, http://www.business2.com/content/magazine/indepth/2000/09/29/20134?template=article_pf.wm

Grappa, M.: "Promises, Promises", Business 2.0, November 2000

Grebb, M.: "Behavioral Science", Business 2.0, March 2000, http://www.business20.com/content/magazine/marketing/2000/03/01/11103

Green, D.: "Cash Burn May Lead E-Commerce Stars to Crash 'n' Burn", Infowar.com, April 2000, http://www.infowar.com

Greengard, S.: "Establishing Human E-Sources", Business Finance, July 2000,

Grensing-Pophal, L.: "Job Applicants and Perks: What Is Offered, What to Ask for – and When!", HR.COM, 2000

Guest, D.E.: "Employee Commitment and Control", Blackwell Publishers, London, 1992.

Hamer, M.; Champy, J.: "Reengineering the Corporation", London, 1993

Hammer, M.: "Reengineering Work – Don't Automate, Obliterate", in: Harvard Business Review, vol. 4/1990, S. 104 – 112

Hammer, M.; Champy, J.: "Reengineering the Corporation – A Manifesto for Business Revolution", HarperBusiness, New York, 1st edition, 1984.

Hammer, M.; Stanton, St. A.:" The Reengineering Revolution", Harper Business, New York, 1st edition, 1995.

Harold, E.; Means, W.: "XML in a Nutshell: A Desktop Quick Reference", O'Reilly & Associates, January 2001

Harris, B.: "Installing the Virtual Workforce" Installing the Virtual Workforce", Government Technology, 2000

Harry, M.; Schroeder, R.: "Six Sigma – The Breakthrough Management Strategy Revolutionizing the World's Top Corporations", 2000

Harst, E.: "Targeting Consumers", Forrester, February 2000, http://www.forrester.com/ER/Research/Report/0,1338,9126,FF.html

Hayhow, S.: "A Comprehensive Guide to Business Incubation", National Business Incubation Association, December 1995

Heaphy, M. S.; Gruska, G.: "The Malcolm Baldrige National Quality Award: A Yardstick for Quality Growth", Addison Wesley Longman Company, May 1995

Hellweg, E.: "A Global Guide to Y2K", Business 2.0, Jannuary 1999

Hemond-Wilson, L.: "Vortals, Schmortals: They Are Big Business", IBM, June 2000, http://www.as400.ibm.com/developer/ebiz/documents/ecommerce.html

Henderson, B.A.; Larco, J.L.: "Lean Transformation: How to Change Your Business into a Lean Enterprise", Oaklea Press, May 1999

Henningsen, L.: "Effects of E-Business on Human Resource Functions", HR.COM, 2000

Heylighen, F.: "The Prisoner's Dilemma", Principa Cybernetica Web, April 1995

Hill, L.A.; Gabarro, J.J.; Kotter, J.P.: "Leadership for New Managers, Business Fundamentals Series", Harvard Business Review, August 1998

Hodges, J.; Bulik, B.S.: "Dot-Com Hits and Bombs", page 13, Business 2.0, January 2001

Holstein, W.J.: "Big Blue Wages Open Warfare", Business 2.0, April 2001

Hoover's online: "IPO Guide", http://www.hoovers.com/ipo/guide/

Horvath, J.: "New Economy Bubble in No Trouble?", Telepolis, December 2000

Hunt, D.V.: "How to Reengineer Your Business Process", John Wiley & Sons, January 1996

Hurt, E.: "AOL/Time Warner Merger Approved", Business 2.0, January 2001

Ifrah, G.: "The Universal History of Computing: From the Abacus to the Quantum Computer", John Wiley & Sons, October 2000

Intellectual Capital – The New Wealth of Organizations, Thomas A. Stewart, Currency Doubleday 1997

InternetNews: "The Internet as Job Creator", August 2000

Jilovec, N.: "A to Z of EDI, Second Edition", 29th Street Press, April 1998

Jones, G.R.; George, J.M.; Hill, C.W.: "Contemporary Management", Irwin McGraw-Hill, July 1999

Judge, P.C.: "Will Online Ads Ever Click?", FastCompany, March 2001, page 182

Jupiter Research: "B2B Infrastructure Practices", August 2000

Jupiter Research: "Trends and Outlook – Digital Commerce Strategies", February 2000

Kalmbach, C.: "Dispelling the Myths of Alliances", Anderson Consulting, June 2000

Kaplan, R.S.; Lamotte, G.: "The Balanced Scorecard and Quality Programs", Harvard Business Review, March 2001

Kaplan, R.S.; Norton, D.P.: "Having Trouble with Your Strategy? Then Map It", Harvard Business Review, December 2000

Kaplan, R.S.; Norton, D.P.: "Putting the Balanced Scorecard to work", Harvard Business Review, September-October, 1993

Kearney, A.T.: "Importance of IT Technology", June 2000
http://www.atkearney.com/pdfs/CEO_IT_Study2000_S.pdf

Kearney, A.T.: "Strategic Information Technology and the CEO agenda", November 1999, http://www.atkearney.com/pdfs/CEO_IT_Study2000_S.pdf

Kellher, R.: "Group Predicts B2B Market Collapse", The Irish Times, July 14th 2000

Kelly, K.: "New Economy? What New Economy?", Wired, May 1998

Kelly, K.: "New Rules for the New Economy: 10 Radical Strategies for a Connected World", Penguin Books, October 1999

Ketola, J.; Roberts, K.: "ISO 9000: 2000 in a Nutshell, Second Edition", Paton, Jannuary, 2001

Kirsner, s.: "Collision Course", Fastcompany, February 2000, page 119

Kleinsorge, P.: "Geschäftsprozesse", in: Masing, W (Hrsg.): "Handbuch Qualitätsmanagement", Carl Hanser Verlag, München, 4th edition, 1999, S. 49-64.

Klinger, D.: "A Matter of Marketing", CIO Magazine, September 1995, http://www.cio.com/archive/091595_ins_content.html

Knight, J.: "Value Based Management", McGraw Hill Professional Book Group, 1998

Konrad, R.: "Will B2G Become the Next 'Big Thing?'", CNET News.com, June 2000

Kotter, J.P.; Kiechel, W.: "How to Get Aboard a Major Change Effort: An Interview with John Kotter", Harvard Business Review, January 1996

Kotter, J.P.: "John P. Kotter on What Leaders Really Do", Harvard Business Review (Hardcover), March 1999

Krell, E.: "Lessons from the New Economy", Business Finance, July 2000,

Laabs, J.J.: "Expert Advice on How to Move forward with Change.", HR.Com, July 1996

Lambrecht, M.R.; Ivens, P.L.; Vandaele, N.J.: "ACLIPS: A Capacity and Lead Time Integrated Procedure for Scheduling," Management Science, Vol. 44, 1998.

Laurie, D.: “Venture Capitalist: The Five Stages to Explosive Corporate Growth”, Perseus Books, February 2001

Layne, A.: “Architects of the New Economy”, FastCompany, June 2000, http://www.fastcompany.com/feature/design.html

Lea, W.: “CyberStaking: Why Partnerships Matter”, Silicon Alley Reporter, September 2000

Lee, H.S.; Tsai, F.: “A Preemptive Dynamic Job Shop Scheduling System," Proceedings of the IBM International Manufacturing Productivity Symposium, IBM East Fishkill, New York, October 1993.

Lee, J.A.N.: “Great Brains – Konrad Zuse”, The Machine that Changed the World, http://ei.cs.vt.edu/

Lee, K.: “The Diversity Training Group”, HR.COM, 2000

Leed, H.: “Consumers Still Wary of Privacy Concerns”, Ebusiness Advisor, August 2000, http://www.advisor.com/articles.nsf/aid/leedh126

Leonard, B.: “New Ways to Pay Employees”, HR.COM, September 2000

Leonard-Barton, D.; Bowen, H.K.; Clark, K.B.; Holloway, C.A.; Weelwright, S.C.: “How to Integrate Work and Deepen Expertise”, Harvard Business Review, September 1994

Lev, B.: “Knowledge and Shareholder Value”, January 2000, http://www.stern.nyu.edu/~blev/

Lev, B.: “What Value Analysts?”, November 1999

Li, S.; Tang, T.; Collins, D.W.: “Minimum Inventory Variability Schedule with Applications in Semiconductor Fabrication,” IEEE Transactions on Semiconductor Manufacturing, Vol. 9, 1996.

Libert, B.D.; Boulton, R.E.S.; Samek, S.M.: “Learning To Juggle”, Business 2.0, June 2000

Lientz, B.; Rea, K.: “Dynamic E-Business Implementation Management: How to Effectively Manage E-Business Implementation”, Academic Press, July 2000

Lucey, S.: “IPOs in the Breakdown Lane” Redhering.com, June 2000, http://www.redherring.com/ipo/2000/0621/ipo-s1withdrawal062100.html

Lynch, R.P.: "The Practical Guide to Joint Ventures and Corporate Alliances: How to Form, How to Organize, How to Operate", John Wiley & Sons, July 1989

Macharzina, K.: "Unternehmensführung, 2. Auflage", Wiesbaden, 1995

Madden, B. J.: "CFROI Valuation: A Total System Approach to Valuing the Firm", Butterworth-Heinemann, April 1999

Magretta, J.: "Power of Virtual Integration: An Interview with Dell Computers", Harvard Business Review, March 1998

Magretta, J.: "The Power of Virtual Integration: An Interview with Dell Computer's Michael Dell", Harvard Business Review, April 1998

Maître, B.: "Les Business Models de la Nouvelle Économie", Dunod, 1999

Maslow, A.H.: "Dominance, Self-Esteem, Self-Actualization: Germinal Papers of A. H. Maslow", Wadsworth Publishing, Jannuary 1973

Mathis, L. R.; Jackson, J. H.: "Human Resource Management", South-Western College Publishing, July 1999

Matzke, P.: "Challenges for Global E-Business", Whitepaper, 2001

McAffee, A.: "Economic Impact of the Internet Revolution", amcafee@hbs.edu

McDermott, R. E.; Mikulak, R. J.; Beauregard, M. R.: "The Basics of FMEA", Productivity Inc. 1996

McGovern, G.: "The Truths and Myths of the New Digital Age", Chapter 5, Nua Inc., 2000,

McKay, K.N.; Safayeni, R.N.; Buzacott, J.A.: "Job-Shop Scheduling Theory: What is Relevant?" Interfaces, Vol. 18, No. 4, 84-90, 1988.

McLagan, P.: "Competencies: The Next Generation", HR.COM, May 1997

McLaughlin, L.: "Broadband Usage Spikes", Business 2.0, February 2001

McQuillen, K.; Prince, A.: "MVS Assembler Language", Mike Murach & Associates, July 1987

Menard, C.: "Transaction Cost Economics: Recent Developments", Edward Elgar Publishing, March 1997

Moran, S.: "A New Visa Plan", Business 2.0, September 2000, http://www.business2.com/content/insights/dailyinsights/2000/09/08/19857

Moran, S.: "New Visa Plan", Business 2.0, August 2000

Morin, D.: "Retaining High-Performance Employees during Organizational Change", HR.Com, February 2000, http://www.hr.com/HRcom/index.cfm/WeeklyMag/4AE8AF3C-BA7B-11D4-9AB4009027E0248F

Morin, R. A.; Jarrel, S. L.: "Driving Shareholder Value: Value-Building Techniques for Creating Shareholder Wealth", McGraw-Hill Professional Publishing, January, 2001

Morris, D.; Brandon, J.; Re-engineering Your Business, New York,1993

Mosley, D.; Petri, P.; Megginson, L.: "Management – Leadership in Action", 1996 Collins Harper; p. 77

Moss Kanter, R.: "Rosabeth Moss Kanter on the Frontiers of Management (Hardcover)", Harvard Business Review, June 1997

Moss Kanter, R.: "The Ten Deadly Mistakes of Wanna-Dots", Harvard Business Review, January 2001

Mougavar, W.: "Another Play for M & As", Business 2.0, Mai 2000, http://www.business2.com/content/channels/investing/2000/06/28/13613

Mougayar, W.: "New Rules. New Metrics. Keeping Score in the New Economy", Business 2.0, September 1998

Moulton, B.: "GDP and the Digital Economy: Keeping up with the Changes", May 1999, http://www.ecommerce.gov/ede/ede2.pdf

Musciano, C.; Kennedy, B.: "HTML & XHTML: The Definitive Guide", O'Reilly and Associates, August 2000

NACE: "NACE Book of Standards/21805", National Association of Corrosion Engineers, January 1994

Neef, D.: "E-Procurement: From Strategy to Implementation", Prentice Hall PTR/Sun Microsystems Press, May 2001

Neumann, K.: "OR-Verfahren, 3 Bände", München-Wien 1975 - 77

Norris, D.; Hurley, B.: "E-Business and ERP: Transforming the Enterprise", PriceWaterhouseCoopers, July 2000

O'Mera, P.; Mehlinger, H.; Krain, M.: "Globalization and Challenges of the New Century, Indiana University, May 2000

Oakes, C.: "FTC Endorses Privacy Rules", Wired News, July 2000, http://www.wired.com/news/politics/0,1283,37853-2,00.html

Oberndorf, S.: "Sleuthing through Cyber Data", Catalog Age, October 1996

Oden, H.: "Managing Corporate Culture, Innovation and Intrapreneurship", Greenwood Publishing Group, June 1997

Perkins, A.: "The Internet Bubble", Harperbusiness, November 1999

Perry, D.: "Five Questions with David Perry", Business 2.0, August 2000, http://www.business2.com/content/channels/ebusiness/2000/08/11/21845

Peters, T. J.; Waterman, R. U. Jr.: "In Search of Excellence", New York, 1982

Pickering, C.: "They are Watching You", Business 2.0, February 2000,

Pickering, C.: "Boo Who?", Business 2.0, November 2000

Poe, R.: "Next-Generation Wireless: No Panacea", Business 2.0, November 2000

Porter, M. E.: "Competitive Strategy, 9th Edition", New York – London, 1997

Porter, M.; Rivkin, J.W.: "Industry Transformation", Harvard Business Review, October 2000

Porter, M.: "Clusters and Competition: New Agendas for Companies, Governments, and Institutions", Harvard Business Review, July 1999

Porter, M.: "Strategy and the Internet", Harvard Business Review, January 2001

Porter, M.E.: "Competitive Strategy: Techniques for Analyzing Industries and Competitors", Free Press, 1998

PR Newswire: CyberCash Announces Closing of Asset Sale, May 2001

Rafter, M.V.: "Keeping the Peace", TheStandard.com, January 1999

Ransdell, E.: "Portals for the People", FastCompany, May 2000, page 366

Rardin, R. L.: "Optimization in Operations Research", Prentice Hall, July 1997

Reed, P.: "Cisco Speed", The Economist, June 1999, http://www.economist.com/editorial/freeforall/19990626/su7156.html

Reed, P.: "Europe's Internet Drought", The Economist, August 2000

Reich, R.: "Company of the Future", FastCompany, November 1999, http://www.fastcompany.com/online/19/comfuture.html

Reid, H.R.: "Principles of the New Economy", Business 2.0, March 2000

Reuters: "FTSE Bounces back Helped by U.S. Data", November 29, 2000

Robert, M.; Racine, B.; Michel, R.: "E-Strategy, Pure & Simple: Connecting Your Internet Strategy to Your Business Strategy", McGraw-Hill Professional Publishing, December 2000

Robinson, D.: "All about Internet FTP", Library Solution Press, January 1995

Roethlisberger, F.J.; Dickson, W.: "Management and the Worker", Boston, 1934

Rogers, M.: "Enterprise One to One", Currency/Doubleday, 1997

Roy, R.: "Scheduling and Control, Performance Measures and Discrete Event Simulation," Journal of the Operational Research Society, Vol. 49, No. 2, 151-156, 1998.

Sailors, F.: "Reduce the Cost of Employee Turnover", FastCompany, March 1999

Saracevic, A.: "Vulture Capitalists", Business 2.0, November 2000, http://www.business2.com/content/magazine/indepth/2000/10/30/21868

Saultz, K.: "Blue Chip Finds Growth in Service Sector Fueled by High-Tech Industry", Greater Columbus Chamber, 2000

Sawhney, M.: "Go Global", Business 2.0, May 2000

Scheuermann, M.: "Manufacturing & Distribution in the New Economy", speech held at the Marriott Thruway, June 2000

Schiffman, B.: "Dot-Coms Get Necessary Capital Infusions", Forbes, July 2000, http://www.forbes.com/tool/html/00/Jun/0621/mu1.htm

Scott, M.: "Value Drivers", John Wiley & Sons, 1998

Seaberg, J.: "Talent Crunch – IT Workers Benefit from a Tight Labor Market", Business 2.0, September 2000

Seamus, P.: "Who Needs a PC?", Business 2.0, November 2000

Seebacher, U.G.; Welker, C.: "Optimierung der E-Business Aktivitäten durch E-Assessment", Information Management & Consulting, 4/2000, S. 51-56.

Seebacher, U.G.: "Anbindung von Handels und Geschäftskonzepten" Speech at the Management Cycle Event, Frankfurt, April 2000

Seebacher, U.G.: "Performance Measurement and Evaluation", OU Business School MBA Event, Brussels, 1997

Seebacher, U.G.; Büchsenmann, K.: "Mobil Commerce – Synonym für Mehrwert?", Information Management & Consulting, 2001/2, p. 24–27.

Seebacher, U.G.; Büchsenmann K.: "Mobile Rechner für Vertreter", Versicherungswirtschaft 8/2001, p. 580 - 583

Seebacher, U.G.: "Ein dualistischer Ansatz für Change Management", Information Management & Consulting, 1999/1, p. 65-68.

Seebacher, U.G.: Electronic Performance Measurement and Management (E-PMM) zur prozessbasierten Center- aber auch Unternehmenssteuerung", IMC, 1/2001.

Senge, P.: "Through the Eye of the Needle", CIO Magazine, June 2000

Shapiro, C.; Varian, H.R.: "Information Rules – A Strategic Guide to the Network Economy", Harvard Business School Press, 1999

Shiller, R.: "Irrational Exuberance", Broadway Books, April 2001

Shirky, C.: "Toughest Virus of All", Business 2.0, July 2000, http://www.business2.com/content/magazine/breakthrough/2000/07/11/13

Simons, R.; Davila, A.; Kaplan, R.: "Performance Measurement & Control Systems for Implementing Strategy: Text & Cases", Prentice Hall College, June 1999

Slater, D.: "What Is E-Commerce", CIO Magazine, June 2000, http://www.cio.com/archive/enterprise/061599_curve_content.html

Slater, D.: "Whole Is More than Its Parts", CIO Magazine, Mai 2000, http://www.cio.com/archive/051500_vision_content.html

Smal Business Reports: "Effective Managers, Happy Employees", May 1994

Smith, S.F.: "Knowledge-Based Production Management", Production Planning and Control, Vol. 3, 1992.

Spak, J.: "Strategies for Keeping Good People", HR.COM, 2000

Spulber, D. F.: "Market Microstructure – Intermediaries and the Theory of the Firm", Cambridge Univ. Press, 1999

Stackpole, B.: "How I survived my IPO", CIO Magazine, June 2000, http://www.cio.com/archive/060100_ipo_content.html

Stamatis, D. H.: "Who Needs Six Sigma, Anyway?", Quality Digest, 2000

Stamp, D.: "The Invisible Assembly Line: Boosting White-Collar Productivity in the New Economy", American Management Association, 1995

Standish Group International: "The World Wide Scam – Reality Check on Dot.Com Retail Trends", April 2001

Stenzel, J.P.: "PTIIF Electronic Commerce Statement", Telecommunications & Information Industries Forum, 1998

Stephenson, P.: "Investigating Computer-Related Crime – A handbook for Corporate Investigators", CRC Press, September 1999

Sterne, J.: "Protecting Privacy and Making a Bundle", January 1999, http://www.personalization.com/soapbox/contributions/sterne.asp

Stevens, R. W.: "TCP/IP Illustrated", Addison Wesley Professional Computing Series, January 1994

Steward, A.T.: "Intellectual Capital: The New Wealth of Organizations", Bantam Books, December 1998

Stoner, J. A.: "Management, 2nd Edition", Engelwood Cliffs, 1982

Storey, J.: "Developments in the Management of Human Resources", Blackwell Publishers, 1992.

Storfer, P.: "Merging Competencies and Technologies", Speech at the IHRIM, Boston 2000 Snow, 1992

Strittmatter, F. J.: Ich habe meine Firma auf den Kopf gestellt", Impulse, o. Jh., Heft 6, 1994, S. 94 - 105

Sullivan, P.H.: "Value Driven Intellectual Capital: How to Convert Intangible Corporate Assets Into Market Value", John Wiley & Sons, February 2000

Summit: "Making the E-Transformation", Worldwide Information Systems, October 2000

Sviokla, J.: "Customer Information Backlash", CIO Magazine, January 2000, http://www.cio.com/archive/011500_new_content.html

Szuprovicz, B.O.: "Supply Chain Management for E-Business Infrastructures", Computer Technology Research, September 2000

Talwar, R.: "Business Reengineering – A Strategy Driven Approach", Long Range Planning, vol. 6/1993, S. 22 – 40

Tapscott, D.: "Growing up Digital: The Rise of the Net Generation", McGraw-Hill Professional Publishing, June 1999

Tapscott, D.: "Minds over Matter", Business 2.0, January 1999

Tardiff, V.; Spearman, M.L.: "Diagnostic Scheduling in Finite-Capacity Production Environments," Computers & Industrial Engineering, Vol. 32, 1997.

Taylor, F. W.: "The Principles of Scientific Management", New York, 1911

Techrepublic: Network Administrator's Security Ressource Guide", TechRepublic, August 2000

Tennessen, D.J.: "Pooling Resources in the Information Age", Journal of Extension, October 1997

Tischler, L.: "Recipe for Success", Fastcompany, May 2001

Ulrich, H.; Krieg, W.: St.-Galler Management Modell, 3.Auflage", Bern – Stuttgart, 1990

Vairaktarakis G.L.; Lee, C-Y.: "The Single Machine Problem to Minimize Total Tardiness Subject to Minimum Number of Tardy Jobs", Department of Industrial and Systems Engineering, University of Florida.

Venture One: "Venture Capital Industry Report", June 1999

ViralMarketer: "Fellow Viral Marketers!", December 1999 http://www.viralmarketer.com

Waller, S.: "Theories of Economic Growth and The New Economy", University of Missouri, March 2000

Wangemann, M.: "2001: Subcontract Management Manual", Harcourt Brace Professional Publishing, January 2000

Webber, A.M.: "New Math for a New Economy", Fastcompany, September 1998

Weber, M.: Wirtschaft und Gesellschaft – Grundriss der verstehenden Soziologie, Band 1 und 2, 5. Auflage", Tübingen, 1980

Welte, J.: "Be True to Your School", Business 2.0, August 2000

Welte, J.: "Ventro's Hopes for Bailout", Business 2.0, February 2001

White Paper: "Automation of B2G, G2B, C2G, G2C & G2G Payments in the US: The Federal Government Leads the Way", Tower Group, November 2000

White Paper: "Business Survival in the Next Millennium", IBM Library, June 2000,

White Paper: "ERP and Business Continuity", December 2000

White Paper: "Extending the Reach of ERP", IBM library, Mai 2000, www.ibm.com/software/big/papers

White Paper: "Improving the Success of Mergers and Acquisitions with IBM Solutions for Business Integration", IBM library, February 2000

White Paper: "Knowledge Management Solutions with a B2E, B2B and B2C focus", IDC, July 2000

White Paper: "The Value Propositions of Business-to-Business Dynamic Comerce", Moai Technologies, May 2001

White Paper: "Transforming Customer Relationships with Business Integration", IBM library, June 2000

White Paper: "U.S. Venture Capital Industry Overview and Economics", 2000

White, K.P.; Rogers, R.V.: "Job-Shop Scheduling: Limits of the Binary Disjunctive Formulation," International Journal of Production Research, Vol. 28, 1990.

White, Z.: "1999 Fee & Billing Survey of A/E/P & Environmental Consulting Firms", Zweig White & Associates, June 1999

Will, R.: "States Prepare for Net Privacy Fight", USA Today, June 2000, http://www.usatoday.com/life/cyber/tech/cti125.htm

Wilson, A.: "Human Ressources", FastCompany, March 2000, http://www.fastcompany.com/online/29/hrindepth.html

Winfield, G. T.; Lawrence, C. S.; "Designing Systems for Internet Commerce", Addison-Wesley Longman, 1998

Wittrock, R.J.: "Scheduling Algorithms for Flexible Flow Lines", IBM J. Res. Develop., 1985, www.ibm.com/software/big/papers

Xiong, H.H.; Zhou, M.C.: "Scheduling of Semiconductor Test Facility via Petri Nets and Hybrid Heuristic Search, IEEE Transactions on Semiconductor Manufacturing, Vol. 11, 1998.

Yang, J.; Chang, T.S.: "Multiobjective Scheduling for IC Sort and Test with a Simulation Testbed," IEEE Transactions on Semiconductor Manufacturing, Vol. 11, 1998.

Young, I.D.: "Introduction to Risk Calculation in Genetic Counselling", Oxford University Press, September 1999

Zink, K. J.: "Successful TQM: Inside Stories from European Quality Award Winners", John Wiley & Sons, May 1997

Zweben, M.; Fox, M.: "Intelligent Scheduling", Morgan and Kaufman, 1994

Index

3G (third generation) licenses 20

A

Advanced Research Agency Projects Agency Net (ARPANET) 10, 11
Alta Vista 15, 22
Amazon.com 15, 41, 44, 164, 207
AOL 38, 154, 216
Application Architecture 121
Application Clustering 4, 119, 123
Application Service Providers (ASP) 120

B

Babbage Machine 9
BeautyScene.com 39, 40
Bragg-Lattice Sensirs 33
Business angels 16, 44, 199, 210
Business Process Reengineering (BPR) VIII, 1, 2, 3, 4, 21, 51, 53–67, 73, 75, 77, 79, 84, 85, 86, 88, 90, 94, 106, 109, 119, 209, 214, 225
Business-to-Associates (B2A) 16, 22, 26, 38
Business-to-Business Commerce (B2B) 2, 16, 22, 26, 38, 45, 46, 47, 48, 125, 158, 171, 201, 212, 213, 216, 217, 227
Business–to-Consumer Commerce (B2C) 15, 16, 22, 26, 38, 40, 41, 43, 44, 45, 48, 171, 208, 211, 212, 227
Business-to-Employees (B2E) 16, 22, 26, 38, 227
Business-to-Government (B2G) 16, 22, 26, 38, 217, 226

C

Catalysts VII, 51, 143
Change Management 66, 90, 102, 115, 223
Cluster computing 125
CommerceOne (C1) 45
Competences 93, 94, 95, 96, 107, 122, 134, 140, 142, 148, 149, 151
Behavioral 149
Core 95, 137, 138, 148, 149
Components for servicing applications 4
Contingency situation 18, 21, 51, 54, 57, 63, 81, 88, 91, 94, 97, 108, 127, 167, 173, 185, 197, 211
Convergence VII, VIII, 71, 108
CORBA (Common Object Request Broker Architecture) 26
COVISINT 26, 47
Customer Centric Systems 4, 119, 120, 211
Customer Relationship Management (CRM) 6, 35, 47, 58, 113, 119, 121, 122, 153, 166, 167, 168, 169, 208

Cyber Assessment (C-assessment) 6, 155, 160, 176, 178, 179, 184
Cyber Challenge (C-challenge) 2, 35, 36, 48
Cyber Commerce (C-commerce) 1, 2, 3, 5, 6, 7, 21, 32, 81, 82, 83, 85, 90, 91, 92, 93, 97, 98, 99, 100, 107, 108, 109, 120, 125, 126, 139, 155, 166, 168, 169, 176, 178, 179, 180, 184
Cyber Commerce Reframing (CCR)
  Approach VIII, 3, 5, 6, 67, 81, 82, 87, 88, 89, 94, 108, 111, 122, 155, 185, 199
  Galaxy 153, 159, 160
  Horizontals 3, 78, 79, 86, 87, 88, 89, 93, 100, 102, 104, 105, 106, 156, 167, 168, 173
  Paradigm, paradigm shift 1
  Verticals 3, 78, 87, 89, 90, 94, 96, 99, 105, 106, 123, 156, 157, 166
Cyber Economy, C-Economy, New Economy VII, 2, 3, 4, 5, 6, 9, 16, 17, 18, 19, 20, 25, 33, 35, 39, 40, 44, 45, 50, 64, 66, 71, 83, 84, 88, 108, 114–119, 129, 141, 154, 158, 159, 164, 176, 177, 181, 184, 185, 190, 193, 197, 199, 206, 216, 217, 218, 220, 222, 223, 224, 226
Cyber solution (C-solution) 96, 97

D

DaimlerChrysler 26
DHTML 23
Digicash 42
Dimension-Impact Matrix (DIM) 3, 78, 86, 87, 88, 89
Direct commerce 1, 22
Diversity 5, 122, 135, 136, 191, 218

E

EDI (Electronic Data Interchange) 26, 112, 113, 124, 162, 163, 192, 216
EDIFACT (Electronic Data Interchange for Administration, Commerce and Transport) 26
Electronic Action (E-action) 39
Electronic Billing (E-billing) 6, 155, 171, 172
Electronic Business (E-business) 5, 6, 18, 20, 26, 35, 38, 40, 44, 45, 49, 58, 64, 81, 123, 141, 153, 154, 155, 161, 162, 164, 175, 185, 205, 208, 215, 218, 219, 221, 223, 225
Electronic Commerce (E-commerce) 9, 19, 20, 22, 26, 27, 30, 38, 40, 43, 58, 61, 81, 84, 88, 112, 135, 159, 164, 168, 175, 207, 209, 210, 211, 212, 214, 224
Electronic Mail (E-mail) 11, 13, 14, 20, 23, 24, 27, 28, 36, 113, 117, 124, 168
Electronic Marketplace (E-marketplace) 45, 46, 158, 163, 169, 170, 171, 206
Electronic Performance Measurement & Management (ePMM) 100, 223

Electronic Procurement (E-procurement) 6, 26, 32, 35, 36, 153, 155, 159, 160, 161, 162, 163, 164, 171, 186, 187, 188, 192, 194, 196, 220
Collaborative 185
Electronic Retailers (E-retailers) 42
Electronic Selling (E-selling) 6, 36, 42, 43, 153, 164, 165, 166, 171
Electronic Tailers (E-tailers) 43, 44
Enterprise Resource Planning Software (ERP), ERP packages 2, 18, 46, 47, 62, 63, 64, 65, 88, 106, 113, 114, 121, 195, 221, 226
European Organization for Nuclear Research (CERN) 13
European Quality Award 69, 228
Evaluation 7, 89, 92, 93, 99, 100, 101, 105, 107, 150, 151, 163, 167, 176, 177, 179, 180, 181, 206, 223
Operational 151
Strategic 150
eZoka Group 185, 186, 187, 188, 189

F

Failure mode and effect analysis (FMEA) 70, 219
Federal Communications Commission (FCC) 28
Federal Trade Commission (FTC) 47, 221
File Transfer Protocol (FTP) 12, 13, 222
Ford 26, 37, 54, 55, 77
FORTRAN 112, 212
Front-end application management components 4

G

General Electric VII, 37, 70, 73

H

Host-to-host protocol 10
Human capital 5, 17, 127, 128, 139, 140, 141, 142, 145, 147, 151, 199
Human Resource Management (HRM) 48, 49, 66, 219
Human Resources (HR) VIII, 2, 5, 36, 48, 55, 58, 66, 102, 107, 108, 111, 117, 120, 121, 123, 127, 129, 131, 132, 136–151, 156, 163, 164, 211, 214, 215, 217, 218, 219, 220, 224, 225
Hyper text markup language (HTML) 14, 37, 120, 124, 220

I

IBM 15, 37, 113, 125, 215, 218, 226, 227
Incubators 16, 215
Indirect commerce 1, 22
Individual learning 145
Information and payment components 4
Information technology (IT) 1, 4, 9, 35, 50, 59, 71, 111, 182, 207, 217
Initial public offering (IPO) 43, 206, 215, 224
Instant messaging 13, 28, 29, 31

Integration 4, 6, 32, 46, 90, 94, 107, 113, 115, 116, 120, 148, 177, 184, 186, 187, 192, 219, 227
Intellectual capital 131, 133
Interactive TV (ITV) 31
Interlinking packet networks (Internetting) 10
International Standards Organization (ISO) 3, 68, 69, 208, 217
  ISO 9000, ISO 9004 3, 68, 69, 208, 217
Internet Activities Board (IAB) 12
Internet Engineering Task Force (IETF) 12
Internet generation 5, 128, 129, 225
Internet Protocol (IP) 11, 225
Internet Service Provider (ISP) 22
Internet Society (ISOC) 12
Interwoven Inc. 46
Irrational exuberance 37, 223

J

Joint production 135
Juniper Networks 115

K

Key performance indicator (KPI) 96, 150

L

Learning Organization 144, 145, 214
Location-based services 28

M

Macroeconomic factors 4
Malcolm Baldrige Award 69, 215
Massachusetts Institute of Technology (MIT) 10, 72, 212, 213
Microeconomic factors 16, 114, 116, 117
Mobile Commerce (M-commerce) 6, 27, 28, 29, 30, 126
Mobile inventory management 29
MOSAIC 37
Multiplex capability 33

N

NASDAQ 35, 40, 50
National Center for Supercomputing Applications (NCSA) 14
NEMAX 40, 50
Net generation 5, 128, 129, 225
Net present value (NPV) 181, 212
News and exchange components 4
Nortel Networks 115

O

Old Economy VII, 3, 18, 39, 50, 108, 130, 147, 153, 169, 188
Open architecture network 10
Operations Research (OR) 3, 56, 68, 71, 72, 73, 79, 207, 209, 220, 222
Optimization VIII, 3, 6, 55, 58, 63, 64, 65, 67, 68, 71, 73, 74,

75, 77, 78, 79, 84, 161, 193, 222
Organizational boundaries 134, 156
Outsourcing 4, 5, 43, 55, 120, 134, 137, 138, 183, 186, 200, 207

P

Pareto Rule 63, 64, 74
Performance Measurement and Management (PMM) 87, 93, 95, 96, 100, 102, 125, 150, 165, 223
Pervasive Commerce (P-commerce) 20, 22, 25, 27, 32, 33, 172
Pixelpark 37
Portal 15, 26, 29, 38, 156, 169, 222
Proactive service management 29
Product location 29
Profit Impact of Market Strategy (PIMS) 73, 74, 208
Project master plan 7, 179
Project Risk-Value Matrix (PRV-Matrix) 182
Purchase order (PO) 191, 192

R

Razorfish 37
Réseaux Associeés pour la Recherche Europée ne (RARE) 12

S

Security 4, 41, 42, 44, 97, 101, 124, 138, 145, 159, 179, 212, 226
Components 4
Short message Services (SMS) 20, 29
Six Sigma 3, 68, 70, 71, 215, 224
Smart cards 42
Start-up companies VII, 5, 16, 18, 35, 39, 40, 42, 43, 45, 49, 50, 51, 83, 108, 115, 116, 146, 147, 151, 154, 155, 157, 159, 178, 197, 198, 201, 210
Strategic Human Resource Managment (SHRM) 66, 102, 139, 150
SupplierLinx 185, 187, 188
Systems and communication components 4

T

TCP/IP Protocol Suite 11
Television Commerce (T-commerce) 27, 30, 31
Telnet Teletype Network 11, 13
Total Quality Management (TQM) 3, 68, 69, 70, 71, 210, 228
Transaction costs 177, 219
Transmission Control Protocol (TCP) 11, 225

U

Uniform Resource Locator (URL) 39

United States' Defense Advanced Research Projects Agency (DARPA) 10

V

Value Chain 2, 53, 55, 69, 119, 135, 137, 159, 162, 176, 177, 179
Ventro Corporation 45, 185, 226
Venture capitalists VII, 16, 25, 44, 45, 47, 83, 218
Voice Recognition 28

W

Web-empowering technology 9
Webvan 44
Wide area network (WAN) 10
Wireless application protocol (WAP) 30
Wireless data and computing service (WDCS) 30
Wireless portals 28, 29
Wireless reframing 30
World Wide Web (WWW) 1, 9, 11–16, 21, 35, 36, 37, 39, 113, 114, 205, 207
World Wide Web Consortium (W3C) 12

Y

Yahoo! 15, 22, 29, 164

Printing: Strauss GmbH, Mörlenbach
Binding: Schäffer, Grünstadt

MIX
Papier aus verantwortungsvollen Quellen
Paper from responsible sources
FSC® C105338

If you have any concerns about our products,
you can contact us on
ProductSafety@springernature.com

In case Publisher is established outside the EU,
the EU authorized representative is:
Springer Nature Customer Service Center GmbH
Europaplatz 3, 69115 Heidelberg, Germany

Printed by Libri Plureos GmbH
in Hamburg, Germany